PRIVATIZATION AND FOREIGN DIRECT INVESTMENT IN TRANSFORMING ECONOMIES

Privatization and Foreign Direct Investment in Transforming Economies

PAUL J.J. WELFENS
University of Münster

and

PIOTR JASINSKI
Hertford College, Oxford University

Dartmouth

Aldershot • Brookfield USA • Singapore • Sydney

© Paul J.J. Welfens and Piotr Jasinski, 1994

Published by
Dartmouth Publishing Company Limited
Gower House
Croft Road
Aldershot
Hants GU11 3HR
England

Dartmouth Publishing Company
Old Post Road
Brookfield
Vermont 05036
USA

British Library Cataloguing in Publication Data
Welfens, Paul J.J.
  Privatization and Foreign Direct
  Investment in Transforming Economies
  I. Title II. Jasinski, Piotr
  338.925   ᐁ P

Library of Congress Cataloging-in-Publication Data
Welfens, Paul J.J.
    Privatization and foreign direct investment in transforming
  economies / Paul J.J. Welfens, Piotr Jasinski.
      p.   cm.
    Includes bibliographical references and index.
    ISBN 1-85521-487-3 : $59.95 (U.S. : est.)
    1. Privatization–Europe, Eastern. 2. Post-communism–Europe,
  Eastern. 3. Investments, Foreign–Europe, Eastern. 4. Europe,
  Eastern–Economic policy–1989- I. Jasinski, Piotr. II. Title.
  HD4140.7.W45   1994
  388.947–dc20   94-11912
                                                         CIP

ISBN 1 85521 487 3

Printed and Bound in Great Britain by
Athenaeum Press Ltd, Newcastle upon Tyne.

Contents

List of Figures and Tables

Preface

Privatization has been an issue in Economics ever since ADAM SMITH (and even before), but with the systemic transformation of the former socialist CMEA countries the scope of the privatization process has reached new dimensions. Moreover, privatization takes place in a radically changing institutional setting, and this makes the analysis of privatization more complex than in textbook models. Proponents of rapid privatization expect major benefits for society if assets are controlled by private owners and competition. While privatizing individual firms became prominent in the 1980s in many Western economies as one element of supply-oriented economic policies, the post-socialist economies of central and eastern Europe face a much bigger challenge in the 1990s - the privatization of whole industries and the economic system at large. Describing and analyzing the challenge of privatization in the economic transformation of former CMEA countries and evaluating different strategies as chosen in Poland - adopting a transformational shock therapy - the former German Democratic Republic, Hungary and the ex-CSFR is the task of our book. We also raise the question which role foreign direct investment (a major ingredient of economic catching-up in the Newly Industrializing Countries) could play in the transformation process and whether international organizations could support the transition process in a meaningful way.

The collapse of the socialist economic system in central and eastern Europe has destroyed the institutional fabric and the formal and informal networks of production and distribution. To organize an effective and efficient transition to a functional market economy is extremely difficult in central and eastern Europe. Despite country-specific differences in the initial situation and different blueprints of market economy design the post-socialist economies face complex transition problems. The switch to a private market economy requires above all privatizing state-owned industry and opening up emerging markets for domestic and foreign investors. Establishing functional governance in privatized and newly created firms is required but also most difficult in a transition stage with significant bottlenecks in management and only emerging financial markets. Moreover, as long as market institutions are not in place and markets not fully working an optimal division line between firms (vertical allocation scheme) and markets is impossible to find.

Given the unproven new institutional political frameworks and parties in place in the former CMEA area, institutional reforms and consistent economic policies are much more difficult to adopt than in countries in which functional political structures exist and the reputation of key players in the political game is firmly established. Confidence in the stability of the political system and the expectation of smooth political decision-making processes have always been decisive for high private investment. Without political stability there cannot be economic prosperity built upon efficient and sustained investment, but without high investment there can be no prosperity and hence no political stability (interdependence problem). Privatization is part of the problem of transformation but it also is part of the solution to overcome economic stagnation.

High and sustaining investment is needed in central and eastern Europe if the restructuring of the capital stock is to be fast and if the modernization of the economies in line with both the growing aspiration levels of the population and the requirements of world market competition is to occur. Since economic opening up of the economies is so important for all the small economies of the former CMEA the problem of rapid and efficient capital formation plays a core role for successful systemic transformation. Foreign investment is new for the countries in the ex-CMEA countries and it is not surprising that people sometimes find it quite difficult to accept selling industrial assets - in an economically desperate situation - to foreign investors. However, the experience of successful Newly Industrializing Countries clearly points to the benefits of FDI inflows provided that they are coupled with an outward-oriented economic policy and finally followed by FDI outflows which allow the pool of ideas and technologies abroad more directly to be tapped than licensing and imports. Here lie new challenges for management and business in both the OECD countries and in the ex-CMEA countries which, unfortunately, have begun to erect trade and investment barriers within the region.

I contributed two papers as chapters A and E of this book, while Piotr Jasinski's contributions are in chapters B and C. Many views expressed in the books have developed from discussions among the authors and from the exchange of ideas and experiences with German, Polish, Hungarian, Russian, US and British colleagues. We joined our intellectual forces because we both consider the theoretical and practical challenges of privatization and foreign investment - chapter D - as decisive for successful systemic transformations in central and eastern European economies. My interest in socialist economies is reflected in many research projects and publications.

We consider privatization and foreign direct investment as two keys to successful systemic transformation in central and eastern Europe. There are other key elements in the transition process, most notably the requirement to establish a stable monetary regime and to introduce foreign economic liberalization in a progressive and sustainable manner. A growing presence of private domestic and foreign investors certainly will influence the course of economic policy both with respect to the monetary regime chosen and the scope of external liberalization pursued. The political economy of systemic transformation will be directly affected by private and foreign investors - not always in a way that lets one expect Pareto-optimal outcomes for society.

We do hope that our book raises central issues of the privatization debate in central and Eastern Europe. Since - in the area of practical economic policy - our focus is (almost) exclusively on the privatization strategies of Germany/the former GDR, Poland, Hungary and the CSFR, we cover only a limited group of the former CMEA countries. The economic collapse of the former USSR has impinged the process of economic restructuring in the small ex-CMEA countries whose trade had been dominated by the USSR. The CIS and the newly emerging countries within the former USSR might have hoped for successful transformations in some of the smaller ex-CMEA countries in order to focus the internal transition on a set of success-promising transition models. However, neither a basic role model for the former USSR is readily available nor can the smaller countries hope for a rapid economic restructuring of the CIS. We will focus only briefly on these linkage problems in systemic transition in the ex-CMEA area. The issues raised and the alternative strategies analyzed may, nevertheless, be fairly general. We emphasize that economic and political problems are closely interrelated in the transition. I am very grateful to Tim Yarling, Washington DC, and Cornelius Graack and Markus Anlauf, Universität Münster, for editorial and technical support.

Paul J.J. Welfens
Münster, October 1993

Introduction

Let me start with a rather personal remark. When I came to Oxford in 1987 to read P P E (*i.e.* The Honour School of Philosophy, Politics, and Economics), my - admittedly rather impatient - answer to the question "Why economics?" was that I wanted to learn how the Polish economy should be privatized. At that time nobody was really interested in teaching me that and first things had to come first anyway. Half way through my course I went to Poland for Christmas and there met Stefan Kawalec, Janusz Lewandowski and Jan Szomburg, who had just one month earlier, at a conference in Warsaw, presented the first two blueprints for privatizing East European economies. Having received their papers (Kawalec, 1989, Lewandowski and Szomburg, 1989), I decided, encouraged by Prof. Wlodzimierz Brus, who supervized my undergraduate thesis, to analyse critically these two proposals, confronting them with Western, mainly British, theories and experiences. However, by the time I finished my thesis and published it (Jasinski, 1990a), what had at first looked like science fiction had almost become an event in a distant past. Privatization had turned into reality and started not only in Poland, but all over Eastern Europe.

My interest in privatization survived this shock therapy, so, apart from the thesis mentioned above, I also tried to take part in the Polish debate on these issues (Jasinski, 1990b, c, d, 1991a, b, 1992a, b, c, d, Jasinski and Lisiecki, 1990), which eventually led me to two observations which constitute, as it were, the starting points of Chapters B and C. First, if one looks at Western debate on privatization, one can find, on the one hand, books like Letwin (1988), Pirie (1988), or Veljanovski (1987), which had adequately been labelled "privatization evangelism". They are closer to political rhetoric than to economic analysis. On the other hand, more serious economic literature on privatization was surprisingly ambiguous, and not only because of policy errors in the British privatization programme at that. The economists seemed to be looking simultaneously at so many issues that they appeared unable to provide any unequivocal conclusions. It is true that privatization is a multidimensional process but its very essence consists in the transfer of ownership rights. Yet the ownership transfer aspect of privatization lost its priority to various aspects of pro-competitive and regulatory policies, for which the shape of the public sector in market economies was only partly to blame.

It is true that according to economic theory and applied economics the type and structure of ownership, the regulatory framework, and the degree of competition co-determine the level of economic efficiency, the improvement of which should be the main rationale for transferring ownership rights. But what is surprising is not that the stress on the ownership determinant of economic efficiency is often complemented by a more or less rigorous discussion of the importance of regulation policy and actual and potential competition, but that most papers and books deal with these issues separately. The absence of an all-embracing analytical framework, integrating these three determinants but concentrating on ownership, makes it impossible to analyse, for example, the direct and indirect effects of the transfer of property rights. This in turn makes it very difficult to find some kind of common denominator for different arguments for and against the privatization of a firm in a market economy. Consequently, these arguments are simply listed instead of being weighted against each other.

This observation constitutes the departure points of Chapter B which contains what could be called an attempt to review the existing literature in order to (re)construct such a framework. In other words, Chapter B will try to identify and compare the direct and indirect effects of the transfer of a firm from one sector to another on the internal functioning of the firm and on its relationship with the environment in which it operates, assuming *other things to be equal*. There are, of course, other forms of ownership, but: first, in no economy do they play a really significant role, the only possible exception being Yugoslavia; secondly, until now they were almost completely absent from any debate on privatization; thirdly, this is even more the case in market economies dealt with in this chapter. We shall, however, return to these issues in the next chapter, while discussing the structure of a post-Communist firm in Poland.

The comparative-statics-type results of theoretical analysis will be complemented by a review of empirical evidence on the comparative performance of public and private sector enterprises and on the effects of privatization. At the same time one has to remember that the decision to concentrate our attention on the ownership transfer aspect of privatization - as distinct, for example, from its technique or the financial problems involved - does not imply that all the rest is considered completely irrelevant. An equally detailed discussion of measures that could and/or should accompany - but are not inherently connected with - ownership transfer in order to improve the regulatory regime and/or optimize the degree of competition is an issue in itself and addressing it would simply take us too far.

One more basic assumption of Chapter B is that, in a sense, all the ingredients of an appropriate analytical framework are already there and that the overall picture simply needs a different focus. The fact that the whole issue requires only such a - one could say, cosmetic - change seems to be one of the most important differences between debates on privatization in market economies and debates on privatization in and of the post-STEs (Soviet-type economies), which are market ones *in statu nascendi* at best.

The case of Poland, with which I am obviously most familiar, is a very good case in point because privatization unexpectedly appeared on the economic agenda of the Mazowiecki government or, more precisely, as one of the main elements of the stabilization and transformation plan, named after its author, Leszek Balcerowicz. Although the market direction taken by the first non-Communist government was in a sense self-evident and will not be questioned here, presenting privatization as an equally obvious choice was indeed, from the point of view of the preceding economic debate which culminated in the round-table talks agreement in April 1989, something of a surprise. This unashamedly capitalist option - *to set up a market system akin to the one found in the industrially developed countries*, to cite the programme announced on 9 October 1989 (in: Pejovich, 1990) - was not exactly - and quite understandably - what most top Solidarity activists had in mind when Lech Walesa finally forced them to take seriously Adam Michnik's newspaper article suggesting to the Communists a deal: our Prime Minister, your President (*Gazeta Wyborcza*, July 1989).

Here and now, however, it does not really matter whether Jeffrey Sachs "seduced" and Leszek Balcerowicz "hijacked" the Solidarity movement, or whether privatization was not seriously discussed because it was thought of as politically inconceivable till the very end of the communist rule. Previous experiences justified to a large extent such a programmatic leap. Nevertheless, the necessity of privatization has to be demonstrated and should precede any discussion on how it should be put into practice - otherwise, the only, if by no means absolute, guarantee against taking a step back or even making a U-turn will be to move as quickly as possible to the stage at which ownership transformation becomes by-and-large irreversible.

A comprehensive answer to the question "Why privatize a post-STE?" is necessary because it is only in this way that the essential difference between privatizing a firm in a market economy and privatizing an economy can be shown. This, in turn, is of crucial importance for a right perception of the Polish economy as well as of other post-STEs: the difference between these economies and market economies of, for instance, the OECD countries does not lie exclusively in the depth and complexity of our problems, nor is it only a question of the size of the public sector and of the absence of any market infrastructure. Apart from all this, the post-STEs are (still?) different economic systems. They are organized according to different principles and that is why, if they are to become market economies, they have to undergo a systemic transformation of which privatization is a necessary element. In other words, privatization in the post-STEs is a *transformational privatization.*

This lacuna in the Polish discussions and the risk of misperceiving the role of privatization there constitute the departure points of Chapter C. Our answer to the question "Why privatize?" will be based on an analysis (1) of the "ontological contradictions" of real socialism, (2) of the debate on the socialist calculation, (3) of the theory and practice of market socialism, and (4) of the structure of firms in the Polish economy as well as (5) of their behaviour after the introduction of the Balcerowicz plan.

As in Chapter B, the case for privatization of the post-STEs will be completed with a brief presentation of dilemmas, trade-offs and contradictions involved - apart from answering the question "Why privatize?", it is these that these two chapters want to discuss as comprehensively as possible.

Chapter D, written by both authors of this book together, brings us closer to the reality of privatization processes. In Chapters B and C we have identified the most important dilemmas of privatization in general and of privatization of the post-STEs in particular, namely the unavoidably political character of the process under consideration as well as indeterminacy (from the desire to have an economy dominated by private property one cannot deduce how to get there) and sequencing (what should come first: stabilization or privatization?). Now we can move to more practical - but by no means less important - issues which have to be solved or at least taken into account in designing privatization programmes. In the first part of this chapter we shall discuss, among other thing, monetary and fiscal aspects of privatizing the post-STEs.

Since the discussion on privatization had started in Poland not only before the Mazowiecki government was formed but also before the Round Table talks which made that change of government possible, our presentation of various proposals for privatization will begin with this "prehistoric" debate, *i.e.* with papers written by Stefan Kawalec and by Janusz Lewandowski and Jan Szomburg as well as with their critical evaluation in the light of some Western theoretical writings of the British experience of privatization.

Although the debate which followed the appearance of the practical possibility and political viability of privatization resulted in literally hundreds of conference papers and articles in various journals, the alternative between selling state-owned assets and distributing them free of charge remained valid. Obviously the proposed procedures became ever more sophisticated but it seems that after almost four years of discussion that the most important conclusions that have been reached are that there is an almost continuum of solutions and that these solutions should not be treated as if they excluded each other. Just the opposite, one should use as many of them as possible.

Our presentation of the most important contributions will be, completed with a note on the so-called spontaneous privatization - advocated by nobody and theoretically underdeveloped, but very relevant from the point of view of public opinion's support for privatization.

Chapter D will end with a brief assessment of the progress of privatization processes in individual countries of Central and Eastern Europe. One will have to remember, however, that full account of what has already happened could make up another book and that, even though it is fashionable to express disappointment with the speed of privatization, things are moving ahead and that rather fast.

I am very much indebted to all the people with whom I could work on various projects and discuss my views, approaches and ideas. Special thanks go to Wlodzimierz Brus, Antoni Chawluk and George Yarrow, all from Oxford University, who were particulary generous with their comments on my chapters at various stages of writing them.

Piotr Jasinski, Oxford

Chapter A

Establishing a Private Economic Sector in Post-Socialist Countries

1. Moving from a Socialist System to a Private Sector Economy

The socialist economies of the former Council of Mutual Economic Assistance (CMEA) have collapsed. Instead of state-owned firms in which production is organized within the overarching framework of central planning the new market economies will have to rely on private ownership of capital and decentralized decision-making and coordination. Hence firms have to be privatized and new private business establishments have to be set up; private domestic and foreign owners will play a new role for central and eastern Europe. Private capital and entrepreneurship have to be revitalized in the formerly socialist countries.

Privatizing firms in Eastern Europe is different from the case of Western Europe. This is most obvious from the fact that privatization of big state firms in ex-CMEA countries often would imply the creation of a private monopoly (since socialist firms often were monopolies that were supposed to exploit static economies of scale) which certainly is not in accordance with the goal of creating a competitive economy. In Austrian Economics competition for monopoly positions is considered a useful element of functional competition which encourages innovation and the efficient use of information. Non-price aspects of competition play an important role here and Yarrow pointed this out with reference to privatization in Western market economies (1986, pp. 344-45):

> *On this view, barriers to entry resulting from sunk costs may actually be beneficial. If firms had free access to the information of rivals and could quickly enter the market without disadvantage, there would be no incentive for the discovery of new information... As with contestability theory, this reasoning seems to suggest that state monopolies can be privatized without much concern for the harmful consequences of market power. Again, however, cautionary notes need to be sounded, as the following two points seek to demonstrate. First the Austrian arguments depend heavily upon reasonable freedom of entry at the pro-production stages of the competitive process.*

Applying this argument to central and eastern European economies one should indeed distinguish between the nontradables sector and the tradables sector. If a private monopoly is created in the nontradables sector neither import competition nor (except special cases) foreign investors represent potential rivalry so that a monopoly would be inefficient from an allocation point of view. In the tradables sector a monopoly owned by private domestic investors will not be sustainable if progressive import competition is enforced or if export promotion increasingly helps to focus the firm's efforts to world markets which are open to market entry. This argument shows that there are links between privatization and foreign economic liberalization that typically need to be discussed in the case of OECD countries which are open economies with import competition, world market-oriented firms and two-way flows of foreign direct investment (FDI). If a foreign investor acquires a state monopoly one may presume that the barriers to entry erected by an experienced foreign competitor are higher than those which could be built up in the case that domestic investors had acquired the state company. This raises the question whether the importance of competition policies depends on the mix of private domestic and private foreign investors.[1]

Privatization in Western European economies typically means that individual firms are privatized. Rarely is a whole industry privatized although British Steel or British Airways during the British privatization programme

---

[1] In any case it is clear that economic integration would also put the question of striving for monopoly versus having a monopoly position in a different context. Market widening will weaken at least temporarily existing monopoly positions, while it might intensify the quest for reaching monopoly positions. An interesting question for some OECD countries is whether there can be inefficient patent races by firms that strive for a monopoly position (inefficient in the sense that too many resources are devoted to invention activities and that innovation cycles might be shortened)

under Mrs Thatcher could be viewed in such a way. While the privatization of a single firm already can create economic and political problems, the privatization of whole industries and, in fact, a whole economy spells politico-economic challenges. Legal, organizational, financial and technological changes have to be implemented at the same time in various industries, and this has to be done while there are no experienced domestic consulting firms, banks or managers readily available. State bureaucracies still employ most of the people who had learned to organize a more or less functional socialist state and its state owned industries; with the same people one now has to organize the move away from socialism and towards a functional capitalist system. Outside support is limited to some external resource transfers, for example from the EBRD, the World Bank or the EC/OECD Phare Programme (named after the French word for lighthouse); and international bureaucracies typically are giving only conditional help which sometimes could even impose restrictions that are adverse to further systemic transformation.

A viable private sector can emerge only if an adequate institutional framework is developed, where clear property rights are an important element. Private ownership is the basis for appropriating future residual income from financial or real assets, and these incomes will depend on investments made today and investment options developed tomorrow, where risk-averting individuals will only invest if uncertainty of property titles does not impose additional risks for private investors. Efficient investment decisions are, of course, crucial for the transforming economies because otherwise neither their capital stock - largely rendered obsolete by opening up to the world market economy - can be rebuilt nor can the per capita endowment be raised in an efficient way. Moreover, only with clear property rights can real assets and financial assets be traded, and this is, of course, the basis for their market value. If functional markets for goods and factors be created, private business activities could prosper so that, given specific macroeconomic conditions, a process of self-sustaining economic growth can be stimulated.

The transition to a market economy will require for political reasons that the negative social consequences (unemployment, adverse changes in relative income positions) be kept within critical limits and that favourable prospects for economic growth can be created so that individuals will accept short-term costs of the transition process: for example facing a high risk of unemployment, losses in real income or status, giving up the right to enjoy social services that used to be provided by state firms or facing pressures for qualifying. Prospects for sustained economic growth largely depend on productivity improvements

Privatization and Foreign Direct Investment in Transforming Economies

and these in turn require that resources are optimally used in the economy. Privatization is a very important measure to improve economic efficiency, although we will see that it is only one of the necessary conditions (chapter B).

State firms could - to some extent - play a role for quite some time in the reforming economies since privatization is a complex and time-consuming process. One could argue that theoretical merits justify state ownership in certain cases; *e.g.* a natural monopoly with declining marginal costs is a well-known case from Western economies,[2] and if economies of scope between activity A and B are prevalent one might even have to consider that A&B constitute a natural monopoly case (even if only A or B exhibits falling marginal costs).

Instead of state-owned industry directed by central plans and input allocations to the mostly monopolistic firms, a decentralized system based on private property, decentralized decision-making, individual economic freedom and responsibility as well as a new role for government are to shape the politico-economic system. Establishing private ownership in industrial assets means for the smaller former CMEA countries to reverse a series of nationalizations undertaken between 1947 and the 1970s,[3] but also to transfer ownership rights of newly accumulated capital and newly established firms under socialist centrally planned systems. Privatization would mean for the ex-USSR to reverse more than 70 years of collectivism and command economy structures. At least there is not the problem of re-privatization in the former USSR, but at the same time the interrupted generational link to former capitalism implies that finding competent capital owners and entrepreneurs will be more difficult than in the smaller ex-CMEA countries.

Issues Raised by Privatization
Privatization raises a host of issues. Viewing firms as a nexus of contracts (Williamson, 1985) which allow efficient transactions under functional corporate governance implies that certain legal forms of enterprises are a more efficient way to organize transactions than relying on arm's length transactions via markets; in this comparative perspective the legal framework for markets and the smooth functioning of such markets are then themselves important for privatization of firms as given entities and for unbundling firms or simply substituting production by importing from other regions or countries. To make a

---
[2] From the point of view of post-STEs privatization, privatizing public utilities seems to be a distant option in the short run, but long term policy options will be generally considered here, too.
[3] We will disregard non-European former CMEA countries.

sound assessment is very difficult in the transition stage if the collapse of the political system means that employees or managers have effectively taken of control over a firm without functional outside control - the old centre collapsed and new banks or functional capital markets are not yet in place.

Basically one can distinguish between allocation problems, distributive aspects and fiscal problems, but one can also discern microeconomic aspects and macroeconomic aspects of privatization. The allocation aspects mainly concern the problem of efficiency in production, while distributive aspects relate to the creation of financial and real wealth that is coupled with the mode of privatization chosen (*e.g.* voucher schemes, preferential share prices for employers etc.); fiscal problems concern the question of how much present and future revenue may be generated by alternative ways of privatization, by the scope of privatizing and by the speed of transferring ownership in industrial assets to private agents. A micro-issue is the question whether and when privatized firms are more efficient than state-owned firms, and this question is related to the allocation aspects. Macro-issues concern *e.g.* the question whether factor markets and foreign exchange markets react differently in the case of a dominantly privatized economy than in the case of an economy with mainly state-owned firms.

The supply-side elasticity might well be higher in a (fully privatized) market economy such that the conditions for improving the trade balance via a devaluation are better - according to the Robinson condition - than in an economy with a small private sector.[4] If private firms increase their output faster than state firms in response to a rise of output prices or a fall of input prices at home or abroad, the share of the private sector will be decisive for the impact of a devaluation in currency markets. Moreover, if private firms move faster to the optimum plant size than state firms, the flatter long term supply curve of a given industry is reached more quickly than in the case of dominating state firms. The differential behaviour of state firms might in part result from the tendency of state firms to be big firms, and industries with a dominance of big firms are known to pursue specific collective wage bargaining agreements in Western economies. Relatively high real wage rates in big firms need not be a

---

[4] The Robinson condition states - assuming an initially balanced trade balance T - that T will improve after a rise of the exchange rate e if a specific condition for demand elasticities D_x (elasticity of export demand; x represents exports) and D_{x*} (elasticity of import demand; x* respresents imports) and supply elasticities E_x and E_{x*} is met: $dT/de > 0$ if $[(D_x D_{x*}/E_x E_{x*})(1+E_x+E_{x*})] > 1+D_x+D_{x*}$. The higher the supply elasticities the more one could expect the expression in squared brackets exceed $1+D_x+D_{x*}$. If supply elasticities approach infinity the Marshall Lerner condition is obtained which states that the sum of the absolute values of demand elasticities must exceed unity: $-D_x-D_{x*} > 1$

contradiction to economic efficiency, at least if one follows modern efficiency wage theory.[5] In big firms the control and monitoring costs for employment are higher than in smaller firms, and productivity (efforts) of workers might be particularly stimulated by higher wages in big firms which often show higher than average capital-employee relationships; finally, big firms might realize monopolistic rents that raise profits and are then partly appropriated by well-organized labour unions.[6]

Tax flows generated in an economy with mainly private business could be higher or lower than in a state-dominated economy, and this is not only because state-owned firms tend to be less profitable on average than private firms but also because the effective tax regime imposed on state firms tends to be relatively soft (ex-post granted subsidies for avoiding lay-offs effectively reduce tax rates). Clearly, the rate of innovation could significantly depend on private ownership and state ownership, respectively; if for example the range of innovations considered were smaller in state firms than in private firms or if private firms would bring novelties to the market faster than state firms one would find a lower rate of productivity increase in countries with a considerable share of state-owned firms.

Due to different adjustment speeds at the microeconomic level in the case of private firms versus state firms, one may also expect different adjustment speeds in macro-markets depending on the relative size of the state sector. For example the monetary transmission process could also differ in both cases; this holds even more for fiscal policy to the extent that expenditure programmes might favour state-owned firms over private firms at home and abroad. Finally, the political system and hence economic policy can be expected to look different in a market economy than in a system with a considerable share of GNP produced by state-owned firms. The type of rent-seeking and the attempts by politicians to organize highly paid jobs for themselves in state-owned firms and

---

[5] If big firms would reduce wages to average wage rates there would be efficiency losses according to the efficiency wage hypothesis. The efficiency wage hypothesis assumes that individuals can vary their efforts to some extent without facing immediate lay-offs. Monitoring is costly and wages are set above wage-clearing levels in order to minimize shirking. With a zero unemployment rate shirking - "insufficient efforts" of workers in their work - would imply little risk of negative sanctions: if a worker is fired he/she would immediately find a new job. Shapiro and Stiglitz (1984) pioneered this approach and Akerlof and Yellen (1990) and Solow (1990) made further contributions. Positive empirical evidence from various Western countries was discussed in the literature: *E.g.* Dunn (1986) and Strand (1987). One might also invoke the theory of compensating wage differentials according to which workers doing hazardous jobs - which may be more typical for big firms than for smaller firms - receive higher than average wages as a kind of compensation. However, the empirical evidence for Western countries is negative; see *e.g.* Lorenz and Wagner (1988) and Schmidt and Zimmermann (1990).

[6] See on the case of Western firms Brown and Medoff (1989).

to generate financial election support will certainly differ in the two polar cases that one could envisage.

1.1 Fundamental Problems in Systemic Transformation

New Principles of Systemic Design
Economic systems whose guiding principle of a socialist command economy has been abandoned, while the desired systemic design of a market economy has not yet been reached, will be labelled post-socialist economies (PSE). PSEs are by definition in a transitory stage of institutional development. In addition to this one may expect that attitudes and incentives change significantly. The policy response under such transitional conditions is likely to deviate from that in the desired new market economy regime. Decisions are not yet made and expectations not yet formed in the way in which this would be done in a fully fledged market economy.

What is the basic meaning of "market economy"? A market economy is a decentralized system of decision-making. Each economic actor tries to reach an optimum situation by maximizing profits (firms) or a utility function (households) subject to certain constraints - typically including a price vector of factor prices and output prices. Each actor might then affect some input prices or output market prices so that another round of optimizing decisions throughout the economy will occur: this is "market piecemeal engineering" in the sense that complex problems with many technical and pecuniary interdependencies can be solved in a stepwise way by agents with limited information at each point of time.

Typically, with a given price increase of a certain good the prices of substitutive goods will increase and the price of complementary goods will reduce; present and future profits are affected by price changes as well as by new technologies (or moving down a learning curve in the case of dynamic economies of scale) such that the net worth of individual firms is changing. Owners of industrial assets might then want to sell shares or to buy additional ones, so that the composition of the group of owners is changing over time. In market economies most firms are explicitly subject to the discipline of financial market forces, above all the evaluation by stock markets; almost all firms are evaluated by banks whose willingness to lend depends on the anticipated capacity of the firm to earn interest and principal in the marketplace. In this context it is clear that it is not the mere existence of banks or stock markets which is decisive but the quality of the services provided; in the case of the stock market there could be minimum requirements for good services, namely that a minimum number of firms must be quoted in order to attract a sufficient number of potential investors. Functional financial institutions were still missing in most ex-CMEA countries in the early 1990s.

With open markets all firms are subject to the threat of potential newcomers which might not only carve out market niches but gradually enter existing "standard markets" with supernormal profits - these will then melt away as more firms sell greater output quantities in markets in which the demand curve always is downward-sloping (greater quantities can be sold only at declining prices). The invisible hand of market forces will create - in a competitive environment - the optimal allocation of resources with the result that prices of many goods will fall, process innovations and product innovations are undertaken and an increasing variety of goods and services will be supplied. The visible hand of capitalist national and multinational firms also plays a role in market economies; production is organized in firms, and intra-company shipments may enhance competitiveness in the market for the final products produced. However, in market economies intra-company flows of goods and services are subject to the discipline that outside producers could be additional or exclusive suppliers in the future; according to Coase transaction costs and other aspects shape the firm's decision in this respect, where low market transaction costs should encourage firms to use outsourcing and outcontracting.[7] A competitive set of private firms as alternative sources of supply and alternative ways to organize production, financing and distribution is new for the state-owned firms in the transforming economies where monopolistic suppliers and monopolistic producers were traits of a centrally planned system.

Despite the only rudimentary market economy institutions developed so far, there are some straightforward expectations with respect to the envisaged privatization process. Private firms are expected to grow faster than state-owned firms so that privatization from above combined with privatization from below should generate an increasing share of private industrial and financial activities. Whether industries are - at the margin - characterised by profit-maximizing firms is an open question. Some worker-oriented management behaviour might well shape market dynamics in certain industries, especially in the non-tradables sector.

---

[7] Coase (1937) points out the relevance of transactional costs.

After four decades of an inward-oriented command economy, there will be a switch towards outward-oriented market economies, where firms are embedded into international competition often shaped by multinational companies and growing international trade in goods, services and capital. There is a strong need for theoretical, ideological and political reorientation in Eastern Europe which faces the shattered values of traditional Marxism-Leninism and the unfulfilled claim to bring prosperity and social justice to the people by means of central planning, state-owned firms and inward-oriented economic development strategies.

The East European economies traditionally were not exposed to world market forces and had no foreign direct investment. Even where export-GNP ratios were relatively high and westward orientation of trade flows considerable - as in Hungary and Poland (Schrenk, 1990) - allocation was not decisively determined by international relative prices and innovation dynamics. Since more than 50 per cent of trade was taking place as intra-CMEA trade, the effective degree of economic openness was (from a market economy perspective) lower than suggested by statistically recorded export-GNP ratios. The experience of successful exporters in ex-CMEA countries is of little value under the new conditions of international competition and trade. One also has to take into account that the effective exposure of industry to world market forces was on average certainly lower than suggested by export-GNP ratios. The basic reasons for this were both the institutional separation of domestic production/ distribution and external trade (organized in state trading monopolies) and, more importantly, the lack of price flexibility and competition in the domestic economy. While in market economies international impulses feed directly and indirectly into all markets for goods and services via substitution effects or complementarity of goods, thereby affecting all prices and price expectations, in command economies both the supply side and the demand side of most industries were widely isolated from world markets. Comparing West European and East European economies is misleading if one would simply focus on export-GNP ratios or per capita export (or import) figures in countries of comparable size. Indeed per capita trade in Poland reached only ECU 281 in 1987 which was only about 1/3 of the Spanish figure of ECU 812, with the EC average being ECU 2563 (GUS, 1991). The task of foreign economic liberalization is tremendous in Eastern Europe since one has to catch up with West European per capita trade figures or export-GNP ratios and import-GNP ratios that all increased after 1945. "Indirect openness" in the sense of general market interdependency via flexible supply adjustment and flexible demand response (especially in industry) have to be introduced as well.

As systemic transformation will mean a hardening of the firms' budget constraints, the incentives for substitution - or reactions to price changes of complementary goods or inputs - will not be unaffected by the development of a competitive banking sector and a functional capital market. Establishing a competitive financial market with private banks, insurance companies and investment firms is of prime importance not only for efficient investment but for the whole process of privatizing the existing stock of capital (except for some remaining state firms). Privatizing firms is one key to efficient allocation in the sense of static efficiency criteria; privatization plus competition should generate forces that lead to static and dynamic efficiency, the latter meaning an optimal rate of innovation.

In ex-CMEA countries people have limited financial wealth. There is a lack of entrepreneurial spirit, but nevertheless a desire for rapid catching up with Western Europe. Hence foreign investors will be considered for at least part of the privatization process.

In OECD countries FDI is a two-way form of transferring capital, technologies and know-how as well as a broad avenue for intra-company trade and inter-company trade. In Eastern Europe one may assume that at least for many years inward FDI will - if at all - be the major element of international investment flows. Foreign investors will not only establish new firms (greenfield investment), but will indeed in many cases acquire part of the existing capital stock. This creates a unique situation in Eastern Europe - as compared to FDI in developing economies - because rarely can Western firms or Japanese firms acquire big chunks of the existing capital stock or even whole industries.

1.2 Challenges

The transition from a centrally planned economy towards a market economy is extremely difficult in reality because the point of departure is a very distorted socialist system. Firms in the official economy are poorly organized, the labour morale is low in the official system (while it may be high in the shadow economy), rationing in consumer markets is widespread and huge gaps between official exchange rates and the exchange rate in black currency markets prevail. With the political system so closely intertwined with the official economic system an accelerating economic crisis implies a declining legitimacy for the political system. Given the weakened state authority it then becomes difficult to thoroughly implement new credible rules of the market economy game. Moreover, in a Western market economy model government institutions should rarely interfere in the economic process but rather provide credible institutions and long-term policy schemes that help to coordinate market participants' decisions (for instance banking supervision and medium-term financial planning); government can also act as a neutral arbiter - possibly with a high reputation - in the competition process (for instance anti-trust authorities and the legal system). Credibility and reputation of political actors and institutions are weak in the first transformation stage which makes the transformation much more difficult than a hypothetical transition initiated by a benevolent dictator in an initial situation of a functional socialist system.

There are at least six building blocks of a market economy (see Exhibit 1). Price liberalization and decentralization are core ingredients for the transition to a market economy. However, with price liberalization markets will not clear at competitive price levels - until competition has been established in all markets. As rationing in the official economy is eliminated, "socialist shadow economic activities" will no longer be profitable. In the socialist shortage economy goods from the official distribution system were diverted towards the flexible price shadow economy in which output price levels were much higher than prices in the official economy; moreover, inputs and labour were distracted from the official system so that output plans could not be fulfilled as planned, and this in turn increased the systemic tendency to hoard input factors in socialist firms. These impediments to allocation efficiency should quickly reduce as prices are liberalized. Switching from low state-administered prices (under uncertain conditions of availability of goods for the consumer at the administered price) to market clearing prices will translate into a relative price shock and an "adjustment inflation". Relative price shocks will follow from the tendency of rather drastic price increases and price changes that will reflect relative marginal production costs in a market economy. Relative price adjustments in the short term could also arise because of newly available possibilities of exploiting the monopoly position of various producers.

Under gradually increasing competition the cost structure will strongly diverge from that in the command economy. Since the outgoing communist governments left a monetary overhang in most ex-CMEA countries - from monetary financing of budget deficits and soft credit allocations to state firms - there will be an adjustment towards a much higher price level for newly produced goods; prices of consumer durables could fall in some cases (as in the case of used cars) because rationing no longer exists. Consumers will perceive a double loss: a reduction of real income positions and, possibly, a loss of non-human wealth. The effective real income position will not fall as strongly as suggested by the rise of the price level because a greater variety of goods is available and because transaction costs are equivalent to a rise of the household budget (this argument may be irrelevant to those who are unemployed). In the tradables sector - assuming that the economy is opening up to world markets - absolute prices and relative prices will become equal to world market prices.

The rise in the price level will affect inflationary expectations and this in turn will generate inflationary dynamics that can be curbed only via an anti-inflationary monetary policy. Whether this can be achieved depends on the stabilization policy adopted and, of course, on the institutional setting for the central bank and the two-tier banking system. In any case the transmission process of monetary policy carries considerable uncertainty. Monetary stabilization in the sense of achieving low inflation rates seems to be important because otherwise relative price signals will be distorted by inflationary noise - *i.e.* relative price signals are superimposed by absolute price changes, so that allocation efficiency is reduced. *Ex post facto* some investments will turn out to be unprofitable because relative price errors occurred. Moreover, the capitalization horizon typically is reduced with higher inflation rates such that long term investments might not find long-term financing schemes at favourable rates; in Western market economies average bond maturities fall with higher inflation. A highly inflationary environment is not conducive to fully mobilizing the benefits of privatization. However, there is an interdependency problem because privatization could also help to reduce inflationary pressures; the expansion of credits and the money supply, respectively, will be easier to restrict if the incentive to reintroduce or maintain soft budget constraints in a big state-owned sector has more or less vanished.

Finally, high inflation rates in the presence of limited competition in financial markets (and capital outflow restrictions) could entail distorted, very low - even negative - real interest rates. This, in turn, would encourage investment projects that would not be profitable in an environment of low inflation rates; the investment-output ratio (I/Y) would be higher than optimal allocation in a non-inflationary environment would warrant, and since the marginal product (dY/dK) would have to match only a low real interest rate r the growth rate of output (I/Y times dY/dK) would be lower than otherwise.

Figure A 1: Building Blocks of a Market Economy

Moving from a Socialist Economy   to a Market Economy

BUILDING BLOCKS OF A MARKET SYSTEM

A: Price Liberalization and Decentralization
- enterprise autonomy
- legalise parallel (unofficial) markets
- establish uniform exchange rate
- decentralization of state organization
- freedom of market entry

B: Stabilization
- eliminate monetary overhang
- create competitive two-stage
  banking system that ensures
  a positive real interest rate
- tax-based incomes policies in
  the transition
- low-inflation monetary policy
  (independent central bank)

C: Privatization
- privatization from above (incl.
  dismemberment of big firms and
  unbundling of assets)
- privatization from below and
  establishment of venture capital
  markets
- privatization of real estate
- regulation of natural monopolies

D: Foreign Economic Liberalization
- import competition
- export liberalization/promotion
- remove restrictions for
  foreign direct investment

**E: Competition in Goods Markets,
  Capital Markets and Labour Markets**
- demonopolization
- deregulation
- import competition
- nurture newcomers
- create competitive financial markets
- remove obstacles to regional mobility
- retraining of labour force
- encourage mobility via
  wage differentials

F: Attitudes
- accepting private property
- accepting income differentials
- accepting wealth disparities
- promoting performance-oriented
  remuneration

G: Government
- role of the state in production sphere
- principles of fiscal policy
- scope of supply-side policy
- principles of monetary policy

Privatization and foreign economic liberalization - including the liberalization of foreign investment inflows - are the core of the transformation to a market economy in the real sphere. Privatization will have to occur on a broad scale and in various forms, along with deregulation and, if there are remaining state firms, regulation (state-ownership can, of course, be perceived as an implicit form of regulation).

Import competition will be a first step to expose the so far sheltered sectors to world market pressure. Transitorily imposing tariffs may be necessary to buy time for some industries that are considered to be viable players in long-term international competition. Export liberalization is part of economic freedom of the firm, and would-be private owners will discount remaining export restrictions in their willingness to pay for firms to be privatized. Export promotion would encourage firms to expose themselves to world market pressure by becoming actors in international markets. This could make sense for society if positive external effects for other sectors could be expected - *e.g.* positive spill-over effects that are emphasized in the new growth theory (Romer, 1990). Liberalizing FDI inflows is a step to overcome capital scarcity, to accelerate international technology transfers and to intensify competition in the bidding for firms to be privatized. Finally, competition in goods markets, capital markets and labour markets has to be established, but attitudes must also change in a way that profit-maximizing behaviour is no longer discouraged; government's macroeconomic policy principles also must be defined in new way.

Labour markets will represent special problems in Eastern Europe. The influence of unions is strong in most ex-CMEA countries, and strong unions and monopolistic state firms suggest that there might be very high transaction costs in labour markets; the bilateral monopoly is known to yield ambiguous solutions and game-theoretic analysis also suggests that efficient solutions are difficult to obtain.

Competition-augmenting policies that reduce the role of big firms could therefore be crucial in the transformation process. Increasing labour productivity and controlling unemployment are two tasks that are faced in the transition process but are difficult to achieve at the same time.

Systemic transformation and the improved access to Western technologies (relaxation of CoCom and impact of FDI inflows) could quickly raise labour productivity in industry, but given the high share of industrial value-added in GNP - 10-20 percentage points above West European values which are close to 30 per cent - high productivity growth is likely to translate into a quickly rising unemployment rate. Only if exports and the domestic service industry expand very quickly could one expect that labour market problems remain limited. The fact that about 20 per cent of the labour force in all ex-CMEA countries (except for the CSFR and the ex-GDR) is in agriculture suggests that modernization will entail both problems in industry and in agriculture.

1.3 Dimensions of the Transformation Problem

The countries involved in the East European transition have embarked upon various transformation approaches which differ in scope, resolve and strategy. No country so far has been successful in developing a quick way to systemic transformation and economic recovery. Except for the prospects of an East German economic miracle - of a modest scale - to be expected in the 1990s, no former CMEA country can hope to double per capita output within a decade; the case of the former GDR obviously is a special one that is shaped by West Germany's enormous resource transfer to Eastern Germany where in 1991/92 nearly 60 per cent of incomes are Western resource transfers which are by no means available in Eastern Europe.[8] In 1990/91 West Germany transferred between 5-6 per cent of its GNP to Eastern Germany so that adjustment measures and structural adjustment could be much more radical in the former GDR than in the other ex-CMEA countries. To some extent the imposition of the West German institutions might be considered an advantage for systemic transformation in Eastern Germany because this reduced uncertainty and saved "political consensus capital". However, the very complex network of West German regulations also raised information costs, imposed very costly adjustment costs and prevented Eastern German industry from establishing specific rules, wages and tax laws that would have eased the survival of more firms and more jobs. The 2.5 million jobs lost in Eastern Germany between 1990 and 1992 represented a quarter of all jobs existing in the former GDR; if for example Poland had adopted a similar shock therapy comparable per capita figures would suggest that Polish unemployment would have reached some 6 million in 1992 (actual unemployment was some 2 million).

---

[8] On German unification see Welfens (1992a); Sinn and Sinn (1992).

1.3.1 Economic Distortions, Stagflation and Instability

The formerly socialist countries faced a difficult point of departure when they embarked upon the transition to a market economy in 1989/90. For the CMEA countries the 1980s had been a period of economic stagnation, falling terms of trade, rising monetary overhangs and expanding socialist shadow economies. Most CMEA economies were characterized by economic structures that were biased towards heavy industry - and against modern service industries; the whole economic system was inflexible especially since the socialist command economy consisted of a huge bureaucratic apparatus and a host of sanctions against individual initiatives and spontaneous creativity (including the formation of new firms). Centralized planning requires stable and manageable micro-structures and this also implies another problem, namely that CMEA countries relied on oversized firms. Most employees were working in firms with more than 500 employees, while employment in Western economies is dominated by the many small and medium-sized firms - some of which will, of course, rapidly expand over time.

Table A1 clearly reveals that, except for Yugoslavia, employment in socialist industrial countries was dominated by "big state firms" - not by big business, as sometimes in the case of capitalist economies. Small and medium-sized business establishments - those with 1-499 employees - are the backbone of West German industry and accounted for 48.1 per cent of all jobs in industry in 1990. By contrast, in the GDR the smaller firm sizes 1-500 accounted for only 12.2 per cent of all employees respectively. In the Republic of Korea and Japan the smaller firm sizes 1-299 accounted for 41.8 and 54.7 per cent of all employees.

A bias against small and medium-sized firms was found in all socialist countries. Obviously central planning was facilitated by having a smaller number of bigger firms (as compared to market economies); however, smooth adjustment and swift supply side response require that the leading role of small and medium sized firms be reestablished in the former CMEA area. This is a structural adjustment requirement that has to take place *uno actu* with privatization and reorganization - the latter including a greater role for outcontracting in industry; this process would be partly achieved *en passant* if the switch to a market economy would bring an over-proportionate share of lay-offs for big firms and if new small firms could attract a significant amount of personnel from big companies. This, however, does not seem very likely. If big firms enjoy some market power, they will be able to offer higher real wages than small firms where employees cannot hope to share part of the supernormal profits accruing in monopolistic markets.

The dominance of big firms will be difficult to reverse, especially since labour can be expected to be heavily organized in big firms so that politicians will find it very difficult - and risky for their political careers - to argue in favour of closing down oversized firms, stripping off assets and creating new firms; this unbundling of assets has been done by the Treuhandanstalt to a considerable extent in the East German case. Indeed privatization - including the dismemberment of firms - is only a first round of allocating private industrial property rights. Over time in the process of economic growth and competition the allocation of property rights will change as will the valuation of assets.

Table A1: Distribution of Employment According to Firm Size in Selected Countries

employees/firm	FRG** (1990)	GDR (1988)	Korea (1986)	Ja-pan (1986)	Po-land ('89)	Hung-ary ('81)	USA ('77)	em./firm
1-100	17.9	1.0	41.8	54.7	1.4	7.0	76.7	5-75
						18.7	12.4	76-189
101-200	11.6	2.5	18.8*#	17.4*#	18.2	9.2	3.8	190-243
201-500	18.6	8.7	39.4***	27.9***		65.1		243+
501-1000	13.6	12.2			15.0			
1001-2500	38.3*	25.9			43.1			
2501-5000		22.6						
5000+		27.1			22.3			
	100.0	100.0	100.0	100.0	100.0	100.0	100.0	

* = 1000 +; ** in the FRG class brackets can be defined as running from 0-99, 100-199, 200-499, 500-999, 1000+; *# 100-299; *** >300.
Sources: OECD (1992), OECD Economic Surveys. Poland, Paris., 90, Statistisches Bundesamt, Wiesbaden, own calculations; Song, B. (1991), The Rise of the Korean Economy, Oxford: Oxford University Press, p. 113.

The dynamics of private enterprise in market economies depend much on the market entry of new firms and the expansion of small and medium-sized firms. In the competition process only a small sub-sample of all firms will rapidly expand; typically, the survival rate of newly created business establishments is not higher than 50 per cent over the time span of the first five years. A switch to a market economy would necessarily require replacing the socialist emphasis on big firms and static economies of scale with explicit support for new and small and medium-sized firms which form the backbone of dynamic market economies, namely both as regards structural and regional resilience as well as innovativeness; big firms, however, play a crucial role for both the innovation and diffusion processes. Moreover, these firms can rejuvenate by buying into dynamic and expansive small firms. The interplay of small and big firms in Schumpeterian innovation competition is crucial for economic growth and structural change in market economies.

In the literature there have been extensive debates on the link between the size of a firm and innovativeness (*e.g.* Acs and Audretsch, 1990, 1991; Scherer, 1992). The available evidence for the neo-Schumpeterian hypothesis that big firms are more efficient with respect to innovation than small firms is mixed, and there are certainly cases - namely in newly emerging industries (such as lasers) - where small firms are superior innovators when compared to big firms; if the latter would acquire such new innovative firms early on these firms might indeed lose their innovative drive because they become integrated into the routines of a big established firm. Many big firms in Western Europe have explicitly set up separately capitalized small firms which are expected to pursue very new technological fields. Winter (1984) suggested that industries may have different institutional regimes which are crucial determinants for innovation efficiency; some industries are characterized by an entrepreneurial regime which means that small firms are relatively superior in innovation, while in other industries big firms might enjoy a comparative advantage. In reality only an endogenous learning process might determine the optimal match of firm size and industry. If promoting innovativeness is important for Eastern Europe one may suggest that privatization should aim at unbundling the assets of big firms and thereby creating a considerable number of small-sized and medium-sized firms which then could grow over time (internally or externally). Only in the first stage of privatization is there likely to be an opportunity at all to dismember big firms. At least this should be done in those industries which are known to be characterized by entrepreneurial regimes in innovation. Clearly, innovation - including diffusion - will be extremely important for long term economic growth in central and eastern Europe; in the short and medium term measures to achieve static efficiency could be more important and yield faster results as regards overcoming the economic depression faced in the first transition stage.

1.3.2 Falling Real Incomes and Wealth Losses in the First Transition Stage

The first stage of systemic transformation is characterized by great reductions in output of investment and consumption goods. While the fall in investment output should not be overemphasized because it partly reflects the switch away from very high and excessive investment-output ratios (a reflection of inefficient investment production), the fall of consumption output is crucial; official figures might not always reflect economic reality to the extent that part of value-added will be from the unrecorded value-added of the shadow economy, but transformation causes serious problems for considerable strata of the population. In the poor societies of central and eastern Europe transformation means real hardship for part of the population, and for those who are mobile, skilled and sceptical about the prospects of a quick economic recovery there are strong incentives to move westward to Western Europe or North America. Western Europe - most notably Germany - is already facing a wave of gradually increasing immigration pressure.

Table A2 indicates the sharp fall of real GNP in the first transition stage in the transforming economies. From a phase of slow growth in the 1980s (where Western accounting standards would imply lower official growth figures) real GNP growth turned to negative figures in 1990; in 1991 output decreased by two-digit figures in all ex-CMEA countries except for the CSFR; industrial output declined by an average of 11 per cent for the former socialist countries in central and eastern Europe.

Real wages fell in most reforming countries, where in Bulgaria, Poland, Romania and the CSFR high losses of 330 per cent, 220 per cent, 43.0 per cent and 41.5 per cent, respectively, were recorded in 1991.[9]

---

[9] The loss of real wage income was probably lower than indicated in these statistics because a considerable number of individuals might have had income from the newly emerging and expanding shadow economy; the gradual elimination of shortages in official markets implies that effective price levels - including transaction costs and a premium for uncertainty with respect to the availability of goods - were not as high as indicated by traditionally defined price indexes.

Table A2: Growth Rates of (g_Y) Real GNP, (g_w) Real Wages and (g_m) Real Money Balances in Socialist Countries

(*real wage increase = nominal increase minus consumer price inflation*)

		1981–86	1987	1988	1989	1990	1991	(Ind. Prod.)
CSFR	g_Y	2.3	2.4	2.6	1.4	-0.4	-16.0	(-23.0)
	g_w	-0.2*	1.9	2.2	0.8	-6.3	-41.5	
	g_m	4.6*	-	11.0	3.1	-16.2	-16.5	
Hungary	g_Y	1.5	4.1	-0.1	-0.2	-3.3	-8.0	(-19.0)
	g_w	0.4*	0.7	-5.5	0.0	-8.3	-11.5	
	g_m	-1.0*	-	-10.2	-2.6	-3.1	-6.8	
Poland	g_Y	-0.8	2.0	4.8	0.3	-11.6	-9.0	(-12.0)
	g_w	-4.3*	-3.7	23.8	31.9	-220.0	6.1	
	g_m	-6.4*	-	-3.7	-6.0	-32.5	-7.0	
Bulgaria	g_Y	3.7	6.1	2.6	-1.9	-11.8	-23.0	(-28.0)
	g_w	2.3*	1.6	5.3	2.4	9.7	-330.0	
	g_m	-	-	-	-	-	-	
Romania	g_Y	3.6	0.7	-0.5	-5.9	-7.4	-13.5	(-22.0)
	g_w	-0.2*	0.0	-0.4	3.4	5.9	-43.0	
	g_m	-	-	-	-	-	-	
USSR	g_Y	3.0	1.6	4.4	2.5	-2.3	-17.0	(-8.0)
	g_w	1.4*	2.3	7.8	7.5	9.5	-25.0	
	g_m	-	-	-	-	-	-	
Average**g_Y		3.0	1.8	3.7	1.7	-4.1	-16.8	(-11.0)
OECD	g_Y	2.7	3.3	4.4	3.3	2.6	0.9	(-0.5)

* 80-85; ** weighted average for Poland, CSFR, Hungary, Albania, Bulgaria, Yugoslavia, Romania, USSR

Source: Bank of International Settlements (1992), 62nd Annual Report, based on OECD, UN Commission for Europe, IMF and Vienna Institute for Comparative Economic Studies, p. 51/52, own calculations.

This inflation-induced fall of real wages certainly reduced the pressure for redundancies in state firms as well as in private firms.[10] Family income losses were often aggravated further by unemployment; hence even a rise of real wages might not have allowed the real family income levels to be maintained in many cases, namely if the employee lost the job. In countries with hyperinflation in 1990/91 real wages fell even stronger than real output, and on top of this there were significant reductions of domestic real balances - for instance in Poland by about 1/3 in 1991. These developments will, of course, affect savings and labour supply behaviour. Individuals faced additional hardship in the form of rising unemployment and higher anticipated unemployment risk.

Table A3: Inflation Rates and Unemployment Rates in Reforming Countries of Central and Eastern Europe

	1989	1990	1991	1992.I*	1989	1990	1991	1992**
	Umemployment Rate				Consumer Price Inflation***			
CSFR	0.0	1.0	6.6	6.5	1.5	10.0	58.0	10.8
Hungary	0.6	1.7	7.5	8.9	17.0	28.3	35.0	24.7
Poland	0.1	6.1	11.5	11.9	251.1	585.0	70.4	38.1
Bulgaria	0.0	1.5	10.1	12.5	6.4	26.3	480.0	73.3
Romania	0.0	0.4	3.1	4.6	0.6	4.7	165.0	265.0
USSR	–	–	0.8	–	2.0	4.7	95.0	>900****
Yugosl.	15.4	17.8	20.5	20.8	1240.0	583.0	118.0	303.0

* first quarter; ** preliminary; *** official consumer prices; **** own estimate
Source: BIS (1992), 62nd Annual Report, Basle.

In the CSFR and Poland real money balances were reduced by about 1/3 in 1990/91, where the Polish case was clearly characterized by hyperinflation which, causing a strong currency devaluation, might have caused some offsetting capital gains for those households which held foreign currency balances. Considerable redistribution effects probably already occur in this monetary adjustment process, and the privatization process could add to the existing disparities in income and wealth.

---

[10] In some cases high real wage losses in 1991 offset very high real wage increases in previous years (sometimes still accorded under socialist government.

Table A3 indicates that open inflation and unemployment played an increasing role in the first stage of transition. Overmanning and the hoarding of factor inputs, typical for socialist economies, are no longer adequate firm strategies in the new market economy environment. The dishoarding process might have brought some welcome additional cash flow for firms struggling to survive, but this was only a one-time effect and could at best help to postpone the real adjustment process. To the extent that monopoly profits were possible at least transitorily adjustment pressure was also reduced temporarily for the existing monopolies, but at the same time barriers to entry for newcomers were erected thereby.

Hyperinflation in all former CMEA countries - except for Hungary and the ex-CSFR - has probably prevented Overmanning under socialism from translating fully into lay-offs. With real wages falling during hyperinflation the pressure for introducing capital-intensive technologies is reduced, but it is not clear that this is an advantage in technologically backward countries. Productivity growth is strongly related to capital-embodied technological progress. Falling real wage rates are also likely to depress savings - namely to the extent that the savings rate is rising with real income and that hyperinflation brought windfall capital gains for owners of real capital, land and foreign exchange.

For those enjoying such windfall gains the gap between desired wealth and actual wealth will have reduced and this would suggest - with a Metzler-type savings function - that savings will reduce. The ability to quickly reduce inflation rates to one digit figures might therefore not only be important in terms of macroeconomic stability; it might indeed be important for the type of modernization (capital intensive vs. labour intensive) pursued. If countries with low inflation rates can also open up the economy more quickly to the OECD countries and the NICs than high inflation countries, the low inflation countries might enjoy a double initial benefit - stronger pressure for capital intensive modernization and hence faster labour productivity growth, but at the same time, increasing FDI inflows and rising export potentials due to early modernization in line with OECD product and technology standards.

Given the strong fall of real incomes in the late 1980s and early 1990s in Eastern Europe, in contrast to West European economic growth, one may anticipate a transitorily rising intra-European economic divide in Europe. This is surprising in the sense that one might expect inefficient centrally planned economies (CPEs) to rapidly improve static and dynamic efficiency (thereby raising growth rates) by switching to a market-based factor allocation. What we observe in reality is a sharp reduction of economic growth rates in the initial transformation stage. Moreover, predictions by many experts suggest only moderate economic growth in the medium term. Even in the case of the GDR, where official unemployment rates reached 17 per cent in early 1992 and then slightly declined there are no prospects of reducing unemployment rates quickly, and only moderate growth rates are expected in the 1990s. Only under favourable circumstances will a doubling of real output be possible in the ex-GDR in the 1990s. Since other ex-CMEA countries can not mobilize comparable external resource transfers it is all the more important that adjustment measures taken spur productivity increases and real output growth.

At the outset it seems clear that only a growth-oriented strategy of systemic transformation offers prospects for sustaining the transition. The new political competition among new parties in Eastern European economies naturally is conducive to extreme party programmes developed to gain profile in political competition; middle-of-the-road political programmes will be an exception in Eastern Europe as long as economic prosperity cannot be reached and the number of parties is not reduced to a few competitors.

Modernization Needs

There is a strong need to modernize the capital stock and upgrade the stock of public infrastructure to accommodate a widening network of exchanging goods and services as well as to provide for a redirection of trade flows primarily towards Western Europe (instead of the formerly dominating East European trade orientation). The age structure of capital equipment in industry deteriorated in most CMEA countries in the 1970s and the 1980s; the share of assets under five years of age fell in Hungary from 41 per cent in 1980 to 29 per cent in 1988; in Poland the share dropped from 35 per cent in 1980 to 19 per cent in 1988; in the CSFR from 32 to 23 per cent. These figures and the figure of 29 per cent in the GDR in 1988 are clearly worse than in Western Europe, where the FRG recorded 40 per cent for the percentage share of equipment in industry under five years of age in 1988 (see Table A4). State firms in central and eastern Europe obviously suffered from declining reinvestment activities in the 1980s.

It is well-known that CMEA countries suffered from inefficient investment selection mechanisms. With investment-output ratios of 30-40 per cent which were 15-20 per cent above Western economies (with top values in Portugal and Spain: 29 and 25 per cent, respectively, in the early 1990s) socialist economies should have grown much faster than EC countries. Reality showed the contrary. Moreover, there were serious problems with the type of investment preferred which caused increasing environmental degradation. While in OECD countries about 1.5 per cent of GNP was devoted to pollution control devices in the 1980s, the ex-CMEA countries hardly reached 0.5 per cent, while emission levels were much higher than in Western market economies; in the ex-GDR environmental damages were higher than the absolute increase in net material product in the 1980s which suggests that effective value added was falling (Welfens, M. J., 1993). The socialist legacy of overinvestment and inefficient investment will be a burden for transformation for many years to come.

Table A4: Age Structure of Capital in Industry in Selected Countries
(per cent of capital equipment under five years of age)

	1975	1980	1985	1988
Hungary	41	41	28	29
CSFR	31	32	25	23
GDR	42	35	17	19
FRG	–	39		40

Source: UN Commission for Europe and Statistisches Bundesamt: OECD (1992), OECD Economic Surveys. Poland, Paris, 89.

Privatized firms can be expected to modernize capital equipment much faster than state-owned firms. Fear that the introduction of newer vintages of capital means rapidly rising unemployment is likely to delay the modernization of equipment in state-owned firms. However, facing increasing international competitiveness and aiming at increasing exports the countries of central and eastern Europe have to upgrade product quality and reduce costs by employing more modern capital equipment so that the amount of profitable output and exports can increase in the long term; the creation of new jobs and of more productive and better paid jobs is essential for a successful transformation process. In countries in which privatization proceeds rapidly one can anticipate faster modernization and higher as well as more productive investments than in slowly privatizing countries. To the extent that modernizing capital equipment requires rising imports of capital goods there is some risk that the trade balance transitorily could deteriorate since imports will rapidly rise, possibly before exports of more refined and diversified products will pick up significantly. Whether the political system can generate a comprehensive privatization programme and provide a framework under which foreign investment inflows will become a major contribution to gross capital formation depends on various aspects, some of which are directly related to the political system itself.

Political Distortions

Political distortions and conflicts can play a serious role since the starting point of transformation is an economy in which economic decisions were politicized very much.[11] The fundamental consensus in transforming economies is - given the lack of role models and the shock of transition - naturally weak and this together with political competition which is still emerging weakens the effectiveness of political control. This weak consensus basically calls all the more for a comprehensive role of market coordination.

A crucial bottleneck in Eastern Europe is the lack of institutions with established reputation. This means considerable uncertainty with respect to the formation of expectations, the size of information costs and the effectiveness of economic policy measures. The destruction of socialist institutions and the creation of new market-oriented institutions means that institutional chaos is characteristic in the first transformation stage. Here lies the enormous value of hooking up with existing multilateral institutions (to the extent that this has not happened before) because membership in international organizations serves as an anchor for institution building in the first critical stage of transformation. The faster the destruction of established institutions the greater the loss of natural advantages of domestic firms in their competition against foreign investors who normally have to learn about the complex environment of the host country, while domestic firms are all familiar with this setting.

For institutions to acquire reputation takes time or one would have to rely on imported institutional settings which would allow borrowing reputation by applying foreign models (*e.g.* the Deutsche Bundesbank model which is popular in Eastern Europe). A straightforward way to economize on information costs and save scarce political "consensus capital" is the import of institutional arrangements. One might indeed consider importing Western institutions *en bloc*, similar to the Meiji Japan that imported institutional subsets from Germany as a strategy to modernize its economy. Imitation of evolutionary processes took this *en bloc* form and then saved learning costs but left enough room to develop and adjust indigenous institutions - is there an optimal institutional import? Importing institutional arrangements can be a

---

[11] Fischer and Gelb (1990) emphasized that transformation is comprised of interdependent economic and political factors.

suitable way of reducing learning costs for transforming economies, but there is, of course, the risk that importing from various countries or systems can then lead to an institutional setting which is neither consistent nor efficiency enhancing.

If one would adopt an evolutionary perspective (Nelson and Winter, 1982; Dosi, 1988; Witt, 1990) of system building and thus emphasize on bounded rationality, learning and adjustment costs in an environment of changing technologies and preferences one would indeed find few arguments that suggest that a quick transformation process in the ex-CMEA countries could be possible at all. Before new institutions can be built, the old ones have to be destroyed and before people can successfully make use of new institutional arrangements they have to learn how to use these and how to coordinate and communicate efficiently under the new rules of the game. Finally, creating a market economy is itself a public good, so that nobody can be excluded from (most of) its benefits, but for each individual it is rational to try to avoid bearing part of the transition costs. Therefore one might find a situation in which many would actually like to proceed towards a market economy, while nobody actively supports this goal. Here external institutions - such as the IMF, the EC or the EBRD - are important because they can make financial support conditional on real progress on the way to a market economy, while it is clear for all important groups that, for example, rising imports will be only possible if an effective agreement with international organizations is reached. If the domestic economy is not competitive or (in the case of a small economy) if firms are not encouraged to adopt a world market orientation, requiring high shares of sales abroad and at least potential investment abroad, the benefits of coordination and communication in a market economy cannot be expected to be realized.

2. Subsidies and Distortions as a Core Problem for Transition

The final stage of the command economy is typically characterized by a host of economic distortions; there is a considerable socialist shadow economy, currency substitution and a monetary overhang as well as a thriving black currency market. There is neither a functional capital market able to price and bundle investment risk nor competitive goods markets which would ensure that basic criteria for efficiency are met. In all socialist economies there is also a host of subsidies which distort market allocation and which need to be reduced or eliminated. This reduces government expenditures in the short run but creates in the medium term the need to provide unemployment insurance benefits which will increase public expenditures in a period of falling or at least stagnating government revenues.

In the 1980s the CPEs in Eastern Europe recorded shares of government expenditures to GNP that were in the range of 55 to 60 per cent. Hence they were more than 15 percentage points higher than in Western Europe. If one takes into account that in Western Europe government interest payments amount to 3-5 per cent of GDP, whereas domestic credit financing plays no major role in Eastern Europe so far, the divergence in aggregate expenditure levels of government is even bigger. Moreover, the structure of expenditures is very different, where a crucial difference concerns subsidies.

In West European countries subsidies to enterprises reach between 2-5 per cent of GDP, while in Eastern European CPEs figures three times as high are observed. As the capital intensive industries received the lion's share of state subsidies the basic impact has been to subsidize capital intensive production. Taking into account the low capital productivity in most East European economies there is no reasonable economic justification for this subsidization. The fact that investment-GNP ratios in Eastern Europe were in the mid-1980s about 10 percentage points above the ratios observed in Western European market economies is mainly due to well organized political influences of heavy industry and the military-industrial complex in former CPEs. High and growing subsidies to the enterprise sector were a core problem of socialist economies and have created production structures that are not in line with relative economic opportunity costs.

In 1989 budgetary subsidies as a percentage of GDP ranged from 9.9 per cent in the USSR to 17.8 per cent in Bulgaria (Table A5). Subsidies to the enterprises rose in the 1980s in most former CPEs as did subsidies for foreign trade. Subsidies for consumers rose sharply in the CSFR in the 1980s when political pressure induced the government to hide rising costs behind rising consumer subsidies. With open reform discussions underway in Poland and Hungary, consumer subsidization could be reduced; however, the cases of Hungary and Poland were already extreme because in 1985 consumer subsidies amounted to more than 7 per cent. It is apparent that in the first transformation stage - in the early 1990s - subsidies were reduced. The transition to a market-based system did not induce short-term improvements in competitiveness, leading to reduced costs and lower subsidies; rather prices charged in the new market environment were raised to market-clearing prices (often at monopoly levels) and output was reduced.

Table A5: Budgetary Subsidies* Relative to GDP in Eastern Europe

B/Y = *budgetary subsidies relative to GDP;*
BC/Y subsidies to consumers (relative to GDP)
BE/Y subsidies to enterprises (relative to GDP);

		1980	1985	1988	1989	1990 est.	1991 est.
Bulgaria	B/Y	13.3	11.9	19.1	17.8	23.7	7.4
	BC/Y	1.2	1.4	1.6	1.6	4.2	.3
	BE/Y	12.1	10.5	17.5	16.2	19.5	7.0
CSFR		8.7	11.8	13.0	16.1	12.1	4.7
	BC/Y	2.3	5.5	5.8	7.7	4.9	1.2
	BE/Y	6.3	6.3	7.2	8.3	7.2	3.5
Hungary		19.8**	17.1	14.0	12.6	9.8	6.5
	BC/Y	9.0***	7.1	5.7	7.2	5.7	3.9
	BE/Y	9.7***	9.9	8.2	5.4	4.1	2.6
Poland		28.7	16.5	17.0	17.1	9.8	7.2
	BC/Y	9.8	7.3	9.0	7.4	3.4	2.5
	BE/Y	18.9	9.2	7.9	9.8	6.5	4.7
Average	CPE4	19.5**	14.3	15.8	15.9	13.9	6.4
USSR	B/Y	1.4**	1.8	9.3	9.9	>10	-

* except for the USSR this includes subsidy expenditures of most, or all, extrabudgetary funds. ** refers to 1981; *** refers to 1982; note: subsidies for foreign trade are not shown here.

Source: Holzmann, R. (1991), Budgetary Subsidies in Central and Eastern European Economies, Economic Systems, Vol. 15, 149-176; for the USSR: PlanEcon, Washington, D.C.

Reducing subsidies for existing firms could be not only useful in the sense of helping to make visible the true opportunity cost of production; it would also reduce the problem of government deficits. However, there is the question whether subsidies should not only be reduced but also generally reoriented in favour of the creation of new business enterprises. Competition creates a positive sum game which means that there are positive external effects - the most important positive externality of competition being the creation of economy-wide useful knowledge; i.e. there will be a higher expected future rate of innovation and economic growth if competition is increasingly based on new market entrants. Western experience shows that a dollar invested in smaller firms yields a higher R&D rate of return than big firms (though the latter may be superior in the diffusion process). Given the difficulty of demonopolization from above - i.e. dismemberment of big firms - one might subsidize the creation of new enterprises and hence the spread of Schumpeterian forces. Another step for increasing efficiency would be a competitive private banking system that would no longer show a positive bias in favour of established state-owned firms.

Lack of Adequate Bankruptcy Legislation
Sorting out non-viable enterprises is important for the expansion of efficient firms in ex-CMEA countries. Non-viable firms are a drag on government finance and obtain credits from commercial banks which otherwise would go to new firms. Only Hungary's Law on Bankruptcy which came into force on January 1992 seems to have worked through its clear prevision that companies must declare bankruptcy if they have liabilities that are more than 90 days overdue. Within two months from the beginning of the proceedings, the debtor must convene a "compromising negotiation" meeting among representatives of the company's directors. A Board of Creditors is formed by these representatives which finally decides to accept or reject the compromise agreement. Approval of all members of the Board who are present is a prerequisite for the rehabilitation plan to be approved and then ratified by the court. If an agreement is not achieved within 15 days, the court starts liquidation procedures. In late September 1992 Hungarian courts had registered 7,900 liquidation and 4,500 bankruptcy applications. The new law had induced a wave of bankruptcies whose number sharply increased until mid-1992 but thereafter stabilized at a lower level. Bankruptcies and liquidations filed by late September 1992 were equivalent to 9 per cent of Hungarian firms - 1/3 of employees, 24 per cent of production and 35 per cent of exports. Cases for which legal proceedings had begun represented for industry much smaller figures: 3.8 per cent of the number of firms, 5.4 per cent of net sales, 7.5 per cent of exports and about 10 per cent of employment; construction and industry were most affected, including some larger firms. About 60 per cent of judicially settled bankruptcy proceedings could be finalized through agreements on restructuring and reorganization. Registered liquidations represented about 20 per cent of commercial banks' claims on the business sector; registered bankruptcy cases which have not led yet to the initiation of liquidation procedures account for another 10 percentage points such that the impact of bankruptcies on banks could be serious. Proposals for an amendment of the bankruptcy law - suggesting the softening of the requirement that all creditors

have to agree on a restructuring plan and that financial institutions would be covered as well - are before the Hungarian Parliament (EBRD, 1993).

There is no comparable bankruptcy legislation in other ex-CMEA countries. The Czech legislation was delayed by the velvet divorce and cannot apply before mid-1993. Poland's legislation is unclear and it is also rarely applied because there is no clearly defined time span for overdue liabilities and because work councils can delay the decision of management to file for bankruptcy. Adequate bankruptcy procedures are important for all ex-CMEA countries, but beyond the problem of adequate legislation there is the practical problem of unemployment which could reduce the effectiveness of this legislation. Hence creating new jobs and new firms is quite important, but the initial situation in ex-CMEA countries favours existing firms, especially big ones.

Points of Departure
Eastern Europe is suffering from the shocks of systemic transformation, the collapse of regional trade - 1991 regional trade declined by almost 50 per cent - and the switch to world market prices. There is a comprehensive need for structural adjustment and catching-up with Western Europe. All this must happen in a period of increased global dynamics since international markets play a greater role than ever. Thus, on the one hand Eastern Europe is facing enormous challenges ahead; on the other hand new institutional arrangements for decentralized allocation, bold policy reforms and a sometimes still existing memory of the market economy as well as considerable external support are expected to provide the necessary assets for a successful transformation. The desired situation would be neither of the type encountered in the interwar period, when Eastern Europe also was comprised of new countries and a weakening regional trade network along with insufficient FDI inflows, misalignment and external debt problems (except for the CSFR) nor the type of scenarios akin to those in some Latin American countries in the 1980s. Instead one would hope that after a drastic short-term fall of output and employment sustaining and high economic growth could be reached which would provide jobs and rising economic prosperity. Reality so far is closer to the two unfavourable historical scenarios, except for the case of Hungary.

Basic problems of systemic transformation not only concern the build-up of a coherent set of market institutions, but there are also three fundamental problems:

(1) The switch to a market-based economy requires a new set of rules and institutions that contribute to economic efficiency *and* avoid distributive issues from dominating political decision-making. Changes in agents' economic attitudes are required that are difficult to impose. Profit maximization, flexibility and Schumpeterian entrepreneurship represent attitudes that used to be frowned upon - along with the lack of experienced managers there are major bottlenecks for the transformation to a thriving market economy. High visible income differentials are very difficult to accept for many, even if such differentials may be normal and at least temporarily necessary for capitalist development.

Since we know from Western societies that income conflicts are the more pronounced the smaller economic growth is, one should not be surprised to find that distributional issues could block systemic changes in East European transforming economies with a sharply shrinking cake in the short term and a population highly sensitive to open income differentials. Income distribution issues could block reforms that would improve efficiency and thereby economic growth in the long term. In a transition period with a visibly shrinking economic cake economic growth is quite important and this leads directly to the problem of efficiency. Competition in capital markets (in factor markets) as well as competition in goods markets is a necessary condition to ensure efficiency in an economy built upon private industry. Competition is difficult to organize in an economy whose starting point is a state-owned industry with oversized firms and inappropriate backward- and forward integration; supplier uncertainty in command economies encouraged firms' strategies to provide many services and produce lots of products that would be bought from the market within a functional market economy. While the consumer was in a weak position in CPEs his strong role in market economies will encourage investment of producing firms in an integrated distribution system. A competitive distribution system is important to ensure that the marginal rates of substitution are equal across individuals so that one condition for Pareto optimality is met (individuals are on the contract curve). Open markets and the elimination of monopolies is a second condition for efficiency, namely that output is in accordance with consumer preferences (marginal rate of substitution should be equal to the marginal rate of transformation). The third condition is most difficult to meet, namely to make sure that firms and the economy produce on the transformation curve which requires that factors are rewarded in accordance with the marginal product; in a medium term perspective this would also require that optimum plant sizes are realized. The latter condition clearly implies for Eastern Europe that most firms would be trimmed down and that firms often be split into several ones. However, given the crucial shortage of skilled management, it is doubtful that optimum plant sizes could be reached this way. As a remedy one may consider creating bigger markets and encouraging exports; if management represents a bottleneck factor export promotion might represent a socially cheaper form to adjust the balance between firm size and market size.

(2) High long term growth and favourable medium term growth expectations are a key to sustaining transformation. From this perspective stabilization should be evaluated under the heading "how does this promote economic growth?". There are three keys to economic growth:

a) the quantity and quality of factor endowments; the first is reduced by the partial obsolescence of the capital stock following the switch to new competitive environments and changing relative prices.

b) Economic coordination that is conducive to static and dynamic economic efficiency. Static efficiency would require competition and privatization such that firms would be price takers and the marginal product rule would hold for factor rewards, whereas dynamic efficiency in the sense of an optimal innovation rate would call require specific conditions for entrepreneurship and intrapreneurship; in the latter case, prices then would not be equal to marginal costs.

c) The time horizon of investors is crucial. If the time horizon of market participants is long, it is easier to finance investment projects that will bring about high productivity growth and hence high economic growth. Given political uncertainties and high inflation rates - bound to lead (as in OECD countries) to relatively short average maturities in the bond market - one will typically find short time horizons and many investment projects with no feasible financing. Real capital formation will then be lower and the type of investment less productivity-increasing than otherwise. Moreover, asset prices (irrespective of capital stock growth) will then be lower than in the case of political stability and longer time horizons since each firm is facing a more restricted set of investment options which reduce - following Myers (1977) and Pindyck (1991) - the value of firms. In a portfolio theoretical perspective the implication is that the demand for money will be lower than with higher values of firms such that a given money supply growth is more inflationary than otherwise. A special problem of transformation is that most firms have to be restructured, and in such a situation ordinary capital markets might be relatively inefficient in allocating capital because monitoring of company performance is so important.

Successful restructuring probably can be only monitored from within the firm, and hence banks - represented on the board of companies - might play a particular role in the transition process. This process is obviously burdened with high transaction costs (partly related to transitorily rising uncertainty as new rules are implemented and new institutions created) and very high information costs.

(3) There are crucial links between internal liberalization and external liberalization which have not received much attention so far: a) One may ask to what extent external liberalization can contribute to sustaining economic growth and to what extent risks for economic stabilization emerge at the same time from external liberalization; b) There is the question whether existing external economic relations with market economies can be a catalyst for change towards a market economy in the whole system. In relatively small countries with mobile skilled and unskilled labour, a relatively strong tradables sector could play such a positive role, but mobility requires that housing shortages do not play a major role. Hungary and the CSFR are candidates in this respect, whereas the former USSR clearly is the opposite case. External liberalization can play the role of a partial substitute if import competition can galvanize domestic producers - the role of import competition is certainly limited in the case of nontradables, but foreign direct investment could play a role here.

Among the smaller East European economies only Poland and Hungary had considerable trade links with Western Europe. Hungary was the only country which already in 1985 had some competitive foreign trade - about 300 firms were active then and this number had increased by 1991 to about 19,000, where smaller firms accounted for an overproportionate share of export growth and hence decisively contributed to rising exports. Hungarian entrepreneurs are already creating a network in trade and investment with ethnic Hungarians in neighbouring countries; Hungary could indeed be the only former CMEA country which exports both capital and entrepreneurship to Eastern Europe.

2.1 Capital Shortage, Lack of Entrepreneurship and Inflexibility

A major problem of systemic transformation is that it makes a large part of the capital stock obsolete - somehow similar to the energy supply shocks of the 1970s in the OECD. However, in contrast to the oil price shocks of the 1970s in Western Europe the East European case represents a situation in which new capital goods and innovations cannot be generated mainly from the domestic resource base, but have to be imported. Moreover, there is no option for an easy recycling of petro dollars which could finance a large replacement of capital in central and eastern Europe.

Since more market transactions will occur in combination with a more decentralized and diversified network of firms a much better infrastructure (transportation, telecom etc.) will be needed. Moreover, East European infrastructure was traditionally oriented to the East (towards the USSR), while in the 1990s a strong westward orientation will be necessary. Hence there is an enormous shortage of capital in Eastern Europe, and this has to be financed. Moreover, there is a critical lack of entrepreneurship in all ex-CMEA countries, except - it seems - for Hungary. The lack of entrepreneurship is most crucial in the former USSR. For the whole of Eastern Europe (including the former USSR) there is a strong need for foreign investment in part because it would also bring entrepreneurship to Eastern Europe. The formation and nurturing of a domestic entrepreneurial class is of paramount importance for a growth-oriented systemic transformation. New business establishments will show a high failure rate - as in all market economies (in West Germany 50 out of 100 firms survive the first five years and then have on average 5.5 employees). Nurturing Schumpeterian forces, namely new private firms, will be the more difficult politically, the greater the opportunities are for huge windfall profits during systemic transition. Social conflicts could erode the potential for promoting entrepreneurship; such conflicts could arise if there were several entrepreneurs which grew rich, while the majority of the population suffered from unemployment and real income losses. There are steps to avoid the problem at least partly: reinvestment incentives that would help to avoid visible high consumption of the *nouveaux riches*; competition that would encourage melting away profits from first-movers and the avoidance of government created uncertainties which will raise the risk premium on the side of investors and entrepreneurs. To the extent that gradualist approaches broaden the group of would-be entrepreneurs - because a larger group would be able to learn about gradual changes than those who understand the opportunities of shock reform strategies - one may consider gradualism as a valuable element for a strategy which intends to create a broader based capitalism.

Eastern Europe has to revive its traditions of entrepreneurship and to promote modern management sciences and engineering. This process will take time, but the conclusion to be drawn simply is that one should start early on in the transformation process - and on a broad scale - to invest in the market economy; the founding of new universities, the systematic improvement of locational advantages to attract foreign capital and entrepreneurs as well as the encouragement of citizens to study abroad (although there is a great risk of a considerable brain drain) would be possible measures. Inflexible economic structures are a major problem in Eastern Europe. Modernizing industry means changing economic structures, and this requires regional and structural change. Regional mobility is low in Eastern Europe so far and little can be done in the short run to remedy this problem. A better infrastructure and a boom in the construction industry could lead the way to increasing regional mobility. The inflexibility of attitudes and insufficient willingness of people in the administration to take any risks in decision-making (to prefer doing nothing than doing anything wrong) are serious impediments for the East European transition. Foreign investors will press for reforms in the right direction. However, one cannot rule out that foreign investors could also cooperate in order to restrict competition in host country markets; the automobile industry in Latin America is interesting in this context, where host country governments sometimes have eased the restriction of competition by raising tariffs on imports. Moreover, foreign firms could make investments dependent on obtaining higher import tariffs, and one should indeed anticipate this, if the growth of host country markets is slow and export prospects are limited. An overvalued currency - the government's resistance against a devaluation - can therefore indirectly contribute to increased protectionist pressures. The resilience of the (privatized) industry will influence the propensity to resort to protectionist measures in ex-CMEA countries.

The modern capitalist corporation is no longer the owner-managed firm that many emerging capitalist giants used to be a hundred years ago or so. However, one should not underestimate the advantage of Western economies which enjoy the benefit of firms that have undergone a certain evolution over time and which nowadays are run by management.[12] Moreover, small firms - with capital held by families - still play a very crucial role in many Western economies. The internal capital market of family owned enterprises often replaces in an efficient manner the allocation of financial funds via anonymous capital markets. More long term decisions can be taken, and high productivity gains at the microeconomic level could result from this. The West European tradition of entrepreneurship will be difficult to transfer to the later-industrializing economies of Eastern Europe (the ex-CSFR is an exception). The lack of Schumpeterian family forces and traditions makes it all the more

---

[12] For the relevance of entrepreneurship see e.g. Lydall (1991).

necessary that privatization is organized in an efficient way and that emerging capital markets, tax laws and the framework for trade and international investment encourage efficient long term investment and innovation decisions. Effectively taking advantage of international specialization and technology transfers is another decisive challenge for the ex-CMEA countries.

2.2 Foreign Economic Liberalization in Eastern Europe

Establishing currency convertibility is necessary if the potential benefits from economic opening up are to be realized in central and eastern Europe. In the ex-CMEA area countries face specific problems in moving towards convertibility because convertibility requires that a set of conditions be fulfilled:[13] sound macroeconomic policies are necessary; excess demand situations in the goods markets have to be removed because otherwise rapidly rising imports could lead to a depletion of exchange reserves (hence price liberalization must come first) and the institutional framework of the economy must be such that firms and individuals are encouraged and able to respond to market signals; the latter would imply that a trade deficit stimulates either endogenous adjustments or that policy measures could effectively bring about corrective adjustment impulses so that market participants will not speculate on an ever-widening excess demand in the foreign exchange market.

2.2.1 Convertibility and the Exchange Rate Regime

Convertibility requires in any case that there is an adequate level of foreign exchange reserves so that countries must realize considerable current account surpluses over extended periods of time or external indebtedness has to increase as governments borrow "sufficient liquidity reserves" for their central bank abroad.

All former CMEA countries - except for the CSFR and Romania - are heavily indebted abroad. To the extent that high foreign indebtedness is reinforced over time by modernization needs that have to be financed by commercial foreign credits, there will be specific risks and problems for achieving convertibility and maintaining a stable exchange rate regime;

---

[13] Greene and Isard (1991) emphasize the problem of convertibility.

exchange rate stability will not be the first problem encountered after unifying the exchange rate, but whether a sustainable exchange rate regime can be defined which sets a reliable framework for international trade and capital flows. Private investors need the guidance of world markets, but without clear international relative price signals privatization as well as foreign economic liberalization would yield limited benefits in the transforming economies.

With a considerable monetary overhang in the first transition period and few chances to switch to credible anti-inflation policies in the medium term, a system of fixed exchange rates clearly would be conducive to massive misalignment. There would be a real appreciation of the currency, thereby undermining prospects for increasing exports rapidly. With trade deficits rising massive speculations on a currency depreciation would set in and sooner or later force the central bank either to adjust the parity, to impose import restrictions or capital account restrictions or to switch to floating exchange rates. Fixed exchange rates might have some merits for a limited adjustment period, but it seems clear that the massive need for structural adjustment and the desired emergence of financial markets make a flexible exchange rate the appropriate regime for many years to come. Whether or not a crawling peg - as established in Poland with a maximum monthly devaluation rate of 1.8 per cent (as of October 1991) - is a suitable and stable institutional arrangement is an open question.

External convertibility was established at first in West Europe's post-World War II reconstruction and international integration attempts; internal convertibility - that is allowing domestic residents unrestricted access to foreign exchange - was introduced only in the 1960s, and capital account restrictions remained widespread in Western Europe (the latter type of restrictions increased in the 1970s as a by-product of economic policies reacting to the oil price shocks via selective interventionism). In Eastern Europe internal convertibility will have to be introduced first because otherwise the existing large amount of foreign exchange could not be channelled into the banking system; for highly indebted countries this also can help to ease the official foreign exchange constraint. Moreover, monetary policy cannot be geared towards anti-inflationary strategies as long as foreign exchange still serves as an important medium of exchange in the domestic economy; the effective money supply under currency substitution consists of the domestic stock of money, M, and the amount of foreign exchange in the country M* (expressed in foreign currency units) times the nominal exchange rate e.[14]

The reforming economies may, however, adopt some restrictions as to the type of transactions allowed, and, of course, the governments in central and eastern European economies could impose restrictions on the capital account. At least with respect to FDI inflows this, however, does not make sense. Whether one could attract a significant amount of FDI without allowing repatriation of profits and investments is doubtful. Portfolio investments will have to be restricted at least initially because a broader convertibility of the currency that would include capital flows fully requires that there is a functional domestic banking system which offers an internationally competitive return. Establishing a viable private banking system at home requires time. Moreover, banks and investment houses have to build up reputations, learn the new rules of the game in the emerging market economies and explore the widening opportunities for investment in the economy. Hence convertibility has to be restricted for pragmatic reasons at first in a way that current account transactions are possible, while some capital flows are impaired. But even this modest aim is not easily realized.

With a considerable monetary overhang in the first stage (as in Poland) a fixed exchange rate regime can provide an anchor for monetary policy in the sense that it imposes some discipline on economic policy. However, a high inflationary momentum then will quickly translate into a real appreciation of the currency. This may not be a crucial problem in the medium term if the initial depreciation was very strong (policy overshooting) and if supply side policies increase the supply elasticity of the tradables sector considerably within 1-2 years; what is crucial is that the tradables sector itself must be increased and this is easier with a real depreciation. If disinflation is well underway there seems to be no reason not to switch to flexible exchange rates which are useful in a period of rapid supply side adjustment as well as during considerable changes of asset prices and interest rates. If high sustainable economic growth is achieved there might be impulses for an expansion of the nontradables sector.[15]

---

[14] Hence with $eM*/(M+eM*)$ reaching a magnitude of 20-50 per cent, each nominal devaluation - a rise of e - would raise the effective money supply. Say, the devaluation rate were 100 per cent, then the nominal money supply would increase by 25 per cent if foreign exchange represented 50 per cent of all money balances; and this would occur with M and M* being constant. Since external convertibility is necessary to effectively organize trade that involves foreign firms which expect to be able to legally use their own currency for current account transactions, one has to establish both external and internal convertibility at the same time.

[15] Kravis' and Lipsey's (1988) empirical findings for market economies clearly suggest that with rising per capita incomes the relative price ratio (P^N/P^T) will increase. Promoting industries with static and

Capital Account Liberalization

The liberalization of the capital account is critical in the case of short term capital flows that might be highly volatile and subject to speculative forces both at home and abroad. Some liberalization, required for trade financing, is, however, absolutely necessary. The natural focus of liberalizing the capital account in Eastern Europe concerns foreign direct investment flows (and, relating to the current account, profit repatriation). In Eastern Europe real interest rates were below market-clearing levels and there used to be an excess demand in the loan market, above all in the form of investment projects planned exceeding private households' and firms' savings. The state planning bureaucracy would exploit credit market rationing to some extent and expand bureaucratic powers by discretionary intervention in favour of well-connected firms; part of the excess demand situation would be solved by the state banking system providing subsidized loans - often effectively at zero interest rates which amounts to printing more money. This mechanism of soft credit financing - Kornai dubbed it the soft budget constraint - must change in the course of transformation in which a two-tier banking system with competitive private banks is to be established. As long as most credits still go through state-owned banks even the presence of many foreign banks, as in Poland, can contribute little to building a functional credit market that selects investment projects on efficiency and profitability grounds and thereby contributes to economic growth.

2.2.2 Trade Liberalization

Transformational and Economic Role of Trade Liberalization

Trade liberalization is expected to support the transformation process in three ways:

- Removing import restrictions and export barriers raises economic welfare. Only in the case of a very inelastic demand abroad could the terms of trade weaken so much with rising output that "immiserizing growth", that is a negative welfare effect, would occur.
- Import liberalization could expose the tradables sector to competitive pressure from the world market such that the lack of dismemberment of giant state

---

dynamic economies of scale in the tradables sector - an apparent strategy of Japan's catching up process - could well counterbalance such a tendency working against a sustaining internationalization of industry.

firms or a slow pace in privatization and in the formation of new enterprises would not result in as much monopolistic pricing as otherwise. Imported intermediate goods and capital goods should also allow firms to effectively take advantage of international specialization and to thereby reduce costs and improve product quality or diversity both for domestic and foreign markets.

- Export liberalization could not only allow the exploitation of static economies of scale - much emphasized in the CMEA - but also the possibility to take advantage of dynamic scale economies in R&D intensive industries in which high price cost margins are sustainable in world markets. Dynamic scale economies mean that marginal costs fall as a rising are cumulated output has been generated, where learning effects, such as in the chip or the aerospace industry play a major role. Such dynamic opportunities to improve the terms of trade require that firms move down the respective industry's learning curve relatively fast in order to position themselves successfully in the field of international competitors which all aim to realize big output volumes at home and abroad. Firms from smaller industrialized market economies, such as the Netherlands, Switzerland or Korea, have proved that even firms with a small home market can exploit dynamic economies of scale provided they have a strong focus upon world markets. An export-promotion policy might actually be adequate to encourage many firms from the smaller ex-CMEA countries to expose themselves to international market forces and to thereby improve their entrepreneurial qualities over time; this is not only crucial for exports, but also for the transfer of know-how back to the home country.

The liberalization of trade is not without risk for East European economies since internal convertibility is introduced at the same time and external convertibility is at least envisaged. If liberalization in combination with privatization of industry and hence decentralized import decision-making would lead to imports increasing much faster than exports a strong nominal (and real) devaluation will occur which could mean "imported inflation" and, more generally, a boost to inflationary expectations for which import prices will play an increasing role as import-GNP ratios should rise in the course of economic opening up.[16]

---

[16] Alternatively, the central bank could run down its foreign exchange reserves and hope that other measures rapidly restore export growth or the central bank would raise interest rates to attract higher capital inflows. Higher interest rates would reduce profitable investment and a rising stock of short-term foreign capital would make the country more vulnerable to speculation and, in the case of flexible rates, to exchange rate overshooting that could disturb the real adjustment process.

There is ample theoretical evidence that trade can be an important engine of growth (*e.g.* Riedel, 1990). The developments of exports and imports in Eastern Europe in 1989 and 1990 indicate that large changes are possible in the context of systemic reforms and foreign economic liberalization. Poland's hard currency exports in 1990 increased by almost 40 per cent while imports increased by only 2.7 per cent. However, this does not indicate a sustaining improvement in international competitiveness since at least part of the Polish export boom is explained by the firms' strategy of dissolving hoarded factor inputs which were a system-specific trait of socialist economies; moreover, the collapse of domestic demand and the removal of export restrictions in combination with monopolies in industry can explain the export boom. Hungary also recorded a double digit increase in exports in 1990. It is certainly true that the end of the CMEA encouraged a regional reorientation of trade in all East European economies. Hungary, Romania and the CSFR recorded double digit growth rates of imports.

2.2.3 External Liberalization, Inflation and Fiscal Policy

With the envisaged external liberalization a host of new problems will be faced by East European economies. We will take a look at three major problems: (i) the liberalization of export markets; (ii) the liberalization of import markets; and (iii) the implications of liberalization for economic policy.

If the country liberalizes exports, the monopoly situation in the domestic market is likely to lead to additional price increases as a consequence of opening up the economy. This paradoxical result is easily explained. Each monopoly faces a given world market price p^* which represents marginal revenue abroad; one may, of course, raise the question whether firms - often still strongly influenced by worker councils - maximize profits or whether decision-making is shaped by a more complex set of goals (including safeguarding employment). However, here we stay as simple as possible and assume that profit maximization is the representative characteristic of privatized firms. Indeed, the more firms that have been privatized and the greater the share of foreign investors in overall investment, the more one may expect that profit maximization is a meaningful assumption.

Profit maximization behaviour requires that marginal revenue at home be equal to the marginal revenue abroad. Hence the interception of the world price line p^* with the domestic marginal revenue schedule will be realized so that the new Cournot point implies an increased monopoly price. The Treasury could indeed be interested in maintaining such a situation to the extent that tax revenues from state-owned monopolies could be relatively high under such circumstances. Hence there could be conflicts of interest between the Treasury and the authorities in charge of privatization or of competition policy. Even foreign investors could be more interested in buying a monopoly firm than having the opportunity to buy only a single firm in an environment of considerable domestic competition.

Supply Elasticity and the Role of Momentum
From the theoretical analysis it seems clear that there must at least be a comprehensive scenario for privatization-cum-competition at the beginning of designing a macroeconomic stabilization and liberalization plan in formerly socialist command economies. The experience with trade liberalization in developing countries suggests (Papageorgiou *et al.*, 1990) that a critical minimum momentum is needed to successfully implement liberalization programmes. A similar reasoning holds in a more general sense for Eastern Europe. Only if a comprehensive package of internal and external liberalization measures is adopted in the initial stage of transformation can one expect a sustaining transformation process.

Import Competition
Foreign economic liberalization in socialist economies offers a host of problems. There is a limited range of liberalization models and policy experiences which can be considered as useful.[17] Developing country experience can provide some useful insight; however, one cannot overlook various system-specific problems. Price distortions in socialist economies are much stronger, the role of currency substitution often greater and the problem of big state monopolies more widespread than in most developing countries. McKinnon (1991) emphasized early on the problem of negative value-added evaluated at world market prices, and Hare and Hughes (1991) provide empirical evidence for this phenomenon in Hungary, Poland and the CSFR. The required microeconomic reorganization and the scope of structural adjustment in the economy at large can thus be considerable, and it certainly is time-consuming. With import liberalization the window of opportunities for international outsourcing will increase, and to the extent that the export sector

---

[17] See Köves and Marer (1991) for a collection of different views. For an analysis of the traditional trade organization in the CMEA see Wolf (1988).

can successfully expand the efficiency of the whole economic production process the economy will gain from a better integration into the international division of labour and know-how. Not only imports from Western Europe could rapidly increase but also those from many NICs which provide cheaper products of similar quality to many suppliers from the OECD countries.

As regards FDI in Eastern Europe there are four critical issues:

- (1) Given the fact that FDI in developing countries is heavily concentrated in a few countries one must raise the question how strong the regional concentration of FDI in Eastern Europe could be; improving the infrastructure in the region could even further contribute to regional concentration effects.

- (2) Can FDI significantly contribute to capital formation at all? So far only in Hungary where FDI in 1990 and 1991 accounted for 10 and 15 per cent of new capital formation, respectively, did one have a case of significant FDI (for comparison: Taiwan had a sustaining share of FDI in total investment of 10 per cent in the 1960s). While Hungary recorded inflows of $ 1 billion and $ 1.5 billion in 1990 and 1991, Poland had insignificant inflows of around $ 500 million which looks even worse in a comparison on a per capita basis. The situation in the CSFR was somewhat better, but in Russia, the Ukraine, Romania and Bulgaria FDI inflows were very small on a per capita basis.

- (3) Whether FDI can be attracted to a sufficient degree depends upon the host countries' locational advantages to which stable economic policies, improved infrastructure as well as a competitive domestic supplier industry can contribute. The latter depends much on rapid progress in the privatization of industry and the formation of new firms. A factor determining the acceptable amount is the regional distribution of source countries. For most countries in Eastern Europe a dominating share of German FDI is difficult to accept in the medium term (this might change in the long run), both because of fear of economic dominance by the new Germany and for historical reasons. Only in Hungary are German investors not at the top of the list. A diversified FDI basis would be important for Eastern Europe. This points to the necessity to involve the world's three main sources of FDI, namely the US, the UK and Japan. British and even more so Japanese investments play no significant role in Eastern Europe so far. If from a source country perspective one considers FDI outflows to Eastern Europe as an investment into the formation of market economies one might consider as useful some "managed international capital" flows in the sense of urging Japanese firms to assume a fair share of FDI as part of international burden sharing.

- (4) The relative share of benefits from FDI will be critical for organizing a sustaining and significant share of foreign investment in Eastern Europe. Given long established East European resistances against FDI and the transitorily growing distributional conflicts in the reforming economies, this issue seems to be of particular importance. The traditional analysis (in the MacDougall diagram) suggests that in the capital importing country capital income will fall and workers' income will increase.

3. International Investment, Liberalization and Economic Integration

Western Europe has witnessed in the second half of the 1980s a rising flow of cross-border investments and a new wave of joint ventures. This is partly due to the formation of the single EC markets but this also fits into some more general developments observed in the global economy in the 1980s and early 1990 (UNCTC, 1988; Welfens, 1990a; Economist, 1992). The formation of bigger international firms has its risks with regard to the intensity of competition in the long term. However, in general rising international capital flows suggest that the benefits from regional economic integration are reinforced by economies of scale or scope at the level of the firm.

3.1 Growing Quantitative and Qualitative Significance of FDI

The 1980s witnessed an increasing role of FDI worldwide and some reconcentration of FDI flows on intra-OECD capital flows. In 1990 global FDI outflows reached $ 225 bill. - for an outward stock of $ 1.7 trillion, where Japan, the US, the UK, Germany and France accounted for outflows of $ 48, 21, 35, 23 and 35 bill., respectively (UNCTC, 1992, p. 16). MNCs which were considered with mistrust in the 1970s by host countries have become important and welcome catalysts for modernization, tax revenues, jobs and exports (UNCTC, 1992).

FDI increased three times as fast as world trade and four times as fast as world output in the period 1983-90, and in 1991 the largest 100 MNCs, excluding banking and finance, represented $ 3.1 trillion of worldwide assets, where 1.2 trillion was outside firms' respective home countries (Economist, 1993). Some 35,000 MNCs were recorded in 1990, when the US, Japan, Germany and Switzerland accounted for about half of all MNCs worldwide; in

1970 the UN counted only some 7,000 MNCs worldwide. The 35,000 MNCs had some 150,000 foreign affiliates in 1990. In 1991 central and eastern Europe accounted for 10,900 affiliates, with 2,200 affiliates in Hungary, Poland and the CIS. With 3,527 Romania recorded the highest number, while the CSFR and Bulgaria recorded only 592 and 117, respectively. All these figures will quickly change over time and certainly the number of affiliates should not be confused with the significance of FDI amounts; high Polish and Romanian numbers of MNC affiliates go along with FDI inflows smaller than those in Hungary, and this points to a strong role of small foreign companies as investors and the absence of major MNCs. Reversing decades of investment autarchy central and eastern European countries have started to welcome and support FDI inflows. In early 1992 foreign investment registrations in Hungary reached 11,000 and foreign equity capital of $ 2.1 bill. In the CIS the number of registered foreign investments was 5,400 which represented some $ 6 bill. (UNCTC, 1992, p.30). All other ex-CMEA countries had under $ 1 bill. accumulated FDI in 1992.

Table A6: FDI in Selected NICs in the Second Half of the 1980s

	GDCF**	Private fixed inv.	Assets*	Foreign-owned share in Manufac- turing inv.	Assets* in manuf.	Service assets*
Hong Kong	19	n.a.	18	n.a.	n.a.	n.a.
Korea, R.	2	n.a.	n.a.	19-31***	n.a.	n.a.
Malaysia	10	5-10***	19***	n.a.	n.a.	n.a.
Mexico	9	n.a.	n.a.	n.a.	76***	34
Philipp.	9	n.a.	19***	n.a.	32***	21
Taiwan	4	4***	n.a.	6	n.a.	n.a.
Thailand	5	4-10***	16	n.a.	83	43

* 1986-89, ** 1986, *** 1984-86 (for Malaysia: 1988; for Philippines: 1987, Taiwan: 1987-88, Thailand: 1986-88)

Source: UNCTC; Lee/Ramstetter and Schive/Ju, both in Ramstetter, E., ed. (1991), Direct Foreign Investment in Asia's Developing Economies and Structural Change in the Asia-Pacific Region, Boulder: Westview.

In the 1970s and the 1980s FDI played a very important role as an engine of growth not only in OECD countries, but in some developing countries as well. There are various caveats as regards suggesting analogies between NICs' economic catching-up and potential catching-up in transforming economies of the ex-CMEA area. One may, however, try to draw at least some tentative conclusions from the contrast between inward-oriented Latin American development strategies which were all outright failures as regards technological modernization and the success of outward-oriented Asian NICs.[18] Particularly the Asian NICs benefited from FDI inflows which accounted for 5-10 per cent of gross capital formation in selected NICs (see Table A6); Hong Kong with a foreign share of 20 per cent and Korea with a share of 2 per cent represent two polar cases, where the Korean case probably understates the role of foreign capital because weak forms of foreign ownership - especially subcontracting - are not taken into account here. About 20 per cent of assets were owned by foreign MNCs which can be important for both the service industry and manufacturing industry. MNCs' impact on productivity growth, rising export proceeds and competitive pressure can be much stronger than suggested by the foreign share in gross capital formation. This holds because MNCs typically are active in technology intensive industries and are embedded in international production networks which are conducive to trade and international technology flows.

A study on the role of FDI in the Republic of Korea argues that during the second half of the 1970s the share of the growth of value-added accounted for by foreign production ranged from 5 to 10 per cent, while the foreign share of the growth of value-added in manufacturing was 16-45 per cent (UNCTC, 1992). A recent study on Korea concludes that foreign firms contributed almost half the new capital in those industries - electrical machinery and transportation equipment - in the period 1984-86 which was particularly important for Korea's rapid export-led growth. As regards economic growth and exports it obviously is important that firms with significant export orientation and strong technology spillovers are attracted. Economic policy in Korea was not so much outward-oriented in the sense of encouraging the expansion of the tradables sector as it was supporting technological catching up by state R&D programmes, preferential credit allocation by state-controlled banks and massive investment in higher education (Song, 1991). Similar approaches and a mix of export support and import protection were employed in Taiwan which, like Korea, also benefitted from US aid, while Singapore combined free trade policies and FDI promotion successfully. The question of trade policies and the access to big export markets will be crucial for the growth of private enterprises in transforming economies in central and eastern Europe.

---

[18] For some estimates of the effects of integrating the ex-CMEA into the world economy see Collins and Rodrick, 1991.

3.2 Liberalization and Economic Integration

Regional economic integration of the markets for goods and services has been beneficial for Western Europe in particular; the opening up of service industries - occurring only in the framework of the EC 1992 project - is important in EC countries not only because service industries represent such a high share of output and employment, but because it enhances competition and internationalization of banks and other financial intermediaries. This in turn should make financial markets and the market for corporate control more efficient; there is, of course, also some risk that these advantages that will concern both the service sector and the manufacturing industry, could be offset by increased financial volatility or instability. Capital mobility has strongly increased in the 1980s.

Eastern Europe has suffered from regional disintegration and in the case of the ex-USSR from the rise of non-tariff and tariff barriers in trade between CIS members. The downward spiral of regional trade in the ex-CMEA certainly has created negative effects on employment and income. There are no comprehensive attempts to revitalize regional trade in the ex-CMEA area.

Following the new growth theory and traditional arguments for economic integration, one can expect positive effects of economic integration which allows static and dynamic economies of scale to be exploited. Given the positive experience of the EC where up to 1/2 of a percentage point of economic growth is accounted for by integration effects (Coe and Kruger, 1990) one may also raise the question whether or not regional economic integration could play a distinct role in central and eastern Europe. Whether business interests in central and eastern Europe will be supportive of initiatives for regional integration will be interesting to observe. International business interests might well become a counterbalance against the revival of political nationalism that favours disintegration rather than integration.[19]

If there were a rapidly rising private business sector in Eastern Europe this could help to reestablish regional economic links among some ex-CMEA countries. Besides rising trade links emerging within a new spatial structure of specialization and cooperation, cross-border investments could flow into neighbouring countries. For example, Polish firms are already investing in the

---

[19] To some extent disintegration might ease the task of integrating regions into the world economy, namely in the case of the ex-USSR. Huge countries such as the USSR - or China - tend to emphasize the domestic market over the size of the world market, while smaller countries (the Netherlands or Switzerland are examples) are strongly interested in maintaining free trade.

former USSR and Russian firms have some investment stakes in Hungary and Poland. It is not clear whether a private business sector is naturally more protectionist than state-owned firms, but if private firms develop a growing network of international input sourcing and sales, the growth of private internationalized business activities would support lobbying efforts for economic integration rather than for protectionism.

A rising outflow of capital as well as a rising inflow of capital have been observed in some West European countries after privatization. In the 1980s France was an interesting case in this respect. State-owned firms often face restricted asset menus abroad but are also less flexible in selling unprofitable lines of business to domestic or foreign investors. In this respect privatization in Western Europe is of double significance for central and eastern Europe: (i) it provides at least some valuable experiences in privatization, and (ii) it increases the pool of firms that might be interested in joint ventures or FDI in eastern and central European economies.

Integration with Western Europe

The CMEA dissolved in 1991 and at least two ex-CMEA countries themselves have disintegrated: the USSR and the CSFR which emerged under different auspices from the end of World War I. Before 1913 the whole of Europe was a market economy which had a strong East-West divide concerning industrialized countries in western and central Europe (including Czechoslovakia, but excluding Spain and Portugal) and the underindustrialized economies in Eastern Europe. After World War II Eastern Europe - including the then emerging GDR - turned communist (some only in 1948/49). Headed by the USSR the group of communist countries formed the Council of Mutual Economic Assistance which soon became the antipode of the EC which - partly inspired by common fear of Western countries of communism - had been created in 1957 as a political approach to overcome nationalism in Western European market economies. With ups and downs EC integration made considerable progress over time and achieved in 1969 the state of a customs union. The removal of nontariff barriers came on the agenda in 1988 when the Rome Treaties were modified in order to establish the single market - free of nontariff barriers - by 1993. In 1990 the first stage towards monetary integration was undertaken by EC countries whose membership had increased over time as some EFTA countries and later Greece and Spain joined the Community. With the demise of the CMEA and the shrinking of the EFTA the transforming economies of the ex-CMEA are looking for new orientations and trade and investment links in the

EC. Hungary, Poland and the ex-CSFR signed association agreements in November 1991 and in early 1993 Bulgaria and Romania followed. At least some former CMEA countries consider future EC membership as desirable although the Maastricht Treaty certainly has raised the barriers to entry into this wealthy club. The EFTA option is not attractive for most of the smaller countries in the ex-CMEA area because many EFTA countries have submitted applications for EC membership. This concerns Finland, Norway, Sweden and Austria, although not all of these countries might finally join the EC.[20] The EFTA has concluded free trade agreements - liberalizing trade in industrial goods and services - with the smaller ex-CMEA countries, but neither free movement of labour and capital nor common regional policies are envisaged in the relations between EFTA and ex-CMEA countries. Whether Eastern European economies will finally exploit economies of integration by becoming full members of the EC or just "EC satellites" in the European Economic Area orbit is an open question. Membership in the EEA does not give the advantages of participation in the EC political decision-making process, but allows the countries to be an implicit part of the EC single market with the four basic freedoms of free movement of capital, labour, goods and services; there are also some common rules for competition policies, including rules for subsidization.[21]

In the 1980s and the early 1990s Western European countries have indeed reinforced market forces and the role of the private sector as many privatizations and deregulation projects show; initiatives were undertaken both at the national and supranational EC level - sometimes because of ideological or economic motives but after the Maastricht Treaty even more because of fiscal reasons. Unprofitable state firms are a drag on government's resources and two entry requirements for monetary union - a deficit-GNP ratio of not more than 3 per cent and a debt-GNP ratio of not more than 60 per cent - indeed have pushed Italy, Spain, Belgium, France and other countries to study new opportunities for privatization that should ultimately translate into less subsidies and higher future tax revenues. Hence the developments in Western Europe certainly encourage in a general manner the move of ex-CMEA countries to privatizing state firms. However, while privatizing firms in EC countries means doing so in a growing single market, privatization in central and eastern Europe is taking place in an environment of (transitorily) shrinking markets. Integration

---

[20] The Swiss application is politically not effective as the referendum on the membership in the European Economic Area did not turn out to be a majority in late 1992.

[21] See on EC aspects of the transformation process Welfens (1993b).

with the EC would offer better access to the huge West European markets on the one hand; on the other hand, firms in transforming economies would become exposed even more to competitive pressure from EC firms.[22]

The politico-economic situation in transforming economies represents a host of challenges. Privatizing firms in an efficient manner to generate prosperity and stability is still the biggest challenge in the ex-CMEA. Theory should provide a rationale for adequate approaches.

---

[22] Firms in small countries - representing small home markets - may face difficulties to survive independently in huge oligopolistic markets; the crisis of so many Dutch firms in the early 1990s seems to suggest both for Western Europe and for Eastern Europe that a big home market still is an asset in international competition in the tradables industry.

Appendix A

Table A7: Change of Labor Productivity (g_A) in Industry

	g_A			
	1990	1991	1992	1993*
Czech Republic	-0.3	-14.4	-2.3	-1.3
Hungary	-3.9	-10.2	-1.4	13.8
Poland	-20.3	-5.2	13.7	11.0
Slovak Republic	-1.1	-14.6	-10.2	-8.6
Bulgaria	-12.0	-5.5	-7.0	-
Romania	-4.4	-15.0	-13.4	6.8
Russia	3.4	-6.4	-16.5	-
Ukraine	2.6	-2.3	-3.4	-

* January - September

Source: HUNYA, G. et al. (1994), Central and Eastern Europe: Uneven Recovery, Research Paper No. 204, Wien: WIIW.

Chapter B

Why Privatize? The Case of a Single Firm in Market Economy. Theoretical Model and Empirical Evidence

1. Theoretical Analysis of Property Rights Transfer

In this section of Chapter B we are interested in only one of the three possible ways of improving economic efficiency, namely that of changing the ownership structure; that was why we shall start with investigating the direct effect of the transfer of property rights as analysed by **a standard, property rights/agency problem-based theory of privatization** in which the markets for property rights and managers decisively determine the way in which the agency problem is solved.

However, the three determinants of economic efficiency: ownership, regulation and competition, are not independent of each other and even though any directly intended change in the other two is in our case excluded, one can expect that not everything will remain equal once the transfer has occured. It is this unintended - and therefore labelled "indirect" - effects of the transfer of a firm from one sector of the economy to the other that will now be identified and its effect on economic efficiency assessed.

In other words, we shall try to answer the following questions:

- if "positive" means increased social welfare and/or economic (productive) efficiency, will the direct effect of transferring the ownership rights on economic efficiency, *ceteris paribus*, going to be positive?
- And what about its indirect effects, *i.e.* about the effects of such a transfer on the degree of competition and on the efficacy of regulation?
- Will the direct effect be reinforced or weakened by the indirect effects?

1.1 The Model: Its Constitutive Elements[1]

Figure B1 (see next page) presents one of the possible structures which can be used to compare external influences on the behaviour of privately and publicly owned enterprises. At the top it has a (democratically elected) legislature (**the Parliament**) as the body ultimately able to take decisions whether to transfer a firm from one sector to another or to leave everything as it is, subject to any legal or constitutional constraints that may be binding.[2] The members of the Parliament, individually and/or organized into political parties are answerable to voters, which leads to the concept of a **market for votes**.[3]

---

[1] Throughout Section 1.1 it has to be remembered that the model is not supposed to represent institutional arrangements of any country - different from one country to another as they are - but rather the essential structural features following from the very definition of the public sector.

[2] Some authors - and Shapiro and Willig (1990) are just one example - prefer to use the concept of a framer, *defined as a public-spirited agent (...), who originally makes the choice between public and private enterprise* (p. 59). However, since one of the characteristics of any economic-political system is that all decisions are taken within it by applying criteria the perception and importance of which are also determined within the system, their approach can be misleading and dangerous.

[3] This market is, admittedly, a rather imperfect one and that for at least three reasons: *the high cost of obtaining reliable information about the relevant facts, the free-rider problem, and the relatively small sum that is at stake for the average individual* (Eggertsson, 1990, p. 66).

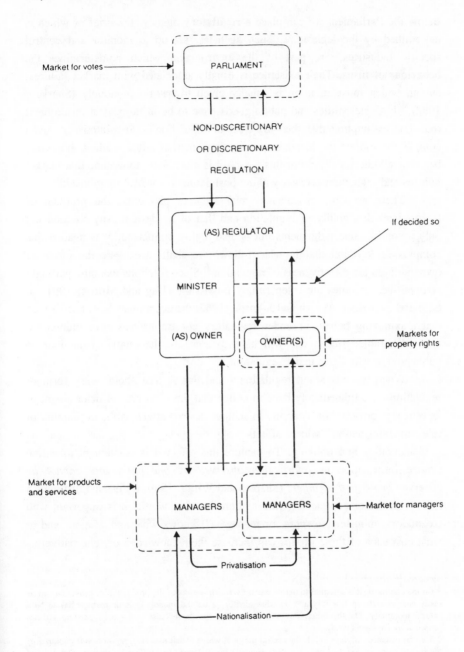

Figure B1: Organizational Structure

Below the Parliament we can place a **regulatory agency**, the brief of which is determined by the legislature. Such agencies, set up to monitor and control specific industries, are part of the environment which co-determines the behaviour of firms. Their existence is usually associated with market failures, among which most attention is usually given to natural monopoly (Sharkey, 1982),[4] but externalities and public goods have to be mentioned in this context too. The assumption that the only goal of regulation is to minimize or even completely remove the losses stemming from market failure cannot, however, be accepted uncritically.[5] For this reason it is much safer to assume that market failures and regulation coexist, without postulating any causal relationship.

There are, in consequence, two separate problems: the problem of (theoretical) desirability of regulation and that of its design. Any solution not only involves value judgements but is also highly politicized. It is against this complex background that in what follows we shall investigate the effect of ownership on the effectiveness of regulation.[6] Since solutions inducing perfectly competitive outcomes are often simply impossible (Hay and Morris, 1991, p. 623) and ever since Averch and Johnson (1962) the economists have been aware that maximizing behaviour under regulatory constraints can have unintended and undesirable effects, one will have to compare the relative behaviour of public and private firms under regulation.

When we talk about regulation - and this is true about every form of regulation - we immediately have to notice that the most crucial determinant of its efficacy, or rather of its ability to achieve desired effects is the availability of relevant information, which affects both the design of regulation and its implementation and policing. To capture this effect it is convenient to define private information as *information observed by one party that cannot be observed or verified by others* (Shapiro and Willig, 1990, p. 59) and distinguish it from public or contractable information. In other words, it is important who (regulators, ministers, owners, or managers?) knows what and whether and at what cost each of these groups can increase their knowledge or, alternatively -

---

[4] On the one hand, it is essential to define precisely which aspects of the production or provision can be really characterized in this way and on what territory a natural monopoly is or perhaps has to be a natural monopoly. On the other, one should consider the "revisionist" view on regulating utilities proposed by Demsetz (1968).

[5] See, for instance, Stigler (1971), the central thesis of which is that *as a rule, regulation is acquired by the industry and is designed and operated primarily for its benefit* (p.1). This thesis was extended and formally presented by Peltzman (1976). Both papers contain some empirical evidence.

[6] Any long run analysis will also have to take into account the possible effects of technological progress, as for example in telecommunication.

e.g. if we assume sequential decision making - when a given piece of information is revealed.

From the point of view of the relationship between the Parliament and the regulator, regulation can be either **discretionary** or **nondiscretionary** (Shapiro and Willig, 1990). The crucial factor is whether the minister (as regulator) or the regulator of private firms operates under - or, respectively, without - restriction put in place by the higher authority.

Public ownership changes the objective function of the firm and therefore is by itself a form of regulation. However, in order to make the fullest possible use of the clause *ceteris paribus* with respect to regulation and competition it is appropriate to distinguish between "**minister-owner**" (in Figure 1: **minister (as) owner**) and "**minister-regulator**" (in Figure 1: **minister (as) regulator**), even though the *de facto* "personal union" eliminates the risk of an informational loss in the process of communication and facilitates access to necessary information. The management depend on the appropriate **minister** or on a governmental body answerable to the Parliament. In the private sector, if a regulatory agency exists, its actions affect those of the **owner(s)** who in turn control(s) the **managers.**[7]

At this level two new markets appear: **market for property rights** and **market for managers**, both assumed to exist only in the private sector, even though in the latter case the difference between the two sectors could be interpreted as one of degree. Their importance follows from the fact that within each firm, regardless of the sector to which it belongs, there are the usual problems caused by the possibility of opportunistic behaviour and by bounded rationality.[8] The degree to which they are solved depends on the quality of the incentive structure and of monitoring, which in turn depends on the incentives of those who are supposed to and/or have right to perform both functions.[9] On the other hand, since these markets imply reasonably efficient working of capital and labour markets, this explains why market economy was mentioned in the title of this Chapter.

One further consequence of our *ceteris paribus* clause is that both types of firm are assumed as operating in the same **market for goods and services**. This can be interpreted as saying that the very transfer does not change the

---

[7] This does not, of course, exclude the case of owners who are managers (or vice versa) nor predetermines the exact legal form of ownership; it simply reflects the fact that the most important distinction is that between internal and external governance of the firm.

[8] These problems are usually discussed under the heading of agency problems (Williamson, 1983), which, in turn, is a special case of incomplete contracts (Klein, 1983).

[9] These issues will be discussed in detail in Section 1.1.4.1.

market in which the transferred firm operates, which is obviously true only in the short run (Yarrow, 1989a).

Finally, it has to be kept in mind that every relationship in this structure is **bidirectional**: although the higher levels of either hierarchy preserve the right to be the ultimate decision makers, it would be naive to expect that lower levels have no influence on the content of these decisions which can be modified further in the process of implementation.

1.2 The Model: Formal Presentation

The most important aspects of the structure described above can be formalized as follows:[10] financial results, *i.e.*, in the public sector, net contribution to the Treasury (revenues, taxes, and subsidies - whatever appropriate), and, in the private sector, profits plus or minus any extra transfer (**T**) from or to the Treasury, depend on the level of activity (**x**) and the level of profitability (**t**). In the first case we shall write it as **PPubl(x,t)**, because it is only the net effect that matters; in the second case **PPriv(x,t)** plus T.

Despite obvious differences between various cases in which it is imposed, regulation can be modelled, following Caillaud *et al.* (1988), in a very general way: the regulator specifies function **T(x)** which reflects the transfer (subsidies, taxes or franchise fees) if action x is chosen. It constitutes the framework within which private investors decide whether to invest and what action to take. Regulatory contract must offer at least a non-negative profit and the decision-maker's commitment must be credible, as otherwise no private firm will enter the industry. Consequently, in our definition of financial results of private firms T(x) will replace T.

It has already been mentioned that when we talk about what determines the efficacy of regulation, *i.e.* the ability of the regulators to achieve their goals whatever they are, one of the crucial distinctions is that between **private and public information**. At this stage of our analysis it is convenient to point out what kinds of private information are likely to appear. They are:

a. information about the **external social benefits** (**f**) which is accessible for both the minister and the ultimate decision-maker;

b. information about the divergence between the public interest and the interests of the public official who oversees the enterprise; we shall denote **private**

---

[10] For a complete list of definitions of symbols used, see end of Section 1.1.

information about private agenda of a public official, observable only to himself, as **e**;

c. information about the **profitability (t)** (*i.e.* about costs and demand), which is unknown to the ultimate decision-maker at the time of decision; he has, however, antecedent beliefs about the interval over which its values are distributed and about probability density and cumulative distribution functions, which allows him to formulate expectations; t is known to the minister and to the owner(s).

The availability of the three kinds of private information modifies our way of representing regulation, which now becomes a function of both the level of activity and the available information: the regulator observes f and e, which is captured by the function **R(f,e)**. What is more, the regulator is assumed to be able to acquire also postinvestment discretion, *e.g.* by offering the private investors a menu of different regulatory schemes [T(x)] identical with T(x,R) equal to T[x,R(f,e)].

1.3 Evaluation Criteria and Decision Structure

Since our ultimate goal in this chapter is to specify and evaluate the difference that is made to the behaviour of a firm by the fact that it belongs either to the public sector or to the private one, it is self-evident that even a most detailed discussion of various distinctions present in our model could only tell us that the behaviour of the two would most likely be different. In some cases we could even determine - as we are going to do - this difference more specifically, but we would not be able to achieve our goal without answering the question which and why one of these patterns of behaviour should be judged as superior or simply more desirable. In other words, we now have to decide according to what (uniform set of) criteria we are going to evaluate each and every possibility. There are many possibilities,[11] but we need not only well defined and measurable criteria, but also criteria which could be hierarchically ordered.

The most obvious candidate is, of course, economic efficiency but, as is well known, "economic" can mean either productive or allocative or a

---

11 One example of a very complicated structure of criteria can be found in Savas (1987), who, following his own definition of privatization, calls them *factors in evaluating arrangements*. His list reads as follows: service specificity, availability of producers, efficiency and effectiveness, scale, relating benefits and costs, responsiveness to consumers, susceptibility to fraud, economic equity, equity for minorities (effects on jobs and services), responsiveness to government direction and the size of government (p. 95 - 107).

combination of the two. *Productive efficiency requires that whatever is done should be achieved at minimum cost; allocative efficiency implies that what is done meets consumer needs at prices which reflect the costs of provision* (Kay *et al.*, 1986, p. 10) and the two do not have to coincide with each other. What is more, although both sorts of efficiency co-determine the level of economic efficiency, they are hardly comparable because allocative efficiency is a general equilibrium concept and productive efficiency refers to what is going on within multi-person economic units (*e.g.* a firm) as well as to the appropriate rate of innovation.[12] Nevertheless, the concept of economic efficiency could still be useful in our context because the very transfer of property rights, assuming, as we do in this thesis, other things being equal, will not affect directly allocative efficiency.[13]

Production possibility frontier, on which a productively efficient firm should be based, cannot, however, be really estimated (Rees, 1988);[14] moreover, a cost-efficient firm should be at the right point of this curve, which, assuming non-homogeneity of the factors of production, is a rather tall order. If we assume that individuals within organization are also utility maximizers, as seems plausible to do, the relationship between financial indicators and the technology used, and efficiency becomes ambiguous and the first two become a very imperfect proxy for efficiency.[15] If economic efficiency cannot be measured directly, a whole series of other variables must be introduced, as for example total factor productivity, profitability, rate of return etc., both in the short and in the long run plus rates of growth of each of them. The best we can get is some panel data. In consequence, this route seems to be more appropriate for gathering empirical evidence (see Section 1.2 and 1.3) than for constructing a model.

Another strong candidate is social welfare, traditionally used in similar situations, which could be defined as a function of weighted sum of profits and

---

[12] In this sense the very concept of productive efficiency is a critique of neoclassical economics, which does not distinguish between single- and multi-person firms, which is of key importance because at the same time it is assumed that economic variables are, from the point of view of an individual, neither the only maximands nor the most important ones and even the maximization itself is tainted with inertia (Leibenstein, 1978b).

[13] However, there will be an indirect effect in the sense that any improvement of productive efficiency will alter allocative efficiency, especially if such improvements do not happen, as it were, across the board but only in some industries or even in individual firms. On the other hand, since such an expected effect will surely be much smaller than the share of the privatized firm in the economy, this effect can be safely ignored.

[14] Pollitt (1991) tries to show that this is not necessarily true.

[15] This difficulty is well exemplified by the discussion between Leibenstein and Stigler and other property rights economists - see, *inter alia*, Leibenstein (1966, 1978a, 1978b), Stigler (1976) and De Alessi (1983).

consumer surplus. Following Shapiro and Willig (1990) it could be further specified as follows: in the public sector, regardless of what, if anything, the Parliament really maximizes, the social welfare, **W**, understood as some kind of an accounting principle and not as a real world maximand, contains, apart from scaled profits, where the scaling factor (**k**) reflects the unit cost of raising public funds (distortionary effect of taxation etc.), the external social benefit associated with action x and the information about it, **S(x,f)**. So, in the public sector:

(1) $W = kPPubl(x,t) + S(x,f)$.

In the private sector, the social welfare function takes the following form:

(2) $W = S(x,f) + PPriv(x,t) - (k-1)T(x,R)$.

As far as the **decision structure** is concerned, we shall assume that, given the information available, the decision about the investment (a yes/no choice) is taken first, to be then followed by an attempt to determine x, the level of activity. Yet, regardless of what the ultimate decision maker maximizes or wants to maximize, the decision taken has to be implemented. In this process it is the minister (or the regulator) who has the last say: his or her objective function **V** has two elements: W and his private agenda, which in turn is a function of x and e: **J(x,e)** and is then scaled by **a** which reflects the quality of the political system as well as the strength of short-term political pressures:

(3) $V = W + aJ(x,e) = S(x,f) + kPPubl(x,t) + aJ(x,e)$.

In the private sector, the regulator's objective function takes a similar form:

(4) $V = W + aJ = S(x,f) + (k-1)T(x,R) + aJ(x,e)$.

1.4 Analysis

At this point let us assume - which seems in principle plausible - that the Parliament, as the ultimate decision maker, wants to improve economic efficiency. This objective - not always, mildly speaking, at the very top of the list of politicians' priorities - can be achieved, according to economic theory and practice, by actions which can have three different but not mutually exclusive objects: property rights structure, regulatory policy, and the degree of competition. They can be deliberately combined - and most real world privatizations pursued precisely this option - but even if it is only, for instance, the property rights structure that is changed, this action will have an effect on the other two determinants of economic efficiency. Therefore the effect of the transfer of ownership will have to be decomposed into its direct and indirect elements. In the latter case economic efficiency will change because of the effect of this transfer on the efficacy of regulatory policy and on the degree of competition. It is only in this way that we shall be able to answer the question we are most interested in: to privatize or not to privatize? In other words, keeping everything else constant, *i.e.* the kind of goods produced,[16] the regulatory framework, the degree of competition (within the economy and from abroad), the kind of externalities present, the informational structure, and the evaluation criteria (and their mutual connections), we have to ask ourselves about the full extent of the change which is introduced when ownership rights are transferred.

If we look at Figure B1 it becomes evident that talking about a transfer of ownership rights means that we deal with a horizontal movement of the lowest boxes: privatization or nationalization changes the institutional environment in which a given firm operates. Markets for products and services remain the same but the privatized firm enters, as it were, the market for property rights and, perhaps with a smaller degree of novelty, the market for managers. What is more, the minister (as) owner is replaced by the owners. The other function of the minister in question may be taken over by a regulator or be simply dropped out. Referring to a situation like this, Shapiro and Willig (1990) write that *simply privatizing a public enterprise (...) will typically have a substantial effect on the allocation of resources, for the simple reason that an unfettered private company will seek to maximize shareholder profits* (p. 58). Is it only the allocation of resources that will be affected? How substantial is the effect? Does it improve economic efficiency? - these are the question that we are now going to answer.

1.4.1 The Direct Effect of Ownership Transfer

Any analysis of the direct effect of ownership transfer has to start with extending the utility maximization hypothesis to all individual choices under constraints. In contrast to the standard approach, the set of relevant constraints should include institutional restrictions and transaction cost (Demsetz, 1966, De Alessi, 1983).

Individuals aim at increasing their welfare through specialization and exchange (De Alessi, 1987). Among institutional arrangements a particular role

---

[16] Savas's (1987) approach to privatization is based on the distinction between different goods which are classified according to whether they are consumed individually or jointly and whether exclusion in their consumption is more or less feasible.

is played by property rights. They are defined *as the sanctioned behavioural relations among men that arise from the existence of goods and pertain to their use* (Furubotn and Pejovich, 1974, p. 3). In the case of private property an individual's rights to the use of the resources he owns are by and large exclusive and voluntarily transferable. It means that the owner has the exclusive right to receive the income generated from the use of his resources and to exchange his property rights with those of other individuals at mutually agreeable prices (De Alessi, 1980). On the one hand, since these rights can be partitioned, so that different individuals may concurrently hold different rights to the use of a particular resource, they can be attenuated (for instance in the case of mutual property or government regulations) or replaced by other institutional arrangements (such as public ownership) (De Alessi, 1983). On the other hand, because transaction costs are positive (information costs as well as costs of defining, allocating, and policing), on pure optimality criteria some rights will not be fully assigned, enforced, or priced (De Alessi, 1980).

This set of assumptions helps to explain the existence of firms and at the same time allows to identify the most important problems which are connected with proper functioning of this kind of economic organization. One set of problems to be solved, as it were, within the firm is usually called the agency problem: it arises because the desire to maximise one's utility - and government employees are no exception - is constrained by the distribution of property rights and transaction costs. Since firms can have many different ownership structures (two polar cases being a firm owned by its manager or managed by its owner and firms publicly owned) one can assume that the way in which the agency problem is solved depends to a large extent on the type and structure of ownership of as well as on the external factors among which one of the most important is the degree to which various aspects of any economic activity are subject to the discipline of relevant markets.

All of this constitutes the background of what could be called **a standard, property rights/agency problem-based theory of privatization** in which the markets for property rights and managers decisively determine the way in which the agency problem is solved. One can summarize it as follows:

Within the private sector owners can be different and numerous and property can be transferred from one (group of) owner(s) to another. Property is tradeable and even acknowledging the unrealistic character of some assumptions of the Coase theorem, certain degree of adjustment towards the best use of broadly understood resources can be expected as long as, well defined and assigned, they can be freely exchanged in a competitive market and transaction costs of exchange are nil (or minimal), even though the degree of initial misallocation will determine the extent of redistribution resulting from such adjustments (Coase, 1960 and Cooter, 1989).

Specialization in ownership becomes possible. First, the decision to be a public company can, in principle, be taken by any firm and it is not irrevocable. Another kind of specialization in ownership can be achieved through takeovers[17] or mergers, of which only the latter is possible in the state sector. What is more, the financial environment is also different, *i.e.* private owners can have other resources, can issue equity or bonds, whichever they find more appropriate, to finance the growth of their firms instead of engaging in political process of bargaining for resources which, regardless of the future returns, here and now represent a drain from the Treasury and in the case of an unexpected deterioration of budget deficit are likely to be cut immediately. One of the associated issues is the possibility of bankruptcy from which it follows that creditors will also try to discipline the firms (in this case, both managers and owners).[18]

Capital structure is an important factor in solving the conflict of interest between managers and shareholders since a higher debt/equity ratio increases the likelihood of bankruptcy and therefore puts more pressure on the managers whose reputation - and, consequently, their long-run utility - depends on avoiding bankruptcy (Jensen and Meckling, 1976, 1979). Finally, since the residual profits belong to the owners, this simple fact makes them interested in a better monitoring of the managers and designing better incentive schemes. Dispersed shareholding (in itself a consequence of optimizing risk by adjusting the composition of one's portfolio or, in the case of large British privatization, a result of pursuing the policy of wider share ownership) and "free rider problems" associated with it can attenuate the expected effects.[19] However, the monitoring and incentive design by private claimants of the residual profits, although never perfect in itself, has to be compared with "political monitoring",

---

[17] It is assumed that takeovers are triggered by *deviations in the target management's behaviour from that implied by its optimal incentive contract* (Vickers and Yarrow, 1988, p. 19; see also Grossman & Hart, 1980), but the smaller the degree of shareholders' control over takeover raids of the firms they own, the weaker the link between actual raids and economic efficiency. Empirical evidence is rather mixed: Singh (1971, 1975), Meeks (1979), Firth (1979, 1980). Nevertheless, the role played by the market for corporate control seems to be at least non-negative.

[18] The relative force of this kind of supervision will vary between the Anglo-Saxon and, for example, the German and the Japanese types of capitalism (Bardhan, 1991, Franks and Mayer, 1990).

[19] Although this sounds plausible in theory and has been taken for granted ever since Berle and Means published their book, empirical evidence on the effect of (dispersed) shareholding on the financial results of private firms is not very convincing (Berle and Means, 1933, Larner, 1966, Hessen, 1983, Stigler and Friedland, 1983, Fama and Jensen, 1983a, 1983b, Williamson, 1983).

where the probability of voting a party out of office because of unsatisfactory performance of a single publicly owned enterprise is minimal. Therefore, if no golden shares or other safety nets are introduced in the process of privatization, one can not say that when a publicly owned enterprise is turned into a private one with dispersed shareholding then political discretion is replaced by managerial discretion because the latter was already there and the transfer of ownership to a large extent removes the former.

Many of the solutions to the agency problem applied in the private sector are in principle possible in the public sector but it is a matter of fact, as Murphy (1989) shows, that incentive to provide incentives is substantially restrained, most likely for political reasons. Needless to say, managers in the public sector fall far short of the Morrisonian ideal of "high custodian of the public interest" - one should rather see them as utility maximizers and since the fruits of increased managerial effort have no effect on their remuneration they should not be expected to supply such effort freely. Market for managers (Fama, 1980, Frech, 1980) can also be assumed to be working better in the private sector because different forms of political patronage exist (Sachs, 1991).

Summarizing, to the extent that markets for property rights and for managers are, in their different forms and operational modes, specific to the private sector and to the extent that political markets are less effective than economic ones, one can reasonably expect that the direct effect of the transfer of property rights from the public sector to the private one is going to be, as far as the performance of the firm in question is concerned, positive, *i.e.* both economic efficiency and social welfare should increase.

1.4.2 The Indirect Effects of Ownership Transfer

As has already been said, we are interested in only one of the three possible ways of improving economic efficiency, namely that of changing the ownership structure; that was why we had to start with investigating the direct effect of the transfer of property rights. However, the three determinants of economic efficiency are not independent of each other and even though any directly intended change in the other two is in our case excluded - which is precisely what was meant by the *ceteris paribus* clause - one can expect that not everything will remain equal once the transfer has occured. It is this unintended - and therefore labelled "indirect" - effects of the transfer of a firm from one sector of the economy to the other that will now be identified and its effect on economic efficiency assessed.

1.4.2.1 Competition

The market structure is not only determined exogenously, for example by its size and changes in it, by the available technology and technological progress, and by the legislative framework (on the one hand, statutory monopoly, on the other, antitrust and anticartel laws both at national and international levels) but also endogenously, that is by the behaviour of individual firms (for instance different forms of maximizing and/or strategic behaviour). Is there any relationship between the ownership status of individual firms and the market structure? Will the degree of concentration - and therefore of competition - be affected by transferring property rights?

First of all, privatization is an almost necessary condition for competition understood as rivalry and for firms being really subject to what is sometimes called competitive pressure. Since both usually enforce higher economic efficiency, making them possible in the process of privatization should have a similar effect. Rivalry between state-owned enterprises (SOEs) within one industry is usually only rivalry for resources from the Treasury but not in and for the market (for instance contracts of central and/or local governments). However, two things have immediately to be pointed out. Firstly, statutory monopoly by itself does not imply public ownership nor the other way round, even though a publicly owned firm is more likely to enjoy such a privilege than a private one because, among other things, of the problems with rent dissipation and with writing complete contracts. Secondly, the situation changes if we deal with firms which are owned publicly but by governments of different countries. For example, this is often the case with airlines and increasingly so with local government contracts in the United Kingdom (Paddon, 1991). In this context, however, it is not public ownership that is of primary importance but rather, as it were, its international character.

What is more, public ownership of one or more firms in a given market also determines its structure and the possibilities of changing it. This has been demonstrated by Fershtman (1990), who discusses two different markets, both having one incumbent and identical demand functions. The incumbents and the entrant have identical cost functions and the only difference between the two incumbents consists in that one of them is partly or totally nationalized. Under these assumptions, Fershtman's analysis, based on Dixit (1980) and Eaton and Lipsey (1981), where entry is modelled as a two-stage Cournot game, leads to rather powerful conclusions: *The ownership of the incumbent firm affects its incentives and ability to deter entry. In particular, it is possible that a firm is not a natural monopoly while being private but that alteration of its ownership structure so that it becomes partly nationalized can transform the firm to a natural monopoly* (p. 324).[20] In some cases *entry cannot be deterred by a private firm, but it is possible that when the incumbent firm becomes partly nationalized entry deterrence becomes feasible* (ibid.). It means that a profit-maximizing potential entrant prefers to enter a market in which its competitor, *i.e.* the incumbent firm, is private. When these results are applied to our problem, Fershtman (1990) seems to suggest that in oligopolistic (and sometimes even in monopolistic) markets dominated by publicly owned firms privatization itself, *i.e.* the very transfer of ownership rights unaccompanied by any other changes, can create conditions for an increase in competition and therefore implies potential gains both in economic efficiency and social welfare. The intuition behind this result is, first, that the objective function of the firm, *i.e.* its maximand, changes and, secondly, that despite alleged lower productive efficiency, the support and backing of government agencies can in practice prove decisive.

Finally, in the case of state-owned enterprises operating in more or less competitive markets we deal in principle only with what we called above the direct effect of the ownership transfer (see Section 1.1.4.1). Since the conclusion derived from our model was that one can expect efficiency and social welfare gains, this sphere of privatization ought to be encouraged as much as possible. There is however one *caveat*: namely it is important who the new owners are - if a publicly owned firm is bought by a private firm already operating in the given industry and both firms control a considerable share of the market, then the degree of concentration will increase and uncompetitive behaviour will become easier.[21] It is precisely in such a situation that privatization would lower the actual level of competition in the markets for

---

[20] Strictly speaking, a natural monopoly is usually defined as an industry in which output can be produced most efficiently by single producer. What Fershtman really means is that if the incumbent firm is publicly owned, the fact that it has a different objective shifts its reaction function away from the origin, which, in turn, increases the critical level of output below which the incumbent can behave like a monopolist and not be vulnerable to entry.

[21] Jones *et al.* (1990) give an example of the sale of the American cargo railroad Conrail in which case the Norfolk Southern, its direct competitor, might have been prepared to pay more than an independent buyer simply because of the resulting change in its competitive position. This is also a warning that sales revenue is not always the best maximand for the government.

products and services. However, since there is nothing necessary about this outcome and it can be easily taken care of, our overall conclusion is that after privatization the degree of competition either remains unchanged or increases.

1.4.2.2 Regulation

As has already been pointed out, in terms of Figure B1 one consequence of privatization is, by definition, a change in the regulatory regime. In order to fully capture this effect, two aspects have to be considered. Firstly, the regulatory aspect of public ownership disappears, *i.e.* the objective function of those ultimately in charge of the firm changes. However, in (perfectly) competitive markets the result of social welfare maximization coincides with that of profit maximization, which implies that if we deal with only this kind of effect, it does not have to be discussed in this subsection at all because there is no indirect effect of the transfer of property rights. In such a case a privatized firm is subject only to general supervision by bodies like, to use British examples, OFT or MMC.[22]

Secondly, regulation as distinguished from public ownership is, instead, inseparably connected with market imperfections. Either it is introduced because of different instances of the so-called market failure or its imposition makes it impossible for competition to develop (see Section 1.1.1). Whatever the real direction of causal relationship between the existence of market failures and regulation, some privatized firms are in fact subject to special control by a regulatory agency (as is the case, for example, of British utilities), most often created in the process of privatization. From our assumption that it is only the ownership status that changes, it follows that if there are going to be any special regulatory arrangements, they will simply replicate the actions of the minister as regulator.

Regardless of whether special regulation is necessary or at least justifiable from the economic point of view, some kind of divide (a communication barrier) between the regulator and the regulated is created, which, obviously, has some impact on the efficacy of regulation and therefore on the behaviour of the privatized firm.[23] In our model such indirect effect of

---

[22] The horizontal dotted line in Figure B1 represents the case of such a general supervision because there is no direct dependence on the regulatory agency.

[23] In Figure B1, where having one box meant that there was no loss of information in the process of communication, this is shown by splitting the box named "Minister (as) regulator and (as) owner" into two parts, namely those labelled "Regulator" and "Owner(s)".

privatization can be analysed, following Shapiro and Willig (1990),[24] in terms of the distinction between privately owned and publicly available (and contractable) information. This in turn allows us to describe this aspect of privatization in a very precise manner: since *the essential difference between public and private enterprise is the location of private information about costs and demand condition,* privatization is an action in which *informational autonomy* is given *to a party who is not under direct public sector control.* It is, therefore, *the <u>deliberate</u> introduction of an informational barrier between the public sector official with responsibility for the enterprise - that is the regulator - and the owners and managers of the enterprise* (Shapiro and Willig, 1990, p. 65).[25]

If regulation is discretionary (see Section 1.1.1), the most general of the conclusions derived by Shapiro and Willig (1990) reads as follows: *if the regulator merely induces the private firm to duplicate the action that he as minister would choose, the framer is indifferent between public and private enterprise* (p. 66). This result obtains when there is no private information whatsoever because taxes and subsidies can in such a situation induce the owners *to operate the enterprise to serve precisely the regulator's objectives in every contingency* (ibid.). In other words, discretionary public enterprise and discretionary regulations are equivalent, which Shapiro and Willig call "neutrality result" - or rather, they would have been equivalent because *in fact, the details of the operation of the enterprise are never commonly known, and thus the nature and identity of the party operating the enterprise can be expected to make a material difference* (ibid.).[26]

Cases in which, firstly, noncontractable private information about profitability is available prior to the investment decision and, secondly, there is concern about the drain on the treasury ($k > 1$) can be analysed as follows:

(6) $V^M = E_t[S(x,f) + aJ(x,e) + kPPubl(x,t)]$,

---

[24] The original intention of their paper was to identify *the impacts of privatization on the operations of an enterprise and its goal was the delineation of various characteristics of an activity's structure and environment that point to either public or private forms of control as the most effective in accomplishing society's aims* (p. 55). However, since, *inter alia,* they discuss only regulated firms and at the same time assume away the agency problem as well as the possibility of "government failure", their analysis, valuable in itself, cannot be considered as reaching its objective. In other words, it has to be placed in a much broader context, which is precisely what has been attempted in this thesis.

[25] As inefficiency is very often associated with such informational barriers, privatization appears as somehow paradoxical reversal of the standard approach. But this paradox is only apparent: as Sappington and Stiglitz (1987) demonstrate, the ease of intervention makes necessary corrections cheaper but also increases the risk of arbitrary interference.

[26] This "neutrality result" holds also in certain situations in which private information is present - see Shapiro and Willig (1990, pp. 66-69).

which gives us the first order condition

(7) $S_x(x,f) + aJ_x(x,e) + kPPubl_x(x,t) = 0$,

and, analogously, for a private enterprise operating under the same regulatory regime:

(8) $V^R = E_t[S(x,f) + aJ(x,e) + PPriv(x,t) - (k-1)T(x)]$,

which in turn gives us the first order condition

(9) $S_x(x,f) + aJ_x(x,e) + kPPriv_x(x,t) - (k-1)h(t)PPriv_{xt}(x,t) = 0$,

where h is the inverse of the hazard rate for t, *i.e.*

(10) $h(t) = (1-F(t))/f(t)$;

the subscripts denote partial derivatives and superscript M and R refer, respectively, to Minister and Regulator.

The optimum regulatory payment schedule that induces the actions leading to the relationship given in (9) is given by:

(11) $E_t[PPriv(x,t) + T^*(x,R)] = E_t[PPriv_t(x(t),t)h(t)] > 0$.

Since $k > 1$, these positive expected values reflect a genuine welfare cost, but under our assumptions about the availability of information these information rents (directly proportional to the level of activity) are a necessary feature of the optimum regulatory mechanism.

Comparing the two formulae Shapiro and Willig (1990) formulate a series of propositions and corollaries which are worth quoting *in extenso*:

Proposition 2: *In equivalent circumstances, activity levels are lower under discretionary regulation than under discretionary public management* (p. 71).

Proposition 3: *In the normal case, the activity level under discretionary public management is more responsive to changes in its marginal value than under discretionary regulation* (p. 72).

Proposition 4: *The public official prefers discretionary public management over discretionary regulation to an extent that depends on the harm associated with treasury and the variability in the enterprise's profitability. Analytically:*

(12) $(k-1)(t-t_0)\max(PPriv_t) > E(V^{M^*})-E(V^{R^*})$

and $E(V^{M^*})-E(V^{R^*}) > (k-1)(t-t_0)\min(PPriv_t)$.

Corollary 1: *If a equals zero, so there is no salient private agenda, then the advantage of public enterprise over regulated private enterprise from the framer's perspective satisfies the same bound as given in Proposition 4 (p. 74).*

Proposition 5: *Suppose that the conditions of the normal case apply and the public official's private agenda places a constant marginal value on increased activity, that is J(x,e) equals ex. As the salience of the private agenda grows, the expected value of the framer's objective function falls faster under discretionary public management than it does under discretionary regulation. Analytically:*

$$(13) \; E[W^P(0)] - E[W^P(a)] > E[W^R(0)] - E[W^R(a)] > 0,$$

where **P** stands for discretionary public enterprise, which simply means that a poorly functioning political system (and/or high short-term political pressures) and/or the absence of substantial private information at the operating level of the enterprise imply that privatization is superior to public enterprise (p. 75).

One last case to be analyzed is that of nondiscretionary governance and regulation, where the room for manoeuvre on the part of the minister and the regulator is simply nil. Hence one faces a kind of trade-off: nondiscretionary governance makes quick reaction to changed conditions impossible but at the same time private agenda ceases to harm public interest. Under these conditions Shapiro and Willig (1990) formulate:

Proposition 6: *Private enterprise subject to nondiscretionary regulation is the best organizational form if there is no private information about public impacts and all private information about profitability is revealed only after the investment decision must be made (p. 76),*

Corollary 2: *Where market revenues equal the gross social benefits of the enterprise's activities, as under perfect competition, private enterprise with a commitment to laissez-faire is the best organizational form (p. 77).*

and   Corollary 3: *Under perfect competition with output externalities,*
       private enterprise with a commitment to laissez-faire and
       externality-correcting taxes is the best organizational form (p. 78).

One can see that regardless of different combinations of when which
information becomes available, **the overall effect ultimately depends on the
particular values of two scale variables: k and a, the unit cost of raising
public funds and the ability of the minister (or regulators) to pursue his or
her private agenda, respectively.** What it means in practice is well illustrated
by the case of the United Kingdom: whether the then governments were
prepared to admit it or not, the role played by the desire to control the PSBR in
the British privatization programme demonstrates, firstly, that it is a very
important factor[27] and, secondly, it works decisively in favour of privatization.
That is, it is a matter of fact that $k > 1$, which in turn suggests desirability of
privatization. As far as the quality/pressure factor a is concerned, instead,
privatization substantially reduces the scope for political interference in and
coordination of economic activities, which, keeping the quality constant, should
curtail the destructive effects of political interference.[28]

1.5 Conclusions

Overall, the results of the above analysis can be summarized as follows: if
"positive" means increased social welfare and/or economic (productive)
efficiency, then *ceteris paribus* the direct effect of transferring the ownership
rights on economic efficiency is going to be positive. At the same time, its
effect on the degree of competition is going to be at least non-negative and its
effect on the efficacy of regulation is going to be rather positive than negative.
Thus the positive direct effect will be reinforced by the indirect effects.

---

[27] See Heald and Stell ([1982], 1986, pp. 71-74) and Veljanovski (1987, p. 66). Outside the British
context, it has to be noted that many government myopically followed the British example and let the
revenues fall into the budget black hole.

[28] On the other hand, this factor not only affects the performance of publicly owned firms but also the
very process of privatization. The effect of a poor political system on privatization can be even worse
than the starting point, which in turn increases the risk of future "expropriation", be it either
straightforward nationalization or changes in the regulatory framework (Vickers, 1991).

<u>List of Symbols:</u>

*	- optimal values
a	- quality of the political system
e	- information about private agenda of a public official
$E_t(.)$	- expectations in time t
f	- information about the external social benefits
h(.)	- the inverse of the hazard rate
J(.)	- private agenda of a minister (or a regulator)
k	- unit cost of raising public funds
M	- minister
P	- discretionary public enterprise
PPriv(.)	- profits of a privately owned firm
PPubl(.)	- net financial result of a publicly owned firm
R	- regulator
R(.)	- regulator's decision function
S(.)	- external social benefit
t	- level of profitability
T(.)	- transfer from or to the Treasury
[T(.)]	- a menu of regulatory schemes
V	- minister's (or regulator's) objective function
W	- social welfare
x	- level of activity

subscripts denote partial derivatives

2. Empirical Evidence on the Effect of a Transfer of Ownership Rights

The model constructed and discussed in Section 1.1 is a theoretical one and the kind of conclusions that can be derived from it are strongly dependent on a stylized representation of the real world. This is a problem which follows from the very nature of any theoretical work. Therefore to answer the title question of this chapter - Why privatize a firm in a market economy? - the theoretical conclusions have to be confronted with the empirical evidence available. Do the differences between the real world and the theoretical model discussed above weaken or strengthen the case for privatization? Do they suggest that it has to be reformulated? These are the questions that we shall try to answer in this section.

Since each theory should be able to point out what kind of empirical evidence could falsify it, the conclusions formulated in Section 1.5 determine to some extent the direction of our search: one has to investigate comparative performance of the public and private sector enterprises as well as the effect of ownership rights transfer on the performance of newly privatized enterprises.[29] Full applicability of our *ceteris paribus* conditions can hardly be expected - no two firms from both sectors are similar enough and privatization is never only a transfer of property rights - but this clause will urge us to look for studies investigating public and private sector enterprises operating in a similar, more or less competitive environment, as well as for examples of privatization in which relatively little has changed as far as the degree of competition and the regulatory framework are concerned. As there are considerable differences between the two kinds of empirical evidence, they will be presented separately.

The pattern of public ownership, in itself an erratic outcome of historic processes, makes our task even more difficult because it has far-reaching consequences for the possibility of producing adequate empirical evidence. This has to be kept in mind in the remainder of Section 2 - because, *inter alia*, as compared with Section 1.1 and anticipating Chapter C, in market economies utilities and the problems associated with them gain disproportional importance.

---

[29] As far as empirical evidence is concerned, a choice of examples has to be made and since we decided to use sources already available - and research done by others is by no means complete - our evidence will quite naturally be drawn above all from the United Kingdom.

2.1 Comparative Performance of Public and Private Sector Enterprises

The above introduction may well be interpreted as a warning against any attempt to compare publicly and privately owned enterprises and to draw any far reaching conclusions from such comparisons. Things become even more complicated - and, for our purposes, a possible source of indeterminacy - when one takes into account what is sometimes called *sociopolitical objectives of state-owned enterprises*, particularly stressed by representatives of the "no comparison is possible" school. Regardless of whether one accepts that such objectives are in fact an important factor and of whether pursuing them is justified (*i.e.* whether there are other, perhaps cheaper and more efficient ways of achieving them), it is a matter of fact that different governments sometimes use the enterprises that they control in this way. They want, for example, to extend social benefits which are external or internal to the state-owned enterprises (such as higher wage levels and perquisites or higher aggregate employment). The former are especially notorious for the degree of difficulty to measure them but even the latter forces a researcher to apply a complicated cost-benefit analysis instead of using relatively straightforward indicators like financial results, various measures of productivity, wage rates, or relative prices.

Nevertheless, despite all these difficulties, the problem of what form of ownership is better - whatever "better" could in this context mean - was considered by many researchers too important to be discouraged by mounting obstacles. Since experiments are of limited availability in economics, students of these issues tried to do their best, leaving at the same time the solutions of most of the problems to those who dared to interpret their tentative results and/or were interested in clear-cut policy recommendation.

One problem with many studies of this issue is, as we have already pointed out, that the requirement to compare similar with similar cannot often be sufficiently met. The availability of appropriate data further restricts the researchable field. In consequence even most imaginative approaches were unable to solve all the problems and that is why most studies are conducted under one or more limitations:
- firms have a natural (spatial) monopoly, *e.g.* water and electric utilities, nonrail transit, fire services, and refuse collection;
- there is a regulated duopoly, *e.g.* airlines, railroads, nonrail transit, financial institutions;

- output is not or cannot be priced by competitive forces: all the above listed cases plus health-related services (Boardman and Vining, 1989).

The classification of different studies presented in Table B1 is a clear confirmation of the aforementioned limitations.[30] Nevertheless, Boardman and Vining (1989) conclude that this Table *suggests an "edge" for the private sector, but the results vary considerably across sectors* (p. 5).[31]

For all those reasons, studies mentioned in Table B1 would require a much more detailed analysis because each of them addresses the issue only in a certain limited context. On the other hand, Table B1 does not seem to contain studies which could directly falsify our conclusions, i.e. studies investigating public and private sector enterprises operating in similar, competitive environments.[32] Boardman and Vining (1989) go even as far as to claim that before their paper was published, *in fact, with the exception of two studies that examine Indonesia and Tanzania, no study had explicitly compared the effect of ownership while controlling for relevant factors*[33] (p. 1). And who would like to make any policy recommendations based exclusively on the evidence from these two countries or following from an analysis of some very special cases?

The cited pessimistic constatation is, however, no longer true. Two studies, published relatively recently, do investigate the differences in performance between the public and private sector enterprises operating in more or less competitive environments of mature market economies. Their relevance in the context of our interests justifies their lengthy presentation.

---

[30] Unfortunately, the cited review does not discriminate between various measures of efficiency used by individual studies.

[31] One thing, however, has to be strongly stressed, namely that *in sectors where there is some evidence of superior public efficiency, (...) there is limited competition or the private firms are highly regulated* (p.5). It contains the most celebrated cases of public sector "superiority", like electricity and water industries in the USA. An interpretation of this kind of evidence as suggesting better performance of SOEs is, however, conditional on optimality of the regulatory regime. We shall return to this kind of issue later on.

[32] The case of public and private enterprises subject to identical regulatory regimes will be discussed separately.

[33] The studies in question are Funkhouser and MacAvoy (1979) and Kim (1981). The former examined the performance of more than a hundred Indonesian public and private companies and found that SOEs had both higher operating costs and lower profit margins than PCs; the latter discovered that public enterprises had lower productivity, overemployment of labour and lower managerial efficiency. In this context one could also mention Lewin (1982), Monsen and Walters (1983), and Ayub and Hegstad (1987), but their major shortcoming is that they used only univariate analysis.

Table B1: Empirical Results on Relative Efficiency of SOEs and PCs

Sector	SOE (Public Corporations) More Efficient	No Difference or Ambiguous Results	PC (Private Company) More Efficient
Electric utilities	Meyer (1975) Neuberg (1977) Pescatrice and Trapani (1980)	Mann (1970) Junker (1975) Spann (1977) Färe et al. (1985) Atkinson and Halvorsen (1986)	Shephard (1966) Moore (1970) Peltzman (1971) Tilton (1973) De Alessi (1974) De Alessi (1977)
Refuse	Pier et al. (1974)	Hirsch (1965) Kemper and Quigley (1976) Collins and Downes (1977)	Kitchen (1976) Savas (1977) Pommerehne and Frey (1977) Stevens (1978)
Water	Mann and Mikesell (1971)	Feigenbaum and Teeples (1983)	Hausman (1976) Morgan (1977) Crain and Zardkooh (1978, 1980)
Health related services		Becker and Sloan (1985)	Clarkson (1972) Rushing (1974) Lindsay (1976) Frech (1976) Bays (1979) Frech (1980) Frech and Ginsburg (1981) Finsinger (1982) Wilson and Jadlow (1982) Schlesinger and Dorwart (1984)
Airlines		Forsyth and Hocking (1980) Morrison (1981) Jordan (1982)	Davies (1971) Davies (1977)
Railroads		Caves and Christensen (1980) Caves et al. (1982)	
Financial institutions		Lewin (1982)	Davies (1981)
Fire services Nonrail transit			Ahlbrecht (1973) Pashigian (1973) Palmer et al. (1983) McGuire and Van Cott (1984)

Note: see Bibliography for complete citations

Source: Boardman and Vining (1989), Table 1, p. 6.

Table B2:   OLS   Regression   Estimates   of   Profitability   Performance Equations

Explanatory Variables	Dependent Variables			
	ROE	ROA	ROS	NI
ME	-12.344 (-2.317	-3.670 (-3.147)	-3.510 (-3.039)	-158.224 (-4.821)
SOE	-11.649 (-3.021)	-1.734 (-2.032)	-2.228 (-2.683)	-52.852 (-2.187)
Sales*	.348 (.541)	.019 (.132)	-.070 (-.503)	23.026 (5.469)
Assets*	-.251 (-.348)	.080 (.500)	.189 (1.209)	19.481 (4.004)
Employees*	-.015 (-.486)	-.009 (-1.319)	-.009 (-1.352)	-2.327 (-9.868)
Employees x food or tobacco*	... ...	... ...	... ...	1.822 (5.792)
Marketshare	.297 (.601)	.160 (1.535)	.150 (1.479)	10.586 (3.585)
Concentr.	.044 (.824)	-.017 (-1.408)	-.002 (-.145)	-.851 (-2.587)
Nonconcentr.	8.323 (1.427)	-.051 (-.039)	1.254 (.998)	-28.553 (-.789)
Follow 14 industry and 6 country dummies				
Constant	1.003 (.110)	1.578 (.774)	-.051 (-.025)	-5.393 (-.094)
R2	.178	.191	.173	.667
F	3.437	3.863	3.405	31.415
N	473.	486.	486.	485.

Note: Parentheses contain $\underline{t}$-statistics

* - Divide these coefficients by 1,000

Source: Boardman and Vining (1989), Table 3, p. 18 - 19.

The first is the already mentioned Boardman and Vining (1989). They maintain that profitability and efficiency measures actually provide information about performance because one could not argue that *greater inefficiency, as opposed to lower profitability, is a costless form of meeting social objectives* (p. 10).

The data used come from Fortune's list of 500 largest manufacturing and mining corporations outside the US, published on 22 August 1983. Among companies for which data were complete, there were 409 private corporations, 23 mixed enterprises and 57 state-owned enterprises - PCs, MEs and SOEs, respectively. The data came from various countries of which six - Great Britain, Canada, France, Germany, Italy and Japan - were singled out in the regression and assigned appropriate dummies; the data were also grouped into fifteen industries.

Using a variant of the standard model for analysis of the relationship between market structure and performance, Boardman and Vining (1989) begin with estimating and reporting the means and the standard deviations of the variables, first separately for each type of enterprises and then for pooled data (seven dependent variables and explanatory variables including, inter alia, all industries and countries Table B2, p. 14 - 16).

After appropriate adjustments (initially standard errors appeared to be not normally distributed and heavy tailed), the final version of the model was estimated by the OLS first for four dependent variables measuring profitability: return on equity (ROE), on assets (ROA), and on sales (ROS), and net income (NI), (Table B2) and then on three other dependent variables measuring efficiency: sales/employee, sales/assets and assets/employee (Table B3). Explanatory variables included two dummies representing ownership (state-owned or mixed companies respectively), sales, assets, employees (each of them once in each regression), market share, concentration, nonconcentration (a dummy equal to one when no concentration measure is available and zero otherwise), industry (14 variables), country (6 variables) and a constant.

As can be seen, *large industrial MEs and SOEs perform substantially worse than similar PCs. (...) The results also suggest that partial privatization where a government retains some percentage of equity, which is occurring in many countries (for example, British Telecom in the United Kingdom), may not be the best strategy for governments wishing to move away from reliance on SOEs* (p. 26). The later phenomenon can be explained by what the authors call *cognitive dissonance* (p. 26), caused by the conflict between public and private shareholders, i.e. their divergent or even contradictory objectives.

Table B3: OLS Regression Estimates of the Efficiency Equations

Explanatory Variable	Dependent Variable		
	Sales/ Employee	Sales/ Assets	Assets/ Employee
ME	-85,445.4 (-1.808)	-.464 (-2.988)	-21,004.0 -.671
SOE	-149,576. (-4.424)	-.438 (-3.891)	-23,940.7 (-1.074)
Sales	... ...	... ...	-.011 (-.733)
Assets	-7.867 (-3.153)	... ...	... ...
Employees*	... ...	-.151 (-1.770)	... ...
Marketshare	3,492.4 (.912)	.006 (.434)	-360.88 (-.141)
Concentration	1,150.2 (2.432)	-.006 (-3.602)	1,384.0 (4.428)
Nonconcentration	54,398.5 (1.036)	-.578 (-3.346)	58,438.3 (1.694)
Follow 14 indusury and 6 country dummies			
Constant	-17,901.3 (-.218)	1.453 (5.334)	20,302.2 (.374)
R2	.582	.325	.553
F	24.525	8.501	21.946
N	486.	487.	489.

Note: Parentheses contain t-statistics

* - Divide these coefficient by 100,000

Source: Boardman and Vining (1989), Table 4, p. 20 - 21.

More specifically, on average the ROE of PCs is 14.5 per cent higher than for SOEs and 18.4 per cent higher than for MEs. For the last two the average return on equity was actually negative. As far as net income was concerned, on average PCs earned $ 57 million, MEs lost $ 17 million, and SOEs lost $ 28 million. The differences were much smaller for returns on assets and returns on sales but the ranking remained valid. PCs also have the highest average sales per asset and only in terms of sales per employee SOEs did better than PCs.

The regression controlling for the factors described above shows that on average SOEs have a return on equity of almost 12 per cent less than PCs; they have a return on assets and a return on sales that are about 2 per cent less than PCs, and their net incomes are $ 66 million less than PCs. MEs performed even worse: the respective figures are: more than 12 per cent, 3.5 per cent and 165 million USD. The most important thing about these results is that although each variable taken on its own has some weaknesses, *the consistent direction and magnitude of the estimates across all equations provides robust evidence that state enterprises and mixed enterprises are less profitable and less efficient than private corporations* (p. 17). Unless one argues that ownership and performance are determined simultaneously, which cannot be rejected on the base of the calculations reported above, this confirms Boardman and Vining's predictions as well as the conclusions reached in our analysis.

The second of the aforementioned studies of the comparative performance of the private and public enterprises is Picot and Kaulmann (1989). They exclude, however, what they call "typical corporations", e.g. railways, PTT, broadcasting, public utilities, hospitals etc., because those kinds of public firms very often operate in regulated markets, which leaves the authors with those companies that act in by-and-large unregulated markets and that are exposed to national and international competition.[34] This is a *conditio sine qua non* for any attempt to check *for systematic differences in performance between the two groups* (ibid., p. 299).

Assuming, as Picot and Kaulmann (1989) in fact do, that similar and market-oriented goals are pursued by all firms, all differences can be attributed to the specific property rights constellation. What is more, even if the public sector corporations have also other ends (employment policy, structural policy), one should be able to estimate what the real cost of changing the priorities is.

---

[34] It seems that as far as competitive environment is concerned there is some kind of asymmetry between private and public enterprises because the former are able to respond to this kind of pressure more actively, e.g. by expansion abroad, diversification etc., which is indirectly confirmed by the behaviour of newly privatized firms in the United Kingdom (Yarrow, 1989a,b).

The data on which this effect was to be estimated were taken from *Fortune 500* - Outside the US, which included companies from six countries - comparing with Boardman and Vining (1989), Japan is replaced by Sweden - and fifteen industries. Computations were made for a pooled sample covering the ten year period (from 1975 to 1984); that is, the paper offers a combination of cross-sectional and longitudinal study. For most regressions the results of one company in two years were treated as separate observations.

Theoretical analysis, heavily drawing on property rights economics, led to the formulation of four hypotheses: government-owned corporations show lower levels of productivity (H1), lower rates of return (H2) and lower ratio of shareholders' equity to total assets (H3) than privately-owned corporations; the increase in the size of firms leads to a smaller increase in profits in the case of government-owned corporations than in the case of private corporations (H4).

Univariate analysis, *i.e.* simple comparison of the appropriate ratios from the two groups - in itself a rather crude method - showed again significant differences with respect to productivity, profitability and the ratio of shareholders' equity to total assets, which seems to corroborate the first three hypotheses.

H1, H2 and H4 could not be rejected by multivariate analysis either, although the inclusion of dummy variables for industry and country usually almost quadrupled R^2 and partially reduced the influence of the ownership variable. H3 could not be sustained because of *a relatively high dependency of the ratio of equity to total assets on industry and country variables* (p. 310). What is also important is that Picot and Kaulmann (1989) felt unable to substantiate the claim that differences in performance should be attributed mainly to special labour market-oriented objectives of government economic policy with the aid of government-owned corporations because *the results of the productivity of capital, a measure that does not contain the number of employees, are as significant as the results of other measures of efficiency* (p. 311).

As far as figures are concerned, it seems to be the case that the cruder the method (in this case, univariate analysis) the more unequivocal the results. Ratios were for sales per employee 65 per cent and sales per assets 40 per cent higher in privately-owned industrial corporations (Table 1, p. 305). The average profitability ratios for private firms ranged, depending on the measure applied, from 2.1 to 7 per cent, while they were all negative in the public sector: net income/equity -0.12, net income/total assets -0.02, net income/sales -0.024 (Table 2, ibid.).

In multivariate regressions with country and industry dummies, instead, the ownership dummy (government $= 1$) had the following statistically significant coefficients:

- 76.36 (standard deviation, sd $= 11.84$) when the dependent variable (DVar) was sales per employee, the other variables (Var) were total assets and the ratio of total stockholder equity to total assets (Lever);

- 0.2266 (sd $= 0.0496$), DVar - sales to total assets, Var - employment and Lever;

- 0.1317 (sd $= 0.0199$), DVAr - return on total stockholders' equity, Var - sales and Lever;

- 0.0303 (sd $= 0.0035$), Dvar - return on total assets, Var - sales and Lever (Tables 4, 5, 6, p. 307 - 309).

The list of determinants which, according to Picot and Kaulmann, should be included in future investigations - duration of government ownership, conditions of takeover by government, intensity of competition, specific information about antitrust policy and government regulation as well as dynamic aspects (*e.g.* growth rates) - is in a sense a catalogue of the shortcomings of their own study. Nonetheless their study even in its present form seems to be a clear indication that both the suggestions of the property rights economics and of the model of Section 1.1 are correct. What is more, the estimated size of the performance differences appears to justify the transfer of publicly owned companies to the private sector. The desirability of the transfer is, however, conditional on whether it is possible to overcome these differences in practice, which may not be the case in the short run. This is a necessary but not a sufficient condition for privatization.

2.2 The Effect of Privatization on Economic Performance

In the 1980s and early 1990s the public sector in the United Kingdom shrank considerably and at the end of this period employed 4 per cent of the workforce and produced less than 6 per cent of the GNP. The privatization programme of the consecutive Tory governments transferred to the private sector assets worth more than £100 bln. One could expect that such a wide-ranging undertaking should provide enough data to answer definitively the question of whether the ownership rights transfer from the public to the private sector fulfilled the promises supposed to justify it. In practice, however, things are extremely complicated and one can doubt whether the problem in question will ever be solved.

Nevertheless, much of the evidence is, at face value, rather encouraging. Cable and Wireless, for example, increased its profits from £64 million in the last year prior to privatization to £300 million in 1986. Similarly, the profit increase at Amersham International from £4 million in 1981, its last year as a public enterprise, to £12.5 million in 1986 represents a sharp outperformance of the norm. National Freight Consortium, where privatization took the form of a management and employee buy-out, shows an even more dramatic improvement from just over £4 million in profits in 1981 to £37 million in 1986. British Airways went from losses in the run-up to privatization to substantial profitability afterwards, although it is difficult to hide that much of the improvement occurred in the process of preparation for privatization. British Telecom, British Aerospace, and British Gas have all shown solid achievements since privatization, while Associated British Ports, which lost £10 million in its penultimate year as a public enterprise, has recorded good profitability in every year since, apart from 1984 when its results were adversely affected by the public-sector coal-mining dispute (Redwood, 1990). Letwin (1988), entitled tellingly *Privatizing the World*, is full of similar success stories.

It all looks so good that one is tempted to look behind such spectacular achievements, even though not necessarily to question them but rather to check on the true message that they convey. The first thing that has to be brought into light is the performance of the British economy as a whole, which after a very severe recession caused by Britain's volunteering to become, to use Galbraith's expression, a Friedmanite guinea pig, did rather well, as compared with other OECD countries. This implies that the results achieved by individual companies improved and there is no reason why newly privatized companies should be an exception. It should also be pointed out that what is very often compared are the results of the last stage of recession (or the first stage of recovery) with the results from the period when boom peaked and it is not even certain whether the numbers were adjusted for inflation. The 1990-1992 recession should very much relativize these achievements.

At the beginning of Section 2.1 it was argued that comparison of the performance of the public and private sector enterprises is almost impossible, which did not, however, discourage us from extracting as much evidence as possible from the available studies. Looking at changes in the performance of newly privatized companies means yet another attempt to compare, this time chronologically, the public and private sector firms. That is why all the above *caveats* have to repeated here and even stressed more strongly.

What constitutes, however, an even more formidable obstacle is the fact that privatization was accompanied by far reaching changes both in the companies themselves (*e.g.* restructuring: some of the privatized enterprises belonged to larger organizations or were taken over by already existing firms) and in their environment (*e.g.* regulatory framework), which, in principle, could either weaken or strengthen what we called the direct effect of ownership transfer. What is more, the preparation for privatization involved laundering of figures and reconstruction of the capital of the firms.

A good illustration of how far this kind of change could go is the electricity supply industry. Nationalization, motivated above all by the desire to exploit economies of scale, transformed a very fragmented industry into a vertically integrated and administered generation and transmission structure. Central Electricity Generating Board (CEGB), which controlled also the high voltage transmission system (the National Grid), had a monopoly in the wholesale market and 12 Area Boards had local monopolies over retail supply.[35]

In the process of privatization the generating plants were divided into three groups, of which two, PowerGen and National Power, were sold to the public (nuclear power stations gathered in Nuclear Electric remained, despite initial plans set out in the 1986 White Paper, in the public sector, mostly because of very high scrapping costs). Transmission in England and Wales (the two Scottish electricity companies preserved their vertically integrated structure) is now handled by 12 Regional Electricity Companies. They also collectively own - "at arm's length" - the National Grid (now called National Grid Company). What is even more important, spot market for electricity has been created and some elements of competition have been introduced, not least because some threats of new entry have materialized and the market has become accessible also for French and Scottish companies. New regulatory regime includes, inter alia, control of transmission and distribution charges and network access for use by third parties (Vickers and Yarrow, 1991). Since one can hardly imagine further-reaching changes, it becomes almost self-evident that any comparison between periods "before" and "after" privatization will at best be very approximate.

---

[35] The 1983 Energy Act tried to introduce some kind of competition by liberalizing third party access to transmission and distribution networks, but it had virtually no effect.

Another case in point is telecommunication: if one wants to go beyond the spectacular increase in profits announced by British Telecom, or BT as it now wants to be called, in May 1991, one has to remember that the history of this company's independence in the public sector was very brief. Till 1981 it was part of the Post Office, which considerably restricts the availability of reliable data which could be used for any comparison. The 25-years licence given to BT after its privatization in 1984 - only 51 per cent of shares were then sold to the public and to financial institutions - included the so-called public-service obligations (*e.g.* emergency services and call boxes) and price regulation[36] which strongly limited its room for manoeuvre as far as its allegedly profit-maximizing behaviour is concerned and made it vulnerable to cream-skimming competition in some spheres of its business activities. Privatization was accompanied by far-reaching deregulation and liberalization with respect to non-network operations. The government licensed another company, Mercury Communication Ltd., which is a subsidiary of Cable and Wireless, to operate and the currently ongoing revision of the structure of telecommunication industry in Britain is bound to further increase competitive pressures by allowing, *inter alia*, capacity resale.[37]

Again, it immediately becomes obvious that any attempt to establish how privatization affected different aspects of BT's operations must run into trouble and any figures produced in this way will be more suitable for political propaganda than for academic discussion. The degree to which British Telecom plc adjusted relative prices charged for different services shows that under the old regulatory system total factor productivity growth could have been strongly overestimated, which in turn implies that the improvement brought about by privatization is in fact larger than the comparison of crude numbers would indicate.

These two examples show very clearly not only that privatization was accompanied by far-reaching changes but also that the extent of these changes differed from company to company, which precludes any comparison across the board. Therefore, the empirical evidence we are interested in can be collected, if at all, only with respect to individual companies. This will not, however, solve all our problems because in most relevant cases, even assuming away all data comparability problems, the available time series are still simply far too short to be used in any serious regressions. One more problem is that the

---

[36] The formula RPI - x was used for the first time precisely in this case.
[37] See Newman (1986), Vickers and Yarrow (1988), Yarrow (1989a,b), and Armstrong and Vickers (1990).

decision when to introduce the ownership dummy has to be arbitrary because the very act of privatization was always preceded by changes, outlined above, which had a large impact on reported results.

Although for these and many other reasons caution is strongly advised whenever performance "before" and "after" privatization is compared, one can still argue that the best - but not necessarily good enough - source of evidence which can be used to test the theoretical results derived above is, like in the previous section, that about these newly privatized companies which operate in more or less competitive markets. This means that we have to look at such companies as British Aerospace, Cable and Wireless, National Freight, Britoil, Associated British Ports, Jaguar and British Airways (Yarrow, 1989a).

Analysing data on these seven companies (Table B4), Yarrow (1989a) identifies three clear success stories: National Freight, Cable and Wireless and ABP.[38] National Freight's privatization was a workers-management buy-out and the incentive effect of employees' shareholding - to be sure, impossible in the public sector or rather achievable there only if even the workers became *high custodians of the public interest* - must have been particularly strong in a company which is in fact a collection of much smaller freight operations (Bradley and Nejad, 1989). Cable and Wireless, which even before privatization was profitable, successfully grasped new opportunities for expansion, opportunities which, on the other hand, under the Government's financial constraints would have been almost surely wasted. Finally, privatization allowed ABP to solve the overmanning problem - one of the typical public-sector diseases, impossible to cure without political embarrassment - which almost automatically improved its performance.

In the case of the other four, as Yarrow (1989a) clearly points out, external pressures, on which the direct effect of privatization is conditional, were strongly weakened by different "golden shares" etc., and by special relationships with the Government - defence orders for British Aerospace, the flag-carrier status of British Airways - which questions the quality of the British privatization programme (or, in other words, shows the strength of political constraints), but at the same time can be interpreted as suggesting that the accompanying changes diminished the effect of the ownership transfer itself.

---

[38] In all three cases what we labelled "the direct effects of ownership transfer" were strengthened by additional factors, but no estimation of their relative importance seems possible.

Privatization and Foreign Direct Investment in Transforming Economies

Table B4: Real Operating Profits (£ Millions in 1980 Prices) and Operating Profits as a Percentage of Total Sales Revenue and Net Assets in Financial Years

	British Aerospace			Cable and Wireless		
	Profits	% of Sales	% of Assets	Profits	% of Sales	% of Assets
1979	87	7.5	15.4	77	28.5	27.3
1980	92	6.5	13.4	70	24.5	24.4
1981	85*	5.7	10.5	26	21.8	19.2
1982	93	5.5	10.6	78	24.8*	18.2
1983	88	4.9	8.9	128	37.4	23.8
1984	124	6.7	11.1	148	28.1	23.6
1985	149	8.0	12.5	181	28.4	23.2
1986	148	6.9	12.3	206	32.5	22.8
1987	142	5.3	11.1	231	37.4	23.8
1988	-	-	-	232	38.2	23.7

	National Freight			Britoil		
	Profits	% of Sales	% of Assets	Profits	% of Sales	% of Assets
1979	-	-	-	131	41.6	-
1980	-	-	-	321	63.4	-
1981	-	-	-	413	55.5	-
1982	20*	3.2	12.8	472*	52.7	57.1
1983	18	4.6	18.8	492	49.9	51.9
1984	21	5.0	18.3	539	46.4	48.6
1985	30	6.2	19.5	534	42.0	46.4
1986	37	7.1	21.4	102	15.2	8.7
1987	43	7.1	22.4	420	35.5	-
1988	-	-	-	275	-	-

	ABP			Jaguar		
	Profits	% of Sales	% of Assets	Profits	% of Sales	% of Assets
1979	34	21.7	17.2	-	-	-
1980	16	11.4	9.4	-44	-26.6	-
1981	-4	-3.7	-3.0	-28	-15.8	-
1982	10	7.5	8.4	8	3.3	9.1
1983	12*	9.5	9.6	40	10.8	46.6
1984	-5	-4.8	-4.5	65*	13.7	50.3
1985	13	13.0	11.9	76	14.4	46.1
1986	18	16.8	15.3	73	12.9	34.3
1987	26	19.6	19.5	56	8.4	25.6
1988	-	-	-	-	-	-

	British Airways		
	Profits	% of Sales	% of Assets
1979	-	-	-
1980	-	-	-
1981	-90	-4.5	-8.5
1982	10	0.5	1.3
1983	150	7.4	19.4
1984	208	10.6	26.0
1985	216	9.9	30.3
1986	138	6.3	21.4
1987	117*	5.4	18.4
1988	154	6.3	14.4

* year in which the first trenche of shares was sold

Source: Yarrow (1989a) Table 9 and 10, pp. 319-320

The British privatization programme is usually associated with very complicated operations, transferring to the private sector utilities worth billions of pounds. This is, however, only one element of the Thatcher revolution. Even more important - although not equally spectacular and surely much less complicated - were, first, the sale of council houses and, secondly, contracting out of different services previously produced "in-house".

Yarrow (1989a) seems to be perfectly right when he writes that *indeed there is a strong case to be made for the proposition that it is the less-heralded changes in local government that are having the larger impact on performance* (p. 305).

Competitive tendering was tried in various cases, like British Telecom coin collection, Ministry of Defence cleaning, Army laundering, or even the carriage of parcel mail to Paris (Pirie, 1988), but local councils and NHS contracts are by far the most important (Ascher, 1987). An impressive example of the success of this kind of privatization is refuse collection.

Cubbin *et al.* (1987) tried to identify the sources of efficiency gains from competitive tendering for refuse collection which, according to Domberger *et al.* (1986), reduced the costs to the local councils by about 20 per cent. Their results seem to reject repeated claims that the main source of savings were lower wages and reduced fringe benefits rather than better management and higher physical productivity of inputs. Using an input-oriented approach to measuring efficiency, first suggested by Farrell (1957),[39] they conclude that the mean technical efficiency for private contractors is 17 per cent higher than for authorities that did not tender, which explains more than three quarters of the cost savings.[40] This was achieved thanks to *the removal of restrictive "task and finish" payment schemes and better deployment of vehicles and crews over geographical areas covered* (p. 54).[41]

A similar story can be written about competition for domestic, catering, and laundry services within the NHS. By 31 March 1988 almost all domestic and laundry services and some 76 per cent of catering services in the NHS had been put out to tender; estimated annual savings generated from contracts

---

[39] It is based on the notion that if a production unit is technically efficient, it must be using the minimum amount of inputs, i.e. labour and capital required to produce any given level of output (Cubbin *et al.* 1987).

[40] For the local authorities which opened for tender the provision of the service but retained it "in-house", technical efficiency improvements accounted for only about 40 per cent of the cost savings, which were smaller anyway (*ibid*).

[41] No wonder that since 1988 all local authorities are under obligation to auction the rights to provide different kinds of services for the provision of which they are statutorily responsible (previously only competition for contract for the supply of goods or materials was compulsory).

awarded for the three services totalled £106 million: £28 million from contracts won by outside contractors and £78 from tenders secured by "in-house" organizations (Fraser, 1988).[42]

This kind of evidence is very important from the point of view of our attempt to verify whether transfer of ownership rights - in this case, of the rights to the residual profits, which perfectly conforms with the definition of privatization proposed in Yarrow (1986) - is likely itself to have any positive impact. That is so because, unlike in almost all other cases of privatization, here we deal with a situation which can be described in terms of other things being equal.

Even though, strictly speaking, the achieved savings could be accounted for by competition rather than by the transfer of ownership rights, this is, first, an example of what we called the indirect effects of privatization, because competition would not be possible without, at least potentially, allowing for the transfer to the private sector of the rights to the residual. We (in Section 1.1.4.2.1) argued that statutory (local) monopoly does not itself imply public ownership nor the other way round, even though a publicly owned firm is more likely to enjoy such a privilege than a private one because, among other things, of the problems with rent dissipation and with writing complete contracts.

Rent dissipation is wasteful regardless of who owns the firms taking part, but in the case of publicly owned firms it is ultimately taxpayers' money that is wasted. Hence one can hardly expect this kind of competition if the given market is closed to private firms.[43] It is in this sense that any gains achieved are an indirect effect of privatization. At the same time consumers and citizens gain from lower prices.

What is more, since in the case of refuse collection we were able to compare three options, i.e. tenders with private winners, tenders preserving "in-house" provision, and no-tenders, we were consequently able, as it were, to separate the effect of competition from that of ownership transfer and, as we could see, the latter was indeed significant.

---

[42] If is sometimes argued that the price paid for such savings were increased divisions among groups of people actually working in hospitals (Cousins, 1990), but one cannot directly compare the two effects.
[43] Social welfare losses resulting from rent dissipation could be offset by the efficiency gains described above.

2.3 Politics of Privatization

This chapter was conceived as a review of relevant literature, but the available empirical evidence, reviewed in Section 2.1 and 2.2, transpired to be not only limited in quantity, but also of limited use for our purposes. What is more, the assumptions of our model are not likely to correspond precisely to the reality nor are they shared by other authors. In a sense the former is true for every theoretical model and that is why more or less complicated interpretations are part of any enterprise of the kind. But when one decides to make use of the already available empirical studies, the whole process of interpretation has to be repeated twice and sometimes the original intention is changed or even reversed in the process.

These two layers of interpretation, necessary as they were, decisively complicated our presentation and have to be kept in mind whenever an attempt is made to express our conclusions in a relatively unambiguous way. The conclusions themselves can be formulated as follows: empirical evidence for the comparative performance of public and private enterprises operating in a similar, by-and-large competitive, environment, as well as for the changes in the behaviour of privatized firms operating in such conditions, confirms the predictions of our model. What is more, we also managed to identify and specify some indirect effects of transfer of ownership rights. The value of efficiency gains, difficult as it is to measure precisely, seems to justify such transfer. However, to anticipate possible misunderstandings as well as to point out possible applications of these results, two things have to be made clear.

If we want to compare these results with the often quoted conclusion from Yarrow (1986, p. 235): *competition and regulatory policies are more important determinants of economic performance than ownership per se*, two points have to be kept in mind. First, one has to remember that in the article "Does ownership matter?" (Yarrow, 1989b), the same author gives a qualified, but in principle affirmative, answer to the question in the title, and this has to be taken into account when interpreting the above quotation. Secondly, one has to go back to what was written above about difficulties inherent in the concept of economic efficiency.

The previous discussion needs to be supplemented to take account of one more distinction, namely that between different levels of economic efficiency in different industries or markets and changes in the levels actually achieved or possible to achieve in the given firm or industry. The quotation from Yarrow (1986) is a general statement about the former and our analysis does not call it in question. Firms operating in (perfectly) competitive markets or under justified and properly designed regulations are likely to be more efficient and one could even say that a publicly owned firm operating in a competitive market will be more efficient than a private monopolistic firm. But our interest was much narrower. We were interested neither in the inter-industry differences in the efficiency levels, nor in the relative importance of the three determinants of economic efficiency, very important though these issues are.

The focus of our interest was on whether the overall effect of the transfer of a firm from the public sector to the private one improves economic efficiency, taking its external (and, in principle,) exogenous determinants like the degree of competition and the presence and design of regulation as given. This again brings into light the very essence, as well as the crucial importance, of the *ceteris paribus* clause, applied throughout the above analysis.

In other words, our conclusion is not that transfer of property rights is the only way to improve economic efficiency,[44] nor is it that such a transfer is the best, the cheapest and/or the most powerful policy tool that can be used to achieve this, and that therefore no other action should be taken, with or without privatization.

The question whether privatization is a *conditio sine qua non* of successful implementation of alternative policies has also to remain open. We did, however, conclude that a transfer of property rights would, other things being equal, improve economic efficiency. Yet to translate this conclusion into a policy recommendation would imply that the gains from transferring ownership rights are comparable, firstly, with other choices available at the same cost and, secondly, with the cost of the transfer itself. Any estimation of this kind, as well as attempts at a solution of all the other aforementioned problems, unfortunately go far beyond our analytical framework.

To avoid another misunderstanding we have to return to the problem of the relationship between ownership and the monopolistic position of the firm (mentioned in Footnotes 31 and 32). Should, for example, public utilities be privatized? Are not private monopolies just as bad or even worse than public ones? The context in which such questions are usually asked is that of the failure to increase competition in the process of the privatization of British utilities, but from this chapter it follows that there is no straightforward answer to this question. On the one hand, in view of what was called the direct effect of the transfer of property rights, *i.e.* the efficiency enhancing pressures coming

---

[44] From this it follows that examples like British Steel or British Coal, where performance improved dramatically without even prospective privatization, are in our context irrelevant.

from markets for property rights and for managers (Figure B1), it does not really matter whether we deal with a natural monopoly or not.

What could matter would be rather the size of the enterprises in question - and most utilities are in fact very large companies - which, for example, limits the possibility of takeover and increases the danger of free-riding by shareholders.

On the other hand, as has been stressed so many times, regulations are an important determinant of economic performance. That is why the question quoted above contains in fact two different problems:
- First, should utilities (natural monopolies) be regulated?
- Secondly, should regulated firms be privatized?

In our context, it is the second question that is relevant. Its importance follows from the fact that everything depends on the particular regulatory policies, and on the criteria used for comparison. Since it seems plausible to assume that the given regulatory regime has different efficiency effects, conditional on the form of ownership (Averch and Johnson, 1962), one could imagine situations where it is precisely the regulatory framework that favours one form of ownership and not the other and "proves" its "superiority". If this reasoning is correct, then one should try to separate this favourising factor from the factor of ownership as such. Yet it is precisely here that our ignorance has to be not only acknowledged, but also declared to be impossible to dispel because the real-life privatizations, which in theory could provide crucial empirical evidence, were accompanied by such far-reaching changes of the regulatory regimes that no comparison is possible.

In short, regardless of whether we agree that private monopolies should not be regulated, those which are not regulated in fact represent too rare a case to be discussed seriously. At the same time, the general question of whether private regulated monopolies are more efficient that public ones cannot be answered conclusively in this form. This ambiguity, which should of course be kept in mind, does however strengthen the case for privatizing the publicly owned firms which do or can operate in by-and-large competitive environments.

In this chapter we have analysed a theoretical model of the privatization of a firm in a market economy. We were interested above all in capturing as fully as possible the effect on the economic efficiency of transferring ownership rights; this resulted in a surprisingly strong case for privatization. Empirical evidence presented and interpreted in Section 2. qualified our conclusions slightly: in regulated industries (e.g. utilities) certain forms of regulation may suggest superior performance of publicly owned enterprises, as measured by standard financial indicators. Nevertheless, this possibility - or danger - only exists in very limited situations and by no means invalidates the whole case for the privatization of individual enterprises in market economies, a case which remains particularly strong in the case of enterprises operating in by-and-large competitive environments. The most general intuition behind this result is that, among other things, the economic markets lead to better results than political ones. This could be seen in a particularly clear way in what was called the "market for property rights" and the "market for managers". The possible gains from depoliticization of competition and regulation, whatever the rationale for the latter (demonstrated in Section 1.4.2) only strengthen this point.

If we look at this conclusion in terms of the structure depicted in Figure B1, we immediately notice the most important paradox present in the case of the privatization of a firm in a market economy: the negative effects resulting from "government failure" can only be remedied by political means. First, the very decision to transfer ownership rights has to be taken by politicians. Secondly, the decision to go ahead with the transfer, in contrast to our model, is usually accompanied by deliberately introduced changes in the degree of competition and/or in the regulatory framework faced by the newly privatized companies.

In most cases, again in contrast to our model, such changes are in fact unavoidable. This is what made any comparison between the periods before and after privatization almost impossible. Furthermore - and this is from where all the problems stem - these changes were discretionary in the sense that even if we assume that they aimed at improving economic efficiency, which is by no means certain (not least because of the many goals that each privatization was supposed to achieve), such an aim did not predetermine unequivocally the option to be chosen. As Yarrow (1986) reminds us, changes in competition and in regulations are of crucial importance. But the decisions in this sphere were exposed to the same dangers (stemming from the political character of the process of taking them) which these decisions were supposed to eliminate. This is true also for the choice of the techniques of privatization, as well as for other strategic choices. In other words, it is only politicians who can (re)establish the priority of economics over politics, but why should they be interested in doing this at all, not to mention doing it properly, if they are, as is plausibly assumed, utility maximizers?

Gains from eliminating political interference and from exposing agents to economic pressures (conditional upon transfer of property rights) may be potentially large, but may remain unachievable within the political processes.

The poor quality of some British privatization programmes illustrates this point very well, the case of British Gas being the "best" example.

Chapter C

Why Privatize? Redefining the Property Rights Structure in a Post-Communist Economy

1. Establishing a Market Economy: Redefining Property Rights

There exists abundant literature discussing the shortcomings of any attempt to organize an economy along the lines of central planning and demonstrating the superiority of market self-regulation and this chapter will not even try to review it. It will rather assume not only that the direction chosen by the Polish government, as well as by other governments in charge of post-communist economies, is correct, but also that in principle there was no other choice. In effect we accept that the desirability or even necessity of re-establishing market mechanisms in what used to be the western outskirts of the Soviet empire is self-evident.[1]

However, as mentioned in the Introduction, there arises the problem of whether the same can be said about privatization. Is the necessity to privatize what amounts to whole economies also self-evident? Does it necessarily follow from the desire to return to the market? The analysis of this chapter is driven by the belief that we need a detailed and exhaustive answer to the question of

---

[1] It has immediately to be noted that so specified an option does not specify institutional arrangements - there is not just one capitalism.

whether and why privatize the post-STEs, *i.e.* whether and to what extent privatization, the case in favour of which, in the context of a market economy, was analysed in the previous chapter, is an indispensable element of the systemic transformation under consideration.

Before the Second World War the public sector share of the GNP in East European countries was relatively high. Nevertheless, the economic systems of these countries could still be classified as market ones, even though the degree of their development, compared with the industrialized countries of Western Europe, was, with the exception of Bohemia, relatively low and differed from one country to another. The war not only resulted in immense destruction of human and physical capital, but also placed these countries in the Soviet sphere of influence. The rejection of the Marshall Plan, forced by the Soviets on their "allies", and the consolidation of Communist power paved the way towards the restructuring of their economies according to the principles which originated from the writings of Karl Marx but found their way to - and, hitherto, the fullest expression in - the real world in the system created by Stalin soon after he gained full control over the CPSU and thus of the Soviet state.

Stalin's death not only allowed for some timid reorganization in the USSR but also ended the most orthodox period of forced reproduction of the Soviet system in Eastern Europe. Nevertheless, from 1953 to 1989 very little changed with respect to the socialist principles of central planning and public ownership of the means of production and at the end of this period all those countries, the Soviet Union including, still had STEs.

As for state ownership, the state administration took care of much of the ownerless property, previously held by the Germans, by those who collaborated with the Nazis, or by the Jews, the majority of whom were exterminated. This process was bound to increase the size of the public sector, and although this by itself implied neither introduction of Soviet style central planning nor full scale nationalization, the latter surely became much easier than it would have been otherwise. There was also some degree of spontaneous nationalization as workers took control of factories and warehouses immediately after liberation, which made it difficult for legal owners to regain control over their property and was used by the state as an excuse for not helping them. The governments themselves argued for the need for emergency control of industry, which prepared the ground for some kind of central planning and could be described as *de facto* nationalization. However, even though it was *safe to affirm that, by and large, the idea of central planning as such met with no serious opposition in eastern Europe, as it entered its socialist period*, it was soon discovered that what really mattered *were methods of planning and the substantive content of the plans* (Brus, 1986a, p. 608). Official expropriation was to follow and it is here that, metaphorically speaking, Stalin did enter.

Stalin provided and legitimized the ideological inspiration of the new regimes established with a little help of Soviet tanks and secret police. Marxist ideology was not in this context an optional extra because it determined the strategic choices regarding the institutional framework of the economies being rebuilt. The new economic and political system was to be socialist and nationalization was perceived and advocated as a necessary step in this direction.

"Socialist" meant in this context that the Soviet implementation of Marx and Engels' ideas was to become the standard. In the aftermath of the October Revolution the ambiguities of the original blueprint were resolved[2] and socialism became a parallel alternative to capitalism instead of being the next stage of mankind's journey to the Communist paradise as originally envisaged. The development strategy used for this purpose (Brus and Laski, 1989, p. 24 - 25) is most adequately labelled as conservative modernization, which suggests that serious problems were to appear sooner or later.

The above remarks only remind us that nationalization of the means of production was, in fact, a necessary element of what was to follow the seizure of power by the Communists, even though it was as a matter of fact conspicuously absent from the programmes of the Communist-led fronts in 1944 - 1945 (Brus, 1986a, p. 596). Nonetheless, all the aforementioned factors contributed to the outcome in which soon the bulk of industry was soon nationalized. The allied countries achieved this state by 1946, while the ex-enemies did so by 1948. The period 1950 - 1953 completed this fast, thorough and radical process as it brought in all countries concerned further changes: *first, a reduction of the legal private sector far beyond all original pledges (in many cases resulting in its almost total elimination), secondly, full subordination of the cooperative sector to the state, amounting to what may be called the "etatization of cooperatives", rendered, that is, entirely subordinate to the state* (Brus, 1986b, p. 7).

---

[2] On the one hand, in Nove and Nuti's reader on socialist economics, the very first sentence of the introduction to Part One reads as follows: *Marx and Engels had no detailed blueprint for the socialist economy* (Nove and Nuti, 1972, p. 17). On the other hand, according to Lavoie, it is possible to find in Marx's writing much more about socialism than one usually expects and, for example, *where 'Das Kapital' offers us a theoretical 'photograph' of capitalism, its 'negative' informs us about Marx's view of socialism.* Therefore Lavoie (1985) concludes that *there is implicit throughout Marx's writing a single, coherent, and remarkably consistent view of socialism (p. 30).*

Once the political decision on nationalization had been taken and nationalization, accomplished by both "legal" as well as patently illegal measures, had started, *the way was open to the planned allocation, and ex ante coordination of economic activity was necessary if nationalization was to be used for macroeconomic objectives* (Brus, 1986a, p. 608). In this way what started with the nationalization of individual enterprises and of some sectors of the economy resulted in a nationalized economy, a full-blooded STE.

The historical background presented above suggests that one can expect an essential difference between privatization in market economies, discussed in Chapter B, and its namesake in the post-STEs. In the former, individual enterprises were to be transferred from the public sector to the private one in order to, say, increase economic efficiency. There were, for example in the United Kingdom, other objectives, mostly political ones or ones that could not always be justified from the logistic and economic point of view, but the macroeconomic effect of these operations was almost exclusively a function of the sheer size of privatized companies and worked above all through the state budget. The economy as a whole was and remained a market one and it is even difficult to say whether privatization really limited the extent of state intervention or only changed its institutional framework.

In the post-STEs too it is individual enterprises that are to be privatized - and it cannot be otherwise - but the problem is not so much their performance, supposedly, to be improved by privatization. The present institutional structure of, for example, the Polish economy makes it still very difficult to estimate the realized efficiency gains, even though from this point of view the situation has much improved since Leszek Balcerowicz started his stabilization and transformation programme. It is the economy as a whole - which does not mean, of course, its homogeneity from the point of view of property rights - that is at stake. Its privatization will be achieved by privatizing individual enterprises and not the other way round. Hence the case for or against privatization of the post-STEs has to be formulated exactly in these terms. The question of which enterprises should be privatized and of where to start is of great practical importance but from the logical point of view a secondary one. In other words, the question "Why privatize?" from the title of this chapter refers above all to "economy-wide privatization" or, even better, "transformational privatization".

2. The Ontological Contradictions of Socialism: Why It Could Not Work

We shall start our search for arguments for or against privatization of the post-STEs with the most abstract considerations, *i.e.* by describing some structural characteristics of what is sometimes called "real socialism" and by specifying their consequences. In this way we shall try to answer the question which will be repeated in each section of this chapter: is privatization a desirable and/or necessary element of the process of transforming the post-STEs into market economies, into - to use the formula from the economic programme of the Polish government - *a market system akin to the one found in the industrially developed countries* (in: Pejovich, 1990, p. 161)?

In the 1980s the systemic contradiction of socialism were extensively analyzed by Jadwiga Staniszkis,[3] a Polish sociologist and political scientist who in 1980 coined the phrase interpreting the Solidarity movement as a self-limiting (or self-restraining) revolution (Staniszkis, 1984).

Staniszkis (1988a) calls the economic system we are interested in the socialist mode of production. This mode of production, established in order to achieve economic rationality and just redistribution, has two inseparable characteristics: property relationships are *par excellence* political and not economic, and ownership is collective.[4]

"Political" is opposed to "economic" because *the state plays a special role not only by substituting itself for economic mechanisms - for example, by transferring funds between sectors as a substitute for accumulation or by creating demand or by setting prices - but also by systematically redistributing the costs and profits of production by administrative measures* (Staniszkis, 1987, p. 53). For example, the state budget replaces capital market and profits become an arbitrary result of an artificially created set of rules which itself is an outcome of bargaining. The decision criteria used in this process cannot be economic because, apart from the physical quantities of goods produced, *there is no universal and reliable standard by which to measure economic outcomes*

---

[3] Staniszkis (1989) is the most complete presentation of her analyses but several articles (1987, 1988a, 1988b, 1990) are equally important. Staniszkis (1987) and (1990) are available in English, the translations of the remaining quotations were done by P. Jasinski.

[4] This follows from the assumption that *a collective legal subject of ownership can be at the same time an economic subject, that the party - a mythicized historiosophic subject - can be simultaneously a political subject* (Staniszkis, 1988b, p. 224).

(Staniszkis, 1987, p. 55). In other words, economics is abolished and everything becomes politics.[5]

The collective character of state property or of what some call national property and the kind of access that there is thereto means that *property is non-exclusive since multiple subjects enjoy various and ambiguous rights to the same assets which are non-transferable on the capital market and non-inheritable* (Staniszkis, 1987, p. 53).

Both characteristics of the socialist mode of production have far-reaching and in fact disastrous implications. The absence of individually and separately owned capital assets makes market for these assets impossible because markets demand numerous and distinct owners. In consequence, the possibility of being guided by economic rationality (and market self-regulation) disappears, but at the same time no alternative universal principle emerges. For example, from the point of view of individuals in charge of various enterprises, investment becomes a kind of consumption, a *sui generis* appropriation in which the legal impossibility of claiming the residual is compensated by acquisition of prestige, power and more or less official perks and privileges. It is therefore no surprise that from the economic point of view production of the means of production becomes an end in itself. This is bad in itself, but in a system which also for structural reasons (Winiecki, 1988, Brus and Laski, 1989) is permanently starved for resources, *i.e.* in a resource constrained system, consequences of this state of affairs are even worse. At the same time it is exclusively the society as a whole that has interest in the reproduction of financial resources and capital assets: every individual is better off by free-riding and a built-in discrepancy between individual utility and social benefit becomes one of the main characteristics of real socialism and continuously upsets its working.

In an economic system embodying such principles, for the legal owner of the major part of financial resources and capital assets, *i.e.* for the state and its organs as well as their political masters, economic control over the sphere of material production becomes impossible despite the fact that they have full administrative control over resources and products (Staniszkis, 1988a). Such a system can therefore be described in terms of ontological contradictions because *the same characteristic which constituted it as a distinct mode of production (state-wide collective ownership) continuously questions and undermines it, segmenting it and creating a gap between the sphere of regulation and that of*

---

[5] The political character of property relationships is not contradicted by the existence of private sector economic activities because there is nothing that could stop intervention by the state, which is in practice the ultimate source of individuals' right to engage in these activities.

material production. In consequence *the basic goal of the socialist mode of production (rationality of control/stabilization) can be realized only by the means of self-limitation (de-articulation) of this mode of production* (Staniszkis, 1988a, p. 172).

Alternatively, one can follow the terminology of Staniszkis (1987), where she writes about the exhaustion of the system which was hitherto growing in an autarchic-symbiotic manner. *It has turned out to be unable to make the transition to an intensive economy or to pay its debts. (...) It has clearly lost all capacity for growth and by itself cannot even maintain levels already achieved. Although it is still able to survive politically, the system seems to have reached a dead end as far as the economy is concerned* (Staniszkis, 1987, p. 57). Attempts to reform it, *i.e.* to shift responsibility within non-exclusive property forms while the principle of non-exclusivity itself remains intact, can only cause the situation to deteriorate and it is no surprise that so many programmes remained on paper and those implemented simply failed to affect the real side of the economy (see section 3).

Briefly, the ontological contradictions of real socialism take time to show the full extent of its disastrous consequences but eventually prove to be a *cul de sac* regardless of how we interpret what the old regimes initially presented as undisputable achievements of the system.

If a solution for these contradictions were to be looked for within the system, it would have to be a dialectical one. What one could, however, observe both in the Soviet Union and in Eastern Europe was evolutionary "de-articulation"[6] of the socialist mode of production, which was supposed to remove or at least postpone the necessity of "ownership reform" (Staniszkis, 1990).

The process of "de-articulation" took many different forms. Firstly, *in order to meet the growing consumer demands originating from within the state sector, more goods in the private sector and the "second economy" have to produced* (Staniszkis, 1990, p. 181). Secondly, dependence on the Soviet Union, itself a consequence of reconstruction and development strategies assumed in the years 1948 - 1956, resulted in low efficiency of the state sector, in the diversion of capital from that sector into obligatory domestic and Soviet projects and in the limitation of the state's property rights in cases where direct

---

[6] In her definition of the concept of "de-articulation" Staniszkis (1990) follows Rey (1969) and Wolpe (1980): *A given mode of production is not fully articulated if the conditions whereby it is reproduced are linked with a second mode of production which entails significant costs in terms of the reproduction of labour* (Staniszkis, 1990, p. 193, note 3).

links between enterprises led to the USSR acquiring some of those rights.[7] Thirdly, both the Polish economy's inability to generate sufficient revenue from convertible currency exports for the purchase of foreign technology and its lack of innovation maintained its technical backwardness and isolation from western markets or even took them still further. The fourth expression of the process of "de-articulation" is the decapitalization of the socialist mode of production in Poland, particularly rapid in the mid-1980s. All four justify an interpretation of Jaruzelski's economic reforms as *"institutionalizing the process of de-articulation" and (...) strengthening (...) the supplementary structures to facilitate the regeneration of the state sector in its present form* (Staniszkis, 1990, p. 182).

Staniszkis (1990) has no doubt that a switch from "de-articulation" to "ownership reform" is highly desirable, even though in the short run its social costs would have been much higher; at the same time, however, she is aware that the change could not be achieved without a political breakthrough, unlikely though it was not only because of the dogmas and vested interests of the ruling group but also because of the inert structure of the Polish society (Staniszkis, 1987).

Elsewhere she describes all previous economic and political crises in terms of their non-transformational character because all demands in the sphere of distribution could only reproduce the system (Staniszkis, 1988b). Yet a breakthrough did happen in 1989 and its causes ranged from economic decline and shortageflation (Kolodko and McMahon, 1987) to perestroyka (Zukrowska, 1990) and the incompatibility between socialism and Polish culture (Herer and Sadowski, 1990). As "de-articulation" of the socialist mode of production is a kind of second-best solution to the problems experienced by the STEs, the formation of the Mazowiecki government in September 1989 opened the door for the first-best solution. Since the logic of the ontological contradictions implies that its removal or overcoming destroys the old system,[8] this, in turn, seems to justify presenting the necessity of recreating the institutional framework for market regulation and privatization as self-evident.

---

[7] The phenomenon of a buyer acquiring some property rights in a producer's assets without actually purchasing them has an interesting analogy in the classical book by von Mises: *All means of production render services to everyone who buys or sells on the market. Hence if we are disinclined here to speak of ownership as shared between consumers and owners of the means of production, we should have to regard consumers as the true owners in the natural sense and describe those who are considered as the owners in the legal sense as administrators of other people's property. This, however, would take us too far from the accepted meaning of the words* ([1932], 1981, p. 31).

[8] *The hereditary and marketable ownership of capital could not be introduced for the obvious reason that this would mean a change of the system itself* (Staniszkis, 1987, p. 58).

But is privatization the only form of "ownership reform" to be considered? Staniszkis's analysis of the contradictions under consideration suggests that what is needed are individualized assets belonging to individuals who can buy and sell them. The ownership of capital assets should be exclusive, inheritable and marketable, and this form of asset ownership should prevail. To this end assets would have to be transferred from state ownership to the private sector, *i.e.* to individuals, owning them directly or indirectly but still in the way characterized above.[9] This is precisely what is meant by privatization.

3. Socialist Calculation Revisited

In a sense it seems that Staniszkis's conclusions should end any discussion of the feasibility of socialism as an economic system based on public ownership of the means of production. Future research should rather be concentrated on explaining why the STEs not only survived so long but also appeared to work and on designing the least painful way of abandoning this experiment.

Nevertheless, one should not forget that Staniszkis has no monopoly on the analytical framework within which inherent problems of socialism can be discussed. The conclusions reached by her can be verified at a less abstract level by reporting the old discussion on the so-called socialist calculation. In this section we shall, among other things, summarize the main arguments put forward in this controversy and reinterpret its results from the point of view of our main interest. This should enhance our knowledge about the necessary elements of the transformation - or, more precisely, of the retransformation - process that the STEs started in 1989.

The starting point of the socialist calculation controversy was a very simple question: is a truly socialist economy at all possible? Is so general a blueprint of a socialist economy as the one that can be found in Marx's writings feasible? On the one hand, the answer, following the Latin formula *ab esse ad posse*, seems quite obviously to be in the affirmative because real socialism as

---

[9] At this stage of our analysis one should note that it is not collective ownership as such that has to be eliminated because group ownership seems to be compatible with market economy as long as there are many groups, independent from each other, and individuals have the choice of whether to join them or not (*i.e.* whether to invest their resources in them or not, becoming in this way materially responsible for the risks that they take). Modern corporations are the best example here, but there is also a theoretical possibility of an economy based on self-management where, unlike in Yugoslavia, employees own all the assets. However, regardless of whether it is feasible or not, it would contradict our definition of socialism because of the essential difference between public and group ownership of the assets.

defined above did in fact exist. The October Revolution, which had been *par excellence* Socialist, initiated it in Russia, and after the Second World War it was imposed on countries which were placed in the Soviet sphere of influence. What is more, an economy claiming to be socialist already existed when the controversy under consideration started.

On the other hand, the conclusiveness of this alleged achievement can be questioned by asking whether socialism is able to generate a relatively stable, long-run equilibrium and whether this economic system offers well grounded hopes for economic growth and development.[10]

Similar question have already been asked (and answered) many times. For instance, Schumpeter's answer to the question of *whether or not there is anything wrong with the pure logic of a socialist economy* ([1942], 1954, p. 172) is in the negative. He also writes, with a strong dose of optimism perhaps still justified in the 1940s: *Can socialism work? Of course, it can* (Schumpeter, [1942], 1954, p. 167). More specifically, to solve the problem of *the pure logic of a socialist economy* one has to answer the following question: *is it possible to derive, from its data and from the rules of rational behaviour, uniquely determined decisions as to what and how to produce or, to put the same thing into the slogan of exact economics, do those data and rules, under the circumstances of a socialist economy, yield equations which are independent, compatible - i.e., free from contradiction - and sufficient in number to determine uniquely the unknowns of the problem before the central board or ministry of production?* (Schumpeter, [1942], 1954, p. 172).

In his answer Schumpeter, whose importance in this context comes from the fact that he *seems to have been the first economist to declare the books closed on the debate over socialism* (Temkin, 1989, p. 33), follows Pareto as well as Barone ([1908], 1935) and claims that they solved the problem of socialist calculation. Hayek, however, calls it a myth because *what they, and many others, did was merely to state the conditions which a rational allocation would have to satisfy, and to point out that these were essentially the same as the conditions of equilibrium of a competitive market. This is something altogether different from showing how the allocation of resources satisfying these conditions can be found in practice* (Hayek, [1945], 1984, pp. 223-4).

This aspect of the controversy is sometimes discussed in terms of the difference between a theoretical possibility and what is in fact achievable in practice. The difference is also that between allocation as a state of affairs and

---

[10] Obviously, since we are talking about real world economies and not theoretical constructs, the only benchmark available is that of market economies, regardless of the extent of state intervention therein.

allocating as a process. That is why Hayek's statement that this is not impossible, *i.e.* that it is not logically contradictory (Hayek, 1935), contains the whole series of "ifs": *If we possess all the relevant information, if we can start out from a given system of preferences and if we command complete knowledge of available means* (Hayek [1945], 1984, p. 211). And although Hayek, unlike von Mises, concentrated his attention on the practical possibility of a general equilibrium type solution, it is wrong to interpret his statements as an admission of a "theoretical" possibility of such a solution, because all the relevant data for the whole society are never given to a single mind which could work out the implications and can never be so given because a modern economy is not only too complex but also continuously changing (Hayek, [1945], 1984, Temkin, 1989). However, the myth that the problem had been solved persisted not least because of Lange's repeated claims that there existed a competitive solution to the practical difficulties.

But the problem is in fact much more serious than this interpretation of the controversy under consideration would suggest: *what they* [von Mises and Hayek - P.J.] *objected to was the transformation of the concept of equilibrium from an explanatory device into a basis for central planning* (Temkin, 1989, p. 34). To see this clearly, one has to go back to the basic facts.

Private ownership of the means of production is of crucial importance because, to quote von Mises, *exchange relations between production goods can only be established on the basis of private ownership of the means of production[;] (...) where there is no free market there is no pricing mechanism; without a pricing mechanism, there is no economic calculation* ([1920], 1935, p. 111-2). Lange's "competitive solution", both socialist and Walrasian in its nature, was a challenge to precisely this claim. *Overwhelmed by the "crystalline beauty" of the Walrasian system, which assured general equilibrium under perfect competition, Lange undertook the task of proving that a centrally controlled economy with state ownership could be made to imitate that perfection* (Temkin, 1989, p. 36).

The promises were impressive: market socialism was to: (1) eliminate monopolistic or oligopolistic pricing, and other practices which prevent the kind of optimum results achievable under perfect competition; (2) internalize external costs; (3) eliminate the ups and downs of the business cycle, thus achieving also employment stability and higher rates of economic growth; and (4) correct inequalities in income distribution (Lange, [1936], 1964).

All of this was to be achieved thanks to envisaging Walras' tatonnement process - which, to use Arrow's expression, was a *clumsy theory* (1968, p. 378)

- as a practical procedure. Minimum cost production and the equalization of price to the (marginal) cost of production, *the two fundamental conditions of an explanatory model of perfect competition* (Temkin, 1989, p. 36), became in Lange's model operational rules.

This kind of epistemological confusion was made even worse by suggesting that imitating could do the trick, which von Mises ridiculed as follows: *they want to organize the socialist utopia in such a way that people could act as if these things [private control of the means of production, market exchange, market prices, and competition] were still present. They want people to play market as children play war, railroad, or school. They do not comprehend how such childish play differs from the real thing it tries to imitate* ([1949], 1966, pp. 706-7).

The relevance of the "competitive solution" is further diminished by the fact that the data are not really constant, which transforms the problem of eventually finding a hypothetical equilibrium into the one of securing more rapid and complete adjustment to the daily changing conditions in different places and different industries. Lange's proposal that price changes be made *at the end of the accounting period* or constantly as he suggested elsewhere were no solutions at all to the latter problem just as within his analytical framework there was no solution to the problem of contract prices (Hayek, [1940], 1948). It was in response to this last criticism that Lange, in a personal letter to the author of "The Road to Serfdom", acknowledged: *I do not propose price fixing by a real central planning board as practical solution. It was used in the paper only as a methodological device* (31 July 1940, cited in: Temkin, 1989, p. 38). What was - and by many still is - considered as a proof turned out to be only a methodological device![11]

Finally but not surprisingly, as in the general equilibrium model itself, the importance of information and incentive was also underestimated. This, from the point of view of the Austrian school, seems to be the most serious flow, a *cardinal fallacy*, in both approaches, *i.e.* in the general equilibrium approach as well as in the socialist one, because *the capitalist system is not a managerial system; it is an entrepreneurial system* (Mises, [1949], 1966, p. 707 - 8). The key word in this quotation is, of course, entrepreneurship. The routine task of a manager can be, at best, reproduced. But *an enterprising man* - writes

---

11 The ultimate position of Lange on these issues is unclear. On the one hand, he refused to revise his original paper (Temkin, 1989). On the other hand, in one of his last papers he wrote *let us put the simultaneous equations on an electronic computer and we shall obtain the solution in less than a second. The market process with its cumbersome tatonnements appears old-fashioned. Indeed, it may be considered as a computing device of the pre-electronic age* (Lange, [1964], 1985, p. 128).

von Mises - *discovers a discrepancy between the prices of the complementary factors of production and the future prices of the products as he anticipates them, and tries to take advantage of this discrepancy for his own profits* ([1949], 1966, p. 711). Yet within the general equilibrium framework there is no room for a theory of entrepreneurial choice and that is why the role of private property is misrepresented.[12] To eliminate, additionally, private property, which follows from the failure to recognize the importance of an entrepreneur, is to eradicate the institution that makes the market work. In other words, it is the entrepreneurship and initiative that makes private property a *conditio sine qua non* of the capital market, without which, in turn, self-regulation of economic activities becomes impossible. When private property is abolished, individuals are unable to take full material responsibility for the decisions they take; even Lange was aware of that when he wrote that *the real danger of socialism is that of a bureaucratization of economic life* ([1936], 1964, p. 109).

In short, the unequivocal conclusion is that private, fragmented property is absolutely necessary for the best possible allocation of resources: without private property there is no initiative and responsibility. This may not sound terribly original but, as one can see, forgetting about it had disastrous consequences.

The Austrian school's discovery approach to the cognitive role of the market[13] is vindicated - and finds its empirical confirmation - when we look at just one aspect of the STEs' operation, namely at their ability to innovate. The detailed study of this issue (Welfens and Balcerowicz, 1988) fully confirms what was known from anecdotal evidence. *In socialist systems the structures conceived as relevant for successful innovation management* [task formulation, organization and control - P.J.] *are difficult to realize. The reforms in some CMEA countries - above all in Poland - that aim to join more flexibility with more elements of market coordination could improve the conditions relevant for innovation management; however, short-run costs of reforms and reorganization make us expect that improvements can be achieved only in the long run,*

---

[12] It is true that even the simplest 2 x 2 x 2 model of general equilibrium is based on exclusive, transferable and inheritable ownership rights but their role is limited to that of an accounting principle which is supposed to individualize the circular flow of incomes.

[13] Lavoie (1990) distinguishes three approaches to the market: computational (*e.g.* Lange, [1936], 1964 and [1964], 1985, which he also calls computopia), incentive (*e.g.* Nove, 1983), and discovery (Hayek, [1978], 1984). The first two seem to be fully compatible with state ownership but Hayek argues that the principal *problem of the utilization of knowledge which is not given to anyone in its totality* cannot be solved without private property ([1945], 1984, p. 212).

especially as attitudes and behavioural patterns would have to change gradually (Dworzecki, 1988, p. 288).

The reasons for this failure are to be seen most clearly in the original, orthodox version of the STEs. There is no incentive to innovate because rivalry and struggle for market shares, absent from the theoretical construct of perfect competition, are incompatible with the constitutive characteristics of socialism. Market shares are allocated to various economic agents and shortages both eliminate the temptation to cheat and guarantee quiet life. Innovations cannot by definition be planned in advance and their implementation disrupts the fulfilment of plans already set up.

In principle incentives to innovate could have been generated by international trade, *i.e.* by competition on international markets but the STEs were closed economies and that in two senses of the word: the share of international trade in their GNPs was relatively small and the practice of *Preisausgleich* and the non-convertibility of their currencies isolated them from pressure towards costs reduction. Again, closedness, in the early stages imposed on the Soviet Union by the hostility of the rest of the world, is a systemic feature of the STEs: in Marxist economics there was no place for the idea of comparative advantage (Wiles, 1975) and the very concept of "economics of shortages" (Kornai, 1980) suggested that exports were a form of impoverishing domestic markets. Hence the only rationale for exports was originally to earn Western currencies to finance necessary imports. Furthermore, since the STEs exported manufactured goods primarily to each other, it meant that internal problems resurfaced at the CMEA level. In general, international trade was unable to encourage innovation.

In the orthodox STEs innovation ran above all against the logic of central planning, and the desire of the centre to modernize the economy (read: to catch up with the West) was shared by lower layers of economic administration only to the extent that it could promise extra funding which in turn could enhance prestige and unofficial appropriation. State ownership of the means of production contributed to this outcome both on its own as well as because of its inseparable link with central planning.

4. Limits of Marketization: Can the Pie of State Property Be Preserved and Eaten at the Same Time? Or: Is Market Socialism a Feasible Option?

The initial, most orthodox implementation of real socialism was a disappointment and the first reforms were attempted almost immediately after the end of the Stalinist period. The idea of market socialism began to agitate the minds of those who thought that return to capitalism was both impossible and undesirable. Careful reading of what the Austrian economists tried to say over decades, reported above, would have helped to notice that what was wrong with socialist economies could not be remedied by attempts to put together central planning and some market mechanisms. Nevertheless some reformers - later called by Kornai "naive" (Kornai, 1986) - did want to have a try.

The degree and persistence of disappointment with economic performance of the STEs is reflected in a number of planned, announced, and attempted reforms.[14] At that time nobody dared to renounce socialism and since, *inter alia*, public ownership seemed to be an either-or issue and markets were deprived of their dominant role but never completely eliminated, the reform designers and their political masters preferred to look for improved ways of organizing the economy, excluding at the same time any ownership reforms. The superiority of state property over any other form of property was argued in *a priori* abstract terms which were immune to empirical evidence (Staniszkis, 1988a, p. 64).

Formidable political and economic difficulties faced by the reformers show up in the fact that all but two attempts, even though many others were endorsed by respective governments (or rather politburos), were either cosmetic or never really implemented. The two which were tried relatively hard - the Yugoslav self-management market socialism of the early 1960s and the Hungarian New Economic Mechanism of 1968 - represent two different possibilities of marketizing the STEs but even they failed to deliver promised results. However, although it is no surprise that changes which have been following the Autumn of the People can no longer be described as reforms but rather as systemic transformations, which is particularly true about Poland,

---

[14] A list of blueprints for reforms proposed by various economist would be even longer but most of them were never taken seriously by politicians and even those which found their way on to the political agenda were very often victims of vested interests (Brus, 1988, Winiecki, 1986 and 1990). One could perhaps argue that these abandoned or ignored proposals would have been able to succeed where others failed, but the very fact that they were disregarded shows the limitations imposed by the political process in Communist countries and this systemic feature must not be assumed away. In the STEs politics and economics were interwoven more than ever.

Hungry and Czecho-Slovakia, the two aforementioned attempts at genuine reforms do not lose their relevance. They can and should be looked at very carefully because they illustrate very well internal contradictions of having the pie of socialism and simultaneously eating the fruits of economic efficiency generated (or at least made possible) by the operation of market mechanisms. If this, in turn, is true, the history of the theory and practice of reforming the STEs will constitute an important contribution to our discussion of the desirability and/or necessity of full scale privatization of the post-STEs.

4.1 Yugoslav Self-Management Market Socialism

The first attempt to apply the ideas of market socialism to practical organization of an economy was triggered by the Stalin-Tito break. It so strongly affected the imagination of Yugoslav ideologists that they discovered that self-management could be a better embodiment of Marx's (and Lenin's?) ideas than following blindly the Soviet example. For the most important decisions one had to wait, however, till 1961, when individual enterprises were given the right to determine autonomously the division of their net income (value added after taxation and social insurance payments) into personal incomes and retained funds. The distributional powers of enterprises were further increased when the tax burden was reduced and the interest payments on the capital assets, with which they had been endowed by the state, were first cut down and then completely abolished.

The reforms of the reforms, introduced in 1973, substituted self-management social planning for still only embryonic markets and marked a change in the direction in which the solutions of economic problems - particular as well as systemic - were looked for. Since market mechanisms were little relied on also in the period between the Stalin-Tito break and the introduction of the reforms, it is the years 1961 - 1973 that can be singled out for evaluation of the Yugoslav experiment with (self-managed) market socialism.

Despite certain positive signs - such as faster growth of labour productivity and an improvement in the balance of payments towards the end of the 1960s - *the overall result of the reforms must be judged as greatly disappointing, not only from strictly economic but also from social and ethnic-national points of view. Deceleration of growth accompanied by accelerated price inflation and rising unemployment, which could not be curbed even though the frontiers were opened for massive migration to Western Europe, bred popular discontent, particularly among the workers. The combination of the shift of economic power away from federal to republican and regional government with the greater role of market forces seems to have favoured the more highly developed parts of the country, thus exacerbating national conflicts* (Brus and Laski, 1989, p. 92).

If one is to learn anything from this disappointing experiment, one has to ask why the Yugoslav economy failed to benefit from and to sustain the market-socialist stage. As usual, diagnoses going in totally opposed directions were formulated: some economists claimed that it was the very idea of market socialism that should have been blamed for the disappointing results (Mihailovic, 1982), while others maintained that this idea was never fully implemented because the decision makers lacked courage and competence (Bajt, 1985).

From the point of view of the extent to which market mechanisms were reintroduced, one has to remember that although the concept of the labour market was ideologically unacceptable and therefore not even discussed, some forms of capital market did appear as early as the 1950s and their role was for some time increasing. Yet the latter market could not develop because workers were only some kind of trustees managing social property and appropriating the residual (custody and usufructus aspects of ownership rights), but at the same time they had to preserve the value of capital assets with which they were endowed.

Workers who were taking a decision to invest a part of the enterprise's net income instead of spending it on wages had to take into account the untransferable character of assets so created as well as the fact that the length of their employment in the given enterprise is uncertain. In other words, invested money was partly lost when a worker retired or simply left his or her firm. A similar loss would have been incurred if the investment had consisted in setting up a subsidiary whose collective afterwards decided to become an independent enterprise. This danger further limited the horizontal mobility of capital. The trade-off between the riskiness of investment and its rate of return was also beyond the control of individual "investors". Hence the decision to invest could only either result from political pressure (usually very strong because of the political monopoly of the Communist Party) or be a consequence of the limited number of more profitable investment alternatives (Furubotn and Pejovich, 1970).

This state of affairs explains why it was bank credit and not retained earnings that was so extensively used in Yugoslavia to finance investment

(Furubotn and Pejovich, 1971, Furubotn, 1974). Banks usually play an important role in the institutional framework of the capital markets, but in Yugoslavia even this route towards increasing allocative efficiency was all but closed because banks were owned jointly by enterprises and local authorities, which not only depressed interest rates, but also replaced commercial considerations by political ones.

In this situation it is no surprise that creating capital markets and making them work proved simply impossible. Consequently, marketization of the Yugoslav economy had to remain partial and the process of allocating resources continued to be a political one. This was not, of course, the only cause of the failure of Yugoslavia's experiment with her own brand of socialism,[15] but without a satisfactory solution of this problem one could not expect a success anyway. The Yugoslav experiment can therefore be interpreted as an indication that even if we reduce what is socialist in a socialist economic system to the dominance of state or social ownership of the means of production, full scale market coordination of economic activities and, in consequence, economic efficiency still remain unachievable.

4.2 Hungarian New Economic Mechanism

The Hungarian Communists, starting in 1968 the process of the implementation of their New Economic Mechanism (NEM) programme, chose a different route towards market socialism. First, the NEM was aimed at increasing economic efficiency and its realization affected the whole economy and not only the state owned sector. Secondly, state enterprises were no longer to achieve obligatory targets set by the centre. Physical allocation of inputs and outputs was abolished too. They were instead *to act as profit maximizers in free contractual relations between buyers and sellers, sensitive to prices and costs, exposed to the discipline of the market, and spurred to innovation and adjustment by the force of competition* (Brus and Laski, 1989, p. 64). The idea was to combine planning with a (regulated) market.

Again, the results, as measured by conventional economic indicators, proved rather disappointing. It seemed that the changes, far-reaching as they

---

[15] More generally, political forces which brought this system into being were also a direct cause of its collapse. *Yugoslav workers never asked for self-management. (...) Self-management is a propaganda slogan, a convenient piece of ideology, hurriedly chosen by the Yugoslav Communists in a critical moment of their history* (Lydall, 1984, p. 114).

were by STE standards, were not enough. And again the question about the cause of the failure has to be asked.

Explanations pointing out that the reform programme was never really implemented (for example because of the resistance of bureaucracy and/or of the vested interests of different groups) or suggesting that in crucial moments goals like maintaining full employment destroyed the consistency of NEM do not seem very convincing, which is not to say that those factors played no role at all. The problem is rather that of "missing" markets for labour and capital, or, in other words, of only partial marketization. The reason for this was that, despite the appearances, the reforms were supposed to preserve the socialist essence of the old system: state ownership of the means of production and a form of planning which would allow the political leadership to pursue their own objectives and impose their own preferences.

The Hungarian NEM was most thoroughly analysed by Janos Kornai and his colleagues at the Hungarian Academy of Science. They concluded, *inter alia*, that the absence of capital markets not only strengthened the position of the centre, substituting indirect for direct bureaucratic control, but also in practice excluded competition. Rivalry among companies having one and the same owner was hard to envisage and freedom of entry and exit was very limited. Attempts to impose so-called hard budget constraints failed for the same reason (Kornai 1980, 1986). Although their analysis of the failure of NEM amounts to a confirmation of what the Austrian school predicted a few decades earlier (Temkin, 1989), books and articles written by Hungarian economists in the 1970s and 1980s fell short of recommending systemic transformation. It was only the sweeping political changes of 1989 that not only made such a recommendation possible but also turned it into a political manifesto (Kornai, 1990a,b).

4.3 Theory of Market Socialism

As we have seen, neither in Yugoslavia nor in Hungary was the absence of capital market the only factor contributing to the failure of reforms; the complexity of the political and economic systems as well as the inherent imperfections of the former make the precise estimation of the relative contribution of different factors impossible. Nevertheless, two things seem to be indisputable: first, market regulation cannot be limited to some markets only, while others, in particular capital and labour markets, are missing and the activities of the state have to take over their functions. In this sense marketization in both countries was halted half-way through. But it could not have been otherwise because, secondly, full-blooded capital markets are simply impossible in an economy dominated by public ownership.[16] That is so because what is needed is full independence of firms and true entrepreneurship and each of these requirements contradicts state ownership rather than can be reconciled with it.

If we view ownership as consisting of rights of custody, usufruct, alienation, and destruction, *the change towards market socialism must therefore mean, first, that most of these rights must be renounced by the state administration in favour of the state enterprise; and secondly, that the latter must be capable of making use of them* (Brus and Laski, 1989, p. 133).

The first problem is similar to that of the separation between ownership and control (Berle and Means, 1933), although it could perhaps be better to have three elements, instead of the traditional two, namely: ownership, management, and entrepreneurship (Brus and Laski, 1989). In the STEs, partly because of their authoritarian political regimes, the three were paradoxically united and exercised jointly by state administration and party bureaucracy.[17] In parliamentary democracies, which are being reestablished in Eastern Europe and in which voters exercise their rights every four or five years and have much more important problems than control of SOEs, the problem of *quid custodiet ipsos custodes?* is far from being satisfactorily solved and their experiences with controlling the relatively small public sectors are not very encouraging. The absence of political accountability in Eastern Europe prior to the changes of 1989 made things considerably worse. Hence, even if the state were to be interested only in the return on and the growth of almost all its assets, which seems to be the minimum requirement, the kind and complexity of the agency problem generated in this way would be almost insoluble and finding a solution would not be helped by the disciplining effect of competition because this in turn would demand *de facto* fragmentation of state ownership into parts, each of them standing on its own: *state enterprises (...) have to become separated not only from the state in its wider role but also from each other* (Brus and Laski,

---

[16] In a sense it is "only" a matter of the size of the public sector - and the figure of 80 or so per cent in Poland in 1989 show how immense this problem is. It is difficult to determine *a priori* in percentage points when quantitative changes turn into qualitative ones.

[17] Individuals' entitlements to the residual were extremely attenuated and most often could be realized only in the form of non-pecuniary gains but they could still generate fierce resistance against any change, including bureaucratic sabotage. At the same time political liberalization and the turbulence of the transition period generated opportunistic behaviour or even simple theft, euphemistically called *uwlaszczenie nomenklatury*.

1989, p. 137). The contradiction between profitability of the totality of the assets and of each the assets separately is all too obvious.

Secondly, as has been shown in Section 2, there are few things that are more incompatible than entrepreneurship and state ownership. Even if the problems of control are solved, creativity, by its very nature, cannot be imposed. Furthermore, nobody will be materially responsible when a venture fails and decision makers, depending on circumstances, *will err either on the side of recklessness or on the side of overcautiousness* (Brus and Laski, 1989, p. 141). They will lack incentive to move resources to their highest value use. They will only pretend that they perform the role of the controlling owners and in this situation even the creation of some kind of horizontal financial intermediation will not help much. Alternative solutions, not tried in practice, like state holding companies, more authentic self-management, contracting out, or Liska's entrepreneurial socialism, do not promise a success either.

For all these reasons the analysis in Brus and Laski (1989) rightly closes with the following conclusions: *the chances of bringing the behaviour of state enterprises closer to the requirements of an effective market mechanism are the greater the further such enterprises are removed from state ownership in the traditional sense* (p. 146).

5. A Firm in the Post-STEs: Internal Structure

The principal message of Sections 1, 2 and 3 is that operational economy-wide market coordination demands the dominance of private property. In the case of the STEs it means that it is whole economies that will have to be privatized. Transferring individual enterprises from the public sector to the private one is "only" a necessary means to a systemic transformation of these economies. In this context, two things have to be stressed. First, had it not been the case, this chapter would have been almost totally superfluous, because the qualified case for privatization of individual state-owned companies has been demonstrated in Chapter B. Secondly, trivial as it may sound, an economy can be privatized only by privatizing single enterprises, either individually or in bundles, which gives rise to such problems as: how to privatize? how fast to do it? which enterprises or industries of the economy to privatize first? The problems of technique, speed, and timetable of privatization have to find solutions which are specific to the post-STEs. Straightforward extrapolation and application of, for example, the British experience, useful as it is, not only seems inappropriate but could also prove disastrous (Jasinski, 1990a). The actually formulated and implemented solutions will depend on the present economic (recession, still relatively high inflation rate, public sector and trade deficits *etc.*), political (the break-down of the consensus that ousted the Communists and a high degree of fragmentation of the first freely elected legislature) and social (patience in the face of falling real incomes as well as the awakening of entrepreneurial skills and attitudes) situation, on available resources (domestic resources and foreign investment), and, last but not least, on the legal structure and organization of the enterprises to be privatized. But the last of the listed determinants is important also at a more general level - the observed further deterioration in performance of state enterprises strengthens the case for privatization of/in the STEs.

In the orthodox STEs enterprises were created and liquidated by the governing state organs, and their assets remained part of the general stock of state socialist property. This orthodox stage did not last in Eastern Europe very long - it was soon followed by an evolutionary process which continued till the end of 1989. Market orientation of attempted reforms led in general to a substantial increase in enterprises' independence, even though the legal changes were unable - and never really supposed - to eliminate the system of political control best exemplified by the institution of *nomenklatura*.

In Poland, for example, the foundations of the final stage of this evolution were laid down by the Law on State Enterprises (25 September 1981). According to the Law a state enterprise could be created by central or local state administrative organs, such as ministries and local and territorial councils. As long as they legally existed, the enterprises were dependent on these founding agencies. Even though merging, splitting, and liquidating of enterprises were the prerogative of the founding agency, such measures had first to be proposed by the workers' council. That was so because within its legally determined sphere of independence internal management was performed by the workers' general assembly, the workers' council, and the director (Law on Self-Management of State Enterprises, 25 September 1981).

The responsibilities of the workers' council, which was elected for a two-year term by all the workers in a secret ballot, lay between those of the director and those of the workers' general assembly, comprising, among other things, the formulation of the enterprise's annual plans, its investment decisions, changes in the scope of the enterprise's activities, approval of the annual balance, and proposals of merger and enterprise liquidation. The director, who acted on behalf of the enterprise, was elected, and could be removed, by the workers' council. This decision was, however, subject to approval by the appropriate founding agency, and possible conflicts could be resolved in courts. In general, the scope of the agency's interference in enterprise management was limited to cases explicitly enumerated by law (Sajko, 1987) but the aforementioned institution of *nomenklatura* used to increase considerably the scope of intervention in the day-to-day running of the enterprises.

As far as the legal status of assets was concerned, according to the Polish version of the doctrine of divided ownership the state was the owner in the economic and public law sense, while the state-owned enterprise's ownership rights over the assets it held went as far as these of any other legal entity. In addition, it was asserted that the liability set out in the Civil Code and in the Law on State Enterprises would be illusory unless the enterprises owned the property (Sajko, 1987).

The attempt to introduce a radical, breakthrough systemic reform, started in the years 1980-1981, was continued in the so-called second stage of economic reform, designed in 1987 and implemented in 1988.[18] A package deal reached during the round-table talks in the spring of 1989 changed the environment in which state-owned enterprises operated, but with respect to the internal structure and external relationships of such enterprises the most relevant change was that of dividing capital assets of a given enterprise into two parts belonging to two different "owners": those acquired before 31 December 1982 (the so-called fundusz zalozycielski) were to belong to the state and those accumulated subsequently (fundusz przedsiebiorstwa) were considered as owned by the company itself. In consequence, apart form turnover and profit taxes paid by each enterprise, it had to pay to the Treasury "dividends" based on the book value of the fundusz zalozycielski and therefore independent of the financial results achieved in the given period of time.[19] Because of high inflation the value of fundusz zalozycielski was recalculated every year. Other important changes included new regulations on price setting, which enhanced the degree of freedom enjoyed by enterprises.[20] The enterprises also gained more room for manoeuvre in their dealing with the outside world as they could

---

[18] The principal proclaimed goals of systemic changes in the 1980s were: monetization, introduction of market relations, enhancement of the role of money and of the banking system, elimination of centralized planning in physical units and the gradual introduction of indicative strategic planning, reinforcement of grass-roots, company level initiative, promotion of workers' self-management.

[19] In the recession which started in 1990 this proved to be a very heavy burden on the finances of some enterprises.

[20] However, at the same time shortages increased and since they were dealt with by central allocation of inputs, much of the newly gained liberty proved rather illusory.

keep some of the currency they earned from exports (ROD).[21] All of this, however, only increased the degree of chaos in the economy which at this stage was neither a centrally planned one nor a market one.

Final touches to the internal structure and external relationships of what we have called a Polish post-communist firm were added after the Mazowiecki government had been formed, but a new law on state enterprise is still being discussed. Yet much more important than these formal changes was the effect on the behaviour of SOEs of the Balcerowicz plan and the impact of that plan on the economic situation in general. One can hardly underestimate the shock caused by a sudden switch to positive real interest rates,[22] by the introduction of internal convertibility, accompanied by very strong devaluation which equalized black market and official exchange rates, by almost complete liberalization of price setting, by the abandonment of any kind of central planning, and by the introduction of tax-based income policies (Blanchard and Layard, 1990; Lipton and Sachs, 1990). Subsidies were cut across the board and only the energy sector and transport were less affected. State firms, especially in consumer goods sector, were suddenly exposed to competition from imports and from the rapidly developing private sector.

This outline of the most recent changes would not be complete without mentioning the effect on the behaviour of enterprises of political changes. Even though many members of the old *nomenklatura* preserved their positions - partly because of the "thick line" policy of the Mazowiecki government and partly because of their near-monopolistic position on the managerial job market - their Communist Party masters all but disappeared from the political scene. At the same time not only did the direction of economic policy change, but so did also the way in which this policy was implemented. Never before did state-owned enterprises enjoy so much independence, but the same could not be said about the room for manoeuvre at the disposal of their managers; that is why the situation within enterprises was described by Prof. Andrzej Zawislak, Industry Minister in the Bielecki government, as some kind of Bermuda triangle: director - self-management - trade unions (Solidarity as well as the ex-Communist OPZZ). The *nomenklatura* past of many managers did not help them to strengthen their position either. In summary, although the internal structure and legal position of and within state-owned enterprises did not change much -

---

[21] At the time this led to the dollarization of the economy and provided a strong inflationary impulse. Once internal convertibility of the zloty was introduced, this arrangement became, of course, completely irrelevant.

[22] For example, in October 1989, according to the Polish Central Statistical Office, the monthly inflation rate was equal to 54.8 per cent while the interest rate was only 51.6 per cent per annum!

which could be interpreted as a failure of the Balcerowicz plan - the environment in which they were to operate was revolutionized.

Keeping all these factors in mind, how can this post-Communist firm be classified? Is it something totally unique, something qualitatively new, a combined result of the terminal stage of the STEs' development and of the initial period of systemic transformation? Or should we look for similarities between the structure of a post-Communist firm and the main types of firms already present in economic theory? What is more, the very existence and the role played by such institutions as, first, the workers' assembly and, secondly, the workers' council points to the Yugoslav self-management system as a principal reference point.[23]

The shortcomings of the Yugoslav system are well known and have been extensively analysed in economic literature.[24] Section 2.3 has very briefly presented and interpreted the way in which the Yugoslav Communists implemented the slogan *The factories to the workers!* (Lydall, 1989, p. 234). From the theoretical point of view, one can refer to two models of the behaviour of a self-managed firm which allow derivation of testable predictions: the so-called Illirian model (Ward, 1957 and 1958)[25] and the one based on property rights economics (Furubotn and Pejovich, 1970).[26]

---

[23] In fact, in 1980-1981, when the direction of economic reforms was negotiated between the Solidarity trade union and the government and the two above-mentioned legal acts, were debated by the Sejm (at the time the only house and at present the lower house of the Polish parliament), the discussion on the structural reform programme was conducted in terms of an alternative between managerial socialism (the so-called Hungarian model, although since then worker participation in Hungary has been substantially enhanced - Pejovich, 1990) and self-management Socialism, drawing strongly on the Yugoslav experiment (the heyday of self-management market socialism was already over but nobody expected the catastrophic economic crisis which began soon afterwards and is still going on) (Kowalik, 1990a and b, Jakubowicz, 1989). The background of the discussion comprised also some experiments with workers' councils introduced after October 1956 but soon afterwards deprived of any practical meaning (Brus, 1988), but one of the strongest factors determining not only the choice of what was thought to be the optimum solution but also the extent of unconstrained discussion of such a solution was politics: real socialism - and therefore a STE in this form or another - was there to stay and the Communists could still count on both the Polish army and police and on fraternal help from Poland's neighbours led by Brezhnev's Soviet Union. One must not forget either that the imposition of the martial law in December 1981 strongly limited the implementation of the most radical measures contained in both documents of 25 September 1981.

[24] See, *inter alia*, Estrin (1983), Lydall (1984), Lydall (1989).

[25] A self-managed, Illirian firm, as compared with a capitalist one, will, *ceteris paribus, reach its optimum with lower output, lower employment and higher capital intensity than the latter [i.e. a capitalist one], because the objective function of a self-management enterprise is maximization of income per worker and not of profit* (Brus and Laski, 1989, p. 97).

[26] Even though it is theoretically possible to conceive of a situation in which, according to this model, it is rational for workers to invest in what they cannot own, the conditions under which it is supposed to happen are rather unlikely to appear in practice.

These two theoretical models *suggest that there are serious difficulties in making even a competitive system of self-management work efficiently* (Lydall, 1989, p. 72). But *the Yugoslav system*, which served as a source of inspiration for Polish reformers, *is not competitive self-management, but Socialist self management* (Lydall, 1989, p. 72). On the one hand, according to Lydall, *socialist self-management has all the weaknesses of competitive self-management (...) but in greater degree* (Lydall, 1989, p. 78). On the other hand, to be genuinely competitive, it would need to abandon the idea that capital assets are owned by the nation as a whole, which in turn would question the socialist character of such a system.

The collapse of the Yugoslav economy discredited socialist self-management. Should one, therefore, try its competitive version? Its introduction would constitute a systemic transformation and amount to yet another grand experiment. In a sense foundations for such an experiment were already laid down in Poland and one could attempt to combine the switch towards multi-party democracy - removing in this way one of the main causes of the collapse of the Yugoslav economy - with allowing workers' councils to fully exercise their rights, as expressed in the laws of 1981. At the same time, the necessity to preserve socialism was no longer a constraint and full property rights with respect to previously state owned assets could be, for example, transferred to the workers, either as collectives or as individuals (Krawczyk, 1990). Apart from the different forms of workforce enfranchisement one could also try to reestablish public ownership in the strict sense of the word, *e.g.* by abolishing self-management. This would not, however, promise much success either, as shown in Chapter B.

A quick look at the history of self-management - or workers' participation, as some prefer to call it - in Poland could throw some light on the dilemmas faced by those in charge of the Polish economy. With or without the Communists in power, self-management was promising to be a solution to many problems of the old system, from guaranteeing independence of enterprises from the centre's interference to the possibility of creating some rudimentary capital market (Dabrowski, 1990). This list could be extended by far more abstract considerations such as the existence and stability of a general equilibrium in labour managed economies (Dreze, 1990). At the same time even Marek Dabrowski, one of the principal advocates of self-management in the late 1980s, acknowledges that the logic of promoting self-management was that of the second best (Dabrowski, 1990). As long as Poland was a member of the Soviet bloc, a form of self-management was supposed to reconcile the demands of market-oriented economic reforms, needed more and more badly, with international and ideological constraints of having to preserve socialism. More precisely, self-management, when initially introduced, was to substitute the control from below, *i.e.* by the employees, for the control from above, *i.e.* by central planners and founding agencies and therefore it is rightly listed among those proposals whose principal rationale was to protect individual enterprises from the politically motivated interference by the centre, made even more arbitrary by the authoritarian character of real socialist regimes. But such a need does not exist any more[27] and therefore the principal justification for the self-management option is no longer valid.

Yet even when the aforementioned rationales and constraints disappeared or at least appeared to be less binding than in the past, it was still thought that a return to full blooded capitalism - including far-reaching privatization - could not get enough public support because, according to an often used cliche, there was no middle class (Dabrowski, 1990; Kolodko, 1990; Staniszkis, 1990). Therefore the fundamental question is whether these social factors are a sufficient reason for sticking to the second best? Should they stop the decision makers from pursuing the first best, *i.e.* from transition towards a market economy dominated by private property? The question can be also reversed: Are there any social forces that would support yet another grand experiment on an economy-wide scale, that is the creation of a competitive self-management economy?

The above analysis suggests unequivocal answers to these questions and its conclusions coincide with the desire expressed by the first non-Communist government in Poland, who in their very first economic programme stated that its goal was to *set up a market system akin to the one found in the industrially developed countries*. As for post-Communist firms, it means that there is no alternative to privatization, not least because of the problems arising from their present internal structure.

There seems to be an analogy between this aspect of the problem "why privatize the post-STEs?" and the British privatization programme. Regardless of the role played by the difficulties which the first Thatcher government experienced with bringing under control the PSBR and regardless of the extent to which these problems were caused by the rather peculiar accounting principles governing the British budget, there was doubtless quite a lot of both

---

[27] At present the attitude of the centre is that of self-restraint and both Tadeusz Syryjczyk and Andrzej Zawislak, Industry Ministers in, respectively, the Mazowiecki and Bielecki governments, were accused of not doing enough and of being unable to formulate industrial policy.

disappointment with the performance of the public sector companies and frustration stemming from failed attempts to discipline them. If this is true, then apart from the long list of objectives openly or covertly pursued by privatization programmes (Yarrow, 1986; Moore, 1986) the transfer of individual companies from the public to the private sector can itself be interpreted as giving up the search for the optimum solution. Similarly, in Poland the problem of what to do with state-owned enterprises demands an urgent solution and one has to choose between experiments with new forms of control of state-owned enterprises (*e.g.* self-management or holdings) and privatization, which solves the problems of state-owned enterprises by getting rid of them. The British governments still had to solve the problem of how to regulate utilities which constituted the major part of the privatized companies. In Poland and other East European countries the situation is much simpler: there are plenty of firms which operate in at least potentially competitive markets. If relatively liberal trade policies are pursued, then these firms do not require any special regulatory framework apart from antitrust policies. This line of argument, certainly powerful as it is, makes the case for privatization in and of the post-STEs stand on the rejection of all other alternatives.

6. The Post-STE Firm and Stabilization of the Economy

It has recently been said that the Communists not only were ruining the Polish economy for the whole period they were in power, but also set fire to it just before they left office. Such a statement could be slightly exaggerated - but only slightly - but there is no doubt that the Mazowiecki government took over an economy in a very deep crisis. The most spectacular illustration thereof was (hyper)shortageflation: inflation turning into hyperinflation and accompanied by increasingly acute shortages (Kolodko, 1987 and 1990). Internal imbalances were made worse by the external one as the country was unable to service its mounting debt. Nobody was really in control of anything.

The Balcerowicz plan, commenced in January 1990, changed drastically the environment in which firms had to operate and the expression "shock therapy" is no exaggeration: almost overnight sellers' markets became buyers' ones (Lipton and Sachs, 1990, Blanchard and Layard, 1990). However, even though the ultimate goal of this plan was the systemic transformation of the Polish economy, in the short run its aim was to stabilize the economy by using macroeconomic policy tools.

Quite obviously, the success of the Balcerowicz plan depended on the extent to which the behaviour of economic agents is modified. Given the dominance of the state sector it was the nature of change within it that was crucial. The stabilization programme assumed that the behavioural patterns of state enterprises would resemble, in large measure, that of privately owned companies in a market system. Do the consequent difficulties in achieving stabilization provide yet another argument in favour of privatization? Later in this chapter the question will be answered in the affirmative.

The behaviour of state-owned enterprises was extensively investigated and is relatively well described. For example, Instytut Gospodarki Narodowej (IGN) surveyed 50 state owned enterprises producing exclusively or mainly consumer goods. They were drawn from seven industries and their employment ranged from 193 to 8000 people. The survey aimed to find out how SOEs responded to radical anti-inflationary elements of the stabilization programme and to sharp decline in demand. Its authors were also interested in the impact of gradually emerging market environment together with the first signs of competition as well as in the influence that the possibility of changes in their ownership status had on their behaviour. The main investigating method employed was that of questionnaire analysis. The survey's findings can be summarized as follows:

The general economic situation increased the level of uncertainty and the political changes affected, *inter alia*, the power structure within enterprises. 80 per cent of directors thought that the workers' council had a large or very large influence on the decisions taken in their enterprises. Sixty-two per cent of them perceived the Solidarity trade union as playing an equally important role, which makes both institutions much more influential than the lower layers of management.

When the managers were asked to identify the most important criteria that were used by the workers' councils and trade union leaders to evaluate their performance they listed: continuous increase of wages (72 per cent), profits (58 per cent), conflictless cooperation with Solidarity (40 per cent) and with the workers' council (28 per cent). In other words, politics was still perceived as an important dimension of the internal functioning of state-owned enterprises.

The decisions themselves, according to those who ultimately took them, were determined to the largest extent by the (new) rules of the economic-financial system. No enterprise complained about interference by its founding agency (in most cases the Ministry of Industry), which constituted the most significant change because it showed that economic instruments finally replaced direct contacts with the centre.

What happened to the enterprises surveyed in the first half-year of the realization of the Balcerowicz plan? Seventy-five per cent of them greeted its implementation with huge price increases - 30 per cent of them by more than 200 per cent, which was a clear sign that the reference point for their price setting decisions was not the level of demand but the current and expected rate of inflation. In their behaviour one could also notice a high degree of inertia because despite a fall in sales experienced by 63 per cent of the enterprises they still wanted to keep the profits at their previous level. This meant, in turn, that the mark-up on costs had to go up, as was indeed the case. Later on some firms recognized initial overshooting in their price setting and prices went down slightly. This is confirmed by the fact that although the rate of return was systematically falling in 1990, by the end of the year its level was still as high as 30 per cent.[28]

The suspicion that state-owned enterprises simply did not want to compete with each other seems well grounded. Complacency, understandable as it is in this situation, is illustrated by the fact that only one out of the 28 enterprises in which this question was answered attempted some kind of marketing of its product instead of trying to sell almost everything to the old wholesale trade centrals.

Sales diminished very quickly but it took time to reduce production. At the end of the period investigated capacity utilization was below 80 per cent for 60 per cent of the enterprises but the managers still did not expect the fall in demand to be permanent. There was some "desperate" increase in exports, facilitated by the strong devaluation of the zloty on 1 January 1990, but nobody felt it necessary to improve their offer by introducing technical changes in the products.

As 94 per cent of the enterprises surveyed had previously enjoyed some kinds of tax exemptions or subsidies, their withdrawal, which was an important part of the Balcerowicz plan, substantially increased the fiscal burden imposed on those firms. Forty-three per cent of them simply tried to make up the losses by forcing customers to pay higher prices. Nevertheless, by the end of June 25 per cent of the enterprises were already indebted with the Treasury and 84 per cent of them did not pay their suppliers on time: penal interest rate was still

---

[28] The whole phenomenon has to be seen in the context of the high degree of monopolization of the Polish economy, the more so as only 26 per cent of enterprises acknowledged that they had to face strong competition, either domestic or from abroad.

lower than the cost of credit. At the same time, in the hypothetical situation of having these debts written off, 67 per cent of the enterprises wanted to use these windfall gains to increase wages.

As far as wages were concerned, all those enterprises had to work in the conditions of very stringent, tax-based income policies. The tax rate on the increase in the wage bill above the announced norm (the so-called "popiwek"), related to the rate of inflation, was as high as 500 per cent if the norm was exceeded by more than 3 per cent. The norm was not "fulfilled", for different reasons, by 62 per cent of the enterprises, but this does not mean that there were no substantial wage increases in money terms.[29] What is equally important is that there were no attempts to adjust wage structure within enterprises.

As for attempts to make their offer more attractive for buyers, 62 per cent of the enterprises surveyed either introduced no changes or the changes that they introduced were of rather cosmetic nature. One has the impression that the enterprises were in general satisfied with what they had been producing previously, which can hardly be interpreted as an expression of entrepreneurship. On the other hand, one must not forget that high levels of uncertainty rarely encourage innovations. Furthermore, if introducing new products demands extra financing, the problem may become insoluble for firms in financial difficulties.

Similar patterns can be noticed in the enterprises' reactions to increased prices of inputs. About 60 per cent of them did not replace the raw materials and intermediate goods they used at that time with cheaper substitutes and 36.2 per cent of the enterprises did this only to a very limited extent. The enterprises did not credit themselves with any relevant improvement in the use that they made of these inputs and of energy. Instead, 84 per cent of the enterprises surveyed simply increased prices. Eighty-two per cent were unable to report any cost-reducing changes in this sphere but at the same time 98 per cent denied that their behaviour was passive!

The enterprises surveyed, as well as all the other state-owned enterprises, were free to decide the level and structure of employment. The determinants of their decisions were both external (*e.g.* falling production and income policies based on the aggregate wage bill) and internal (*e.g.* power structure within enterprises) but the general conclusion is clear: in most cases the number of employees fell by much less than production and even this

---

[29] Despite that fact that the norm worked in a cumulative way, this situation changed dramatically in the second half of the year.

reaction was strongly delayed. What is more, despite universal awareness of considerable overmanning, inherited from the past, a considerable share of employment reduction could be accounted for by autonomous decisions taken by employees.[30] No enterprise was internally reorganized nor was the share of fixed costs (koszty ogólnofabryczne) diminished, which shows once more the negative nature of the adaptation processes. The enterprises wanted simply to survive the difficult period instead of adjusting to the new times.[31]

Summarizing the findings of his team,[32] Professor Jan Lipinski pointed out that the authors of the stabilization policy had expected that the inflationary effect of rising costs would be diminished by a fall in demand. However, enterprises were not prepared to see their profit rates going down and falling demand had no effect on price setting decisions. The introduction of positive real interest rates had in the period under consideration only a weak influence on the level of inventories and investment and was really relevant only as far as the speed of paying outstanding bills to the suppliers was concerned. But the Ministry of Finance, responsible for designing and implementing the stabilization programme, was also partly to blame because non-payment of various taxes and/or dividends did not trigger either bankruptcies or sanation procedures, which brings to mind Kornai's concept of the soft budget constraint. The statutory powers of Izby Skarbowe to control prices charged by monopolists were not used either.

There were also many other factors which led to these disappointing results. Firstly, one of the determinants of the behaviour of SOEs was certainly their perception of the credibility of the government's commitment to reforms. The Balcerowicz plan was neither the first attempt at reform nor the first stabilization programme - the so-called first and second stages of the economic reform as well as the programme of strengthening the Polish currency prepared by the NBP are just a few examples from the 1980s and each of them was initially publicized as something very radical. Hence the enterprises had reasons

---

[30] The workers' councils and trade unions were, of course, partly to blame because they demanded improved results from managers but were not prepared to pay the price, *i.e.* to accept redundancies and lay-offs.
[31] The economists from IGN also asked questions about the attitude towards changes in the ownership structure. The answers are quite revealing as the directors suggested that insolvent and inefficient enterprises should be privatized first but all of them volunteered with their own enterprises. Privatization was for them above all an opportunity to increase financial resources at the disposal of their enterprises as well as to change the power structure within them. No director expected that the remuneration in privatized companies would worsen. There was criticism with respect to the Law on Privatization of 13 July 1990 but no enthusiasm for ESOPs.
[32] Similar conclusions were formulated by other research groups - see Dabrowski *et al.*, (1991), Maj, (1991), Schaffer, (1991), and Mayhew and Seabright, (1992).

to expect that the government would sooner or later back down, so they did act upon their previous experience. It was an error - and an expensive one - on their part because this time the political will and public support did coincide, but it took time to recognize it.

Secondly, in the whole post-war period the managers and directors of SOEs were neither expected to act independently - under central planning this was dysfunctional behaviour and the previous reforms never really dismantled the political safety net - nor forced to do so by the environment in which they operated: the STEs were by their very nature economies of shortages, *i.e.* they were economies where producers sovereignty reigned. Hence the expectation that the decision takers would know how to cope with a completely new situation was based on heroic assumptions and both the lack of appropriate skills and the straightforward ignorance displayed by the managers certainly played an important role.

The behaviour of SOEs in the first half of 1990, as surveyed by IGN, had certain features which can be identified as systemic ones, *i.e.* as either following from their state-owned status and/or being a consequence of the self-management orientation of previous reforms. In this context the question whether and to what extent the Ministry of Finance is to blame is of course important but it does not change the main conclusion, namely that there was a serious discrepancy between the actual behaviour of state-owned enterprises and that which was assumed by, and required for the success of, the stabilization programme.

In itself such a discrepancy suggests that one - or both - of the two should be changed, *i.e.* either the stabilization programme or the behaviour of state-owned firms. We have however from the very beginning assumed (see Introduction) that the STEs are to be turned into market economies. From this assumption it follows that the stabilization programme, absolutely necessary as it was in the autumn of 1989 and in the winter of 1990, had to be a version of what is sometimes labelled IMF orthodoxy or heterodoxy (Kolodko *et al*, 1991). Nobody claims that the programme actually implemented in Poland was designed ideally, but adjusting it in such a way that it could take into account the consequences of the ownership structure of the Polish economy and of the distribution of property rights within it would only have petrified the existing structures. Consequently, the Polish post-STE would perhaps have been stabilized, but the systemic transformation would have had to be delayed or at least considerably slowed down.

If the post-STEs are to be transformed into market economies and at the same time to be stabilized, one has to change the institutional structure of these economies and their ownership structure in particular. More precisely, the umbilical cord of the soft budget constraint and the vicious circle of the internal power structure must both be interrupted. Again, there are many theoretical possibilities, but only those which include privatization combine support of empirical evidence, discussed extensively in this thesis, with relative simplicity. It does not therefore matter to what extent the negative phenomena observed were consequences of state ownership as such and to what extent it was rather particular institutional arrangements that should be blamed. What is much more important is that the degree of pain caused by the stabilization policy itself is likely to considerably weaken public support for systemic transformation, which should be used as yet another argument in favour of radical solutions of existing problems and as quickly as possible at that.

7. Conclusions: Dilemmas, Trade-Offs and Contradictions of Privatizing

The section which ended Chapter B, reminded us, *inter alia*, of the difference between the transfer of ownership rights and privatization as a multidimensional process. It is precisely in the sphere of changes accompanying privatization that various dilemmas, trade-offs and contradictions appeared. Complex and difficult to solve and/or overcome as they are in the case of an individual firm in a market economy, they may appear relatively easy when contrasted with the problems of privatizing the entire post-STEs. Redefining property rights is doubtless much more complicated than transferring them and therefore one can expect many more dilemmas, trade-offs and contradictions to accompany the former.

Staniszkis's analysis of the "ontological contradictions" of socialism (Section 1) showed that achievement of the ideologically motivated objectives of real socialism was prevented by the very nature of the means employed. Her analysis and the Austrian school's demonstration that the price to be paid for breaking the sequence of *private property-free market-pricing of goods-rational economic calculation* is economic rationality (Section 2) show that market self-regulation of economic activities on the one hand and private property on the other are inseparable. The latter is a necessary condition for the former and that is why to overcome the "ontological contradiction" of socialism - and to reestablish economic rationality - one needs "ownership reform". In other words, reestablishing an economy dominated by private property should be the ultimate goal the systemic (re)transformation of the STEs. But so formulated an objective states only what is to be achieved; it implies nothing about the process of achieving it. It is not even certain whether a path from the present state to the desired one really exists, as the jokes about the aquarium and fish soup or about eggs and omelette suggests.

The ontological contradictions of real socialism, as analysed by Staniszkis, implied that "ownership reform" is a necessary condition for the market regulation of economic activities. But if the former is to precede the latter, then what should the length of the transition period be? Can "ownership reform", or more specifically, privatization be achieved at the stroke of a pen? Should the whole process of transformation be completed at one go because any intermediate steps seem to be excluded, *i.e.* should the critical mass of private property be reestablished by a single act of the Parliament? Even the most ambitious programmes of privatization fall short, mainly for practical reasons, of envisaging so much so quickly. In other words, privatization appears not only highly desirable, but also necessary; at the same time there is no doubt that logistically it will be very difficult, if not impossible. Privatization programmes will also have to solve problems of management of SOEs because the transitional period will last years and not months. However, if privatization cannot be achieved instantly, are we not running the risk that our efforts will create yet another form of "de-articulation" of the socialist mode of production?

If one turns to the Austrian school's case for the privatization of the post-STEs, it becomes immediately apparent that the socialist calculation controversy, in which von Mises and Hayek prominently took part, suggests an equally uncomfortable either-or alternative, with no reference to any intermediary state. This is quite understandable because these economists wanted to protect (and ameliorate) the capitalist *status quo* in order not to have to restore it. The experiences with market socialism in Hungary and Yugoslavia demonstrated that private property is necessary for the creation and efficient operation of capital markets. The STEs could successfully reform themselves only by renouncing their essential characteristic: public ownership of the means of production. Socialism may be unreformable but if markets are necessary for the pricing of the assets that are to be transferred, as seems to be the case, then we seem to end up with some kind of vicious circle. In short, in this context privatization may appear as almost a panacea - but also as a Holy Grail.

The so-called privatization from below (Kawalec, 1989; Jasinski, 1990a), *i.e.* allowing unlimited development of the private sector and withdrawing all privileges from other sectors, could be a solution but at the end of the Communist era the state-owned sector was producing about 80 per cent of GNP in Poland and almost all the output in Czecho-Slovakia. This means that to rely exclusively on the growth, however rapid, of the domestic private sector and on foreign investment would make the process of systemic transformation unacceptably long. And how would the economic activities be regulated in the meantime? One should therefore proceed with privatization as quickly as possible, but the question "how?" remains unanswered.

Sections 1, 2, and 3 derive the necessity/desirability of privatization from the necessity/desirability of recreating an economy eventually dominated by private property. An economy is, however, either dominated by private property or not and hence some of the most difficult problems. Section 4 formulated two additional arguments, which can be labelled the "negative" and the "common denominator" arguments. Not surprisingly, each implies difficulties of its own.

The organizational structure of post-STE firms in Poland appeared to justify their privatization because (to sum up our rather long discussion) neither socialist self-management, nor competitive self-management, nor direct public ownership could realistically promise anything better. The first post-Communist governments in Eastern Europe was faced effectively with a choice between setting up *a market system akin to the one found in the industrially developed countries* and therefore having mostly private firms on the one hand and yet another grand experiment on the other.

But if one accepts that *the idea that there is such a thing as private property is shown to be false* and that *what is at issue at all times is the precise "bundle of property rights"* which is created by changes in ownership (Veljanovski, 1987, p. 21), then the whole discussion becomes a discussion on different bundles of property rights which differ from each other according to the degree of their attenuation. Unfortunately very little can be said in advance about whether a given state-owned enterprise should be privatized, for instance, by takeover or by public offer. The problem is not only that of choosing the right technique of privatization. Choosing an appropriate legal form - and, in a sense, the future owners - for a privatized enterprise is equally important and problematic, and the promise of higher economic efficiency is marked - and put at risk - by precisely this fundamental indeterminacy.

The case for privatization (ownership reform, the redefinition of property rights), formulated in this way, is, as was stressed, a negative one. Yet its force is strengthened when we look at the link between privatization and stabilization, as we did in Section 5. The empirical evidence presented there produced a surprisingly clear-cut conclusion: the internal structure of Polish SOEs that needed to be changed for reasons of economic efficiency undermined and frustrated the implementation of the stabilization part of the Balcerowicz plan. But this argument in favour of privatization also has rather disturbing implications. Can a post-STE be really stabilized? If the dominant role played in the Polish economy by SOEs made macroeconomic stability very difficult to achieve, then perhaps privatization should have preceded stabilization. Privatization is, however, a long and complicated process even when only individual enterprises are privatized, and the necessity to privatise a whole economy increases the degree of complexity exponentially, and when the decision was being taken, achieving macroeconomic stability was a matter of great urgency.

It has been argued above that privatization cannot be achieved at the stroke of a pen, although this would be the best solution. It has also been mentioned that the redefinition of property rights is "only" one element of the process of (re)creating an institutional framework of market economies in the the post-STEs and one should at best be able to jump into such a framework once it has been created in its entirety. Now we can see that the problem of the systemic transformation of these economies has one more dimension, namely that of the present economic situation in Eastern Europe. Furthermore, what is to be achieved developed elsewhere in an evolutionary and organic way and therefore long and careful preparation is not really a solution to these problems. Nevertheless, the common denominator of a large share of the dilemmas, trade-offs, and contradictions can be identified as that of *sequencing*. The rest of them follows most likely from what was above called *"indeterminacy"*, *i.e.* from the fact that the solutions of particular problems cannot be deduced from the general case for privatization.

Where does all of this leave us? First, at this stage one can only hope that awareness of how fundamental these problems are will help in solving the practical issues that appear during the process of privatization. In this sense an answer to the question "Why privatize?" will be both academically and practically important. Academically, because it will fill the gap in the literature on these issues. Practically, *i.e.* not only from the economic but also from the political point of view, first, because it will specify the areas in which decisions have to be taken, decisions which by their very nature will have to be more or less arbitrary, and, secondly, because by bringing these problems to light one opens a path for future research which should investigate two main issues: (1)

how the issues outlined above are solved in theory, *i.e.* both in various blueprints for privatization in the the post-STEs and in the law on privatization and governments' official programmes; (2) what judgements can be passed not only with regard to theoretical proposals but also with respect to the achievements (or their absence) of the privatization programmes actually implemented in the post-STEs.

Appendix C

Figure C1: Factors Influencing Property Rights

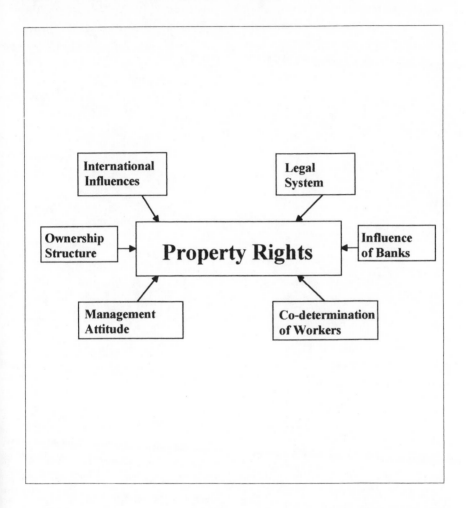

Chapter D

Privatization and Foreign Investment: Proposals, Experiences, Policy Options

1. Recognizing the Benefits of Privatization

To efficiently reduce scarcity and to achieve stability are two major challenges for all economic systems. In backward countries infant industry arguments have often been used to justify a transitory role of state firms; but in reality the transitory period was extended time and again - as in the case of Latin American economies - and infancy of industry was thereby artificially prolonged. In socialist countries state industry was, of course, a systemic trait of the politico-economic system, and ideology maintained that communism could only be achieved after several rounds of nationalizations which wiped out almost all private industrial activities in the former smaller CMEA countries by the end of the 1970s (we disregard the growing unofficial economy here). While OECD countries prospered on private ownership and competition embedded into a growing international division of labour and know-how, countries with state-dominated firms faced gradual and progressive economic decline. Capitalism based on private ownership may be fragile in certain periods and under certain circumstances - as is witnessed by the Great Depression - but typically it is a very complex and productive system of decentralized self-organization of production, investment and consumption; socialist industrialized countries have been unable to generate sufficient and efficient economic growth for the majority of the population in Eastern Europe, and flexibility and innovativeness to adjust to changing external environments and new technological opportunities have been weak, except for some cases in the arms industry to which especially the USSR devoted enormous resources (probably 20-30 per cent of GNP).[1] While two-way foreign investment has been a major source of technology transfer and prosperity in Western market economies, the CMEA countries emphasized autarchic trade and investment policies. Since markets for technological information/innovations are very imperfect markets international technology flows are dominated by technology trade within multinational companies and by cross-licensing; majority ownership typically is crucial for an early and full flow of intra-company technology flows - accepting majority ownership of foreign capital will thus be a crucial challenge in ex-CMEA countries.

Foreign direct investment implies that capital is mobile at least to some extent, and the pursuit of profits drives capitalist firms to combine foreign locational advantages with their firm specific advantages; setting up subsidiaries abroad will also change the locational advantages of the host country itself since technology spill-overs, incentives for host governments to provide public infrastructure goods and possibly changing management and working attitudes will affect at least some traits of the host country's location profile in the long run. Moreover, mobile capital implies a specific type of "voting with one's feet" in the sense that footloose capital will move towards locations which offer political stability, abundant complementary factors, cost advantages and expanding market segments. This international mobility of capital indirectly contributes to controlling the efficiency of competing political systems.

State-owned firms have played an important role for output and employment in all European countries as well as in many developing countries and NICs. While in Western market economies state-owned industrial firms and banks are in a minority position - although they might be more influential than suggested by shares in value-added or employment - and typically concentrated in the utilities industry, arms production and high-tech industry, state firms have dominated economic development and economic structures in central and eastern European countries for decades. In West European economies the rival and often parallel organization modes of state firms and private firms have

---

[1] See on the poor innovation performance of the ex-USSR and the socialist countries in general Schneider (1993) and Balcerowicz and Welfens (1988).

always provided visible alternatives and lessons from which to infer measures to improve economic efficiency over time. Given the insignificance of private sector activities in ex-CMEA countries, there is no viable counterexample to and yardstick for state firms in the early transition stage. Abstract theoretical reasoning and the experience of foreign countries must suffice to guide politico-economic developments towards progressive privatization.

Benefits from Privatization

In Western open economies import competition and the development of export market shares have always served as critical criteria for alternative modes of allocation (privately owned versus state-owned, big companies versus small companies etc.), and in some case the developments in world markets have inspired competition policy and privatization policy even more than domestic economic developments. For example after 1945 France pursued for decades an industrial policy which nurtured big industrial firms - national champions - which in some industries were state-owned for at least some time; the relative failure of such national champions in certain industries, above all in electronics and in the chemical and pharmaceutical industry has encouraged privatization policies. This also encouraged a changing stance of competition policy in which economies of scale and firm size were no longer considered to be the only crucial yardsticks for international competitiveness:[2] Rivalry in domestic markets, outward-orientation of firms (including international M&A orientation), open markets with a strong role of potential competition and the nurturing of new firms - as a necessary element for maintaining rivalry and diversity in established industries - have become more important for French competition policies in the 1980s than in the 1970s. Unfortunately, in the case of central and eastern Europe the transforming economies have just begun to really open their systems towards the world market and hence information and impulses from world market competition are relatively scarce for decision-makers in the business community and in economic policy.

Privatization of firms should make the supply-side more responsive to relative price signals in general and to international relative price signals in particular - at least in the case of tradable goods and services. In ex-CMEA countries privatization is indeed an element of economic opening-up. Sometimes economic opening-up will transitorily imply sharply rising imports and - under certain conditions - serious balance of payments problems. Hence, even if

---

2 See Schanze (1991).

privatization itself might be accepted on political and economic merits the side-effects of privatization might derail the privatization process. Even if privatization is accepted in the short term, some medium term distribution effects, namely very high profits from first mover advantages, monopoly positions and rent-seeking might discredit the transformation to a market economy. It seems clear that a progressive transformation can occur only if visible economic success for the medium strata of society can be achieved in the medium term (and if such strata can be established persistently at all). The technological and economic backwardness of eastern Europe will render the privatization process a very painful one since large technological gaps *vis-à-vis* Western Europe imply the potential for rapid increases in labour productivity and hence considerable unemployment. Moreover, the traditionally oversized manufacturing industry has to be trimmed and a viable service industry be established; both processes require high adjustment and information costs as they will entail unemployment, retraining requirements and structural as well as regional changes.

From a theoretical viewpoint there are many arguments for privatization in Western economies, and, of course, even more so in formerly socialist countries. At the same time resistance to privatization is well organized in big firms and big firms clearly dominate output and employment everywhere in Eastern Europe. Moreover, the benefits from privatization in formerly socialist economies are lower than in an existing market economy because privatized firms cannot immediately exploit the benefit of economy-wide low transaction costs that are typical for a full-fledged market economy. Once a critical minimum of firms has been privatized the additional benefit of reduced information costs and transaction costs can be exploited in the course of further privatization projects. A critical question therefore is how to generate a high momentum in privatization and how to ensure continuous progress of the privatization programme. The speed of the privatization process is also important because a very fast privatization would very much depress asset values in an economy in which savings are quite limited and in which individual retraining as well as learning about news and new opportunities takes time.

The basic challenge of privatization and foreign investment is to achieve economic efficiency and economic catching-up *vis-à-vis* OECD countries. Given the rising aspiration levels of the population in transforming economies a successful catching-up process is of crucial importance for political stability. Ex-CMEA countries have to face the challenge of privatization and foreign investment in a period of rapidly falling output, increasing unemployment and rising economic nationalism. Even for rich West European countries successful transformation steps would be quite difficult under such circumstances.

Facing the Problem of Oversized Firms
Socialist firms were oversized by Western standards, not least because central planners emphasized static economies of scale and found planning easier in an environment of not more than several hundred big companies; firms have been inefficient not only because of disincentives to innovate, but also because of oversized plants. In Poland, the biggest of the small countries, not more than 3,300 firms constituted the manufacturing sector and big firms dominated output and employment (Lipton and Sachs, 1990). The dominance of big firms indirectly is bound to create labour market problems in the new market economies because from Western market economies it is well-known that in industries with dominance of big firms there is very limited wage flexibility and wage differentiation so that excess supply in the labour market is difficult to reduce (König, 1990; Lindbeck and Snower, 1988; Franz, 1991). The efficiency wage hypothesis suggests that firms offer relatively high wages as a signal to attract the relatively better motivated workers. Moreover, in big firms controlling and monitoring costs may be higher than in smaller firms, so that the problem of dominant big firms in ex-CMEA countries in combination with the efficiency wage hypothesis could lead to wage levels much above equilibrium rates. In the first stage of transformation this problem is probably masked by the sharp reduction of real wages rates entailed by hyperinflation or very high inflation rates.

In order to recognize how different Eastern Europe is from Western Europe we take a look at a few figures: while in West Germany 18 per cent of all employed worked in firms with up to 100 employees in the late 1980s, only 1.0 and 1.4 per cent of all employees in the GDR and Poland, respectively, were working in such small firms. Hence privatization is not only the task of finding new owners but also of unbundling industrial assets in a way that optimum plant sizes can be realized. Few capitalist economies ever were up to the task of dismembering big firms.

In terms of property rights privatization ultimately means the transfer of ownership rights to private citizens and thus creating via coupons, vouchers or stocks of another financial asset besides domestic money and (important in Hungary, Poland and Russia in particular) foreign currency. It is clear that privatization will not only have allocation effects and indirect wealth effects that may result - e.g. via exchange rate effects and real interest rate effects - from improved present and future economic efficiency; there will be direct wealth effects that largely depend on the type of ownership transfer chosen. Savings decisions will be affected by wealth distribution as is clear if one models savings behaviour under the side-constraint of changing initial wealth endowments. One should, however, distinguish between the motivation to save and the ability to save. A very even distribution of wealth might reduce the incentive to save; the concentration of wealth in the hands of a minority might imply a higher average savings rate at the macroeconomic level than a relatively even distribution of wealth. However, one should not overlook that adequate tax provisions may well be able to encourage all major household groups - almost regardless of their initial wealth position - to realize a high savings rate.

In countries in which no free allocation of vouchers or stocks is taking place and in which ESOPs with a preferential stock sale to employees (ESOP=employee share ownership programme) are of minor importance privatization is likely to create a very uneven distribution of wealth and income. This holds all the more because the majority of citizens have suffered wealth losses in the process of fading out the socialist system which was a shortage economy. In the socialist shortage economy certain goods, including consumer durables, represented a preferred store of value, but the prices of used consumer durables have fallen relative to newly produced domestic and imported goods (such as cars). Finally, very high inflation rates reduced real balances sharply. With a ratio of the domestic money stock to national output of 30-50 per cent (and foreign exchange accounting for a smaller, but not insignificant value) and given the low savings rate of 2-7 per cent of disposable income, people in ex-CMEA countries lack the necessary funds to buy industrial assets (if West European ratios would hold industrial assets would be two or three times the value of a year's GNP).[3] Several methods have been employed in central and eastern Europe to effect a speedy privatization even under such difficult circumstances. Some countries have auctioned off "leaseholds" instead of ownership in order to make up for the lack of capital (OECD, 1993, p.20).

Since price liberalization, foreign economic liberalization and the collapse of CMEA trade mean that a considerable part of the capital stock and of human capital becomes obsolete - similar to the effects of the oil price shocks

---

[3] In Poland private household's savings rates increased from 2.6 per cent in 1987 to 6.6 per cent in 1991; in Hungary the savings rate increased from 1.8 per cent in 1982 to 6.6 per cent in 1991, while in the CSFR the savings rate hovered around 2 per cent in the 1980s, fell to -0.6 per cent and jumped to 1.6 per cent in 1991; see BIS (1992).

in OECD countries in the 1970s - the amount and the value of economically significant capital are reduced. High debt positions *vis-à-vis* banks and high intra-company debts make the evaluation of company assets additionally cumbersome. In addition to this there are hidden liabilities of socialist production in the form of environmental degradation or the contamination of sites which will reduce the usefulness of industrial assets and in any case require increased future government expenditures for an environmental clean-up.[4] Foreign investors will assess the value of assets quite critically and will discount expected profits heavily if microeconomic risks are coupled with market risks and political uncertainties. Privatization of socialist firms in the sense of transferring well-defined ownership rights to domestic residents and encouraging entrepreneurial people to launch their own business is a major challenge for systemic transformation and raises in itself various theoretical issues.

This chapter is organized as follows: Section 2 analyzes selected proposals in early privatization in central Europe. Section 3 analyzes problems of privatization transforming economies (including country specific experiences); in section 4 the focus is on policy options and the problem of privatization cycles. We argue that privatization of banks is quite important and, indeed, it might be the key to privatizing industry in a way that allows efficient economic restructuring.

2. Proposals for Privatization

In November 1988, a conference was held at the Central School of Planning and Statistics in Warsaw entitled "Proposed Transformations of the Polish Economy". This conference marked the first serious academic discussion of privatization in a Polish context. Two papers were of crucial importance. Stefan Kawalec in "Privatization of the Polish Economy" proposed, broadly speaking, turning state-owned firms into joint stock companies, and selling shares in these companies to the public (Kawalec, 1989). By contrast, Lewandowski and Szomburg, in "Property Reform as a Basis for Social and Economic Reform", advocated some kind of free distribution in shares of state-owned enterprises (Lewandowski and Szomburg, 1989).

---

[4] The costs of bringing East European countries to West European environmental standards has been estimated to reach between 10 and 20 per cent of GNP over an extended time. See Welfens, M. J. (1992).

2.1 The First Two Models

Kawalec's proposals had three main objectives:
(1) to transform the Polish economy into an open, market-type economy, dominated by private firms and having a convertible currency;
(2) to create a broad stratum of shareholders to serve as the political base of the new economic system and ensure its political stability;
(3) to minimize the social costs of the economic transformation, make these changes beneficial for the majority of the population and ensure that the benefits outweigh the losses, both in the long and short term (p. 241).

At the same time it was implied that two kinds of action would be pursued simultaneously:
(1) lifting those barriers which restrict the operation of the market and all current limitations imposed on the functioning of private firms, thereby creating the conditions for PFB through the development of existing and new private firms;
(2) launching of a multi-stage PFA by selling shares in state enterprises, so as to create as broad a group of private shareholders as possible and, incidentally, generate important revenue for the state budget (p. 241).

Kawalec's paper considered PFA (privatization from above), and discussed two issues in detail. The first was that of how best to privatize, a question which he saw as dependent on the question of how to find financial resources. The second issue was that of the benefits privatization would allegedly bring: given an operational free market, privatization would *make the country prosper* (p. 241).

As for PFA itself, three principles were to be respected:
- *the pricing of shares in state companies selected for privatization should make their purchase a very profitable investment for the prospective buyers, but, on the other hand, revenue generated by the sale of a firm must not be too low in comparison with its future market value;*
- *shares should be sold so as to ensure the widest possible distribution;*
- *the employees of privatized companies should be granted the right to buy a certain number of shares at preferential prices* (p. 242).

Next, the following procedure was proposed. Shares of some state-owned firms were to be offered for sale, and the time-table of the future privatization was to be announced. Profitable firms were to be privatized first. In the first stage, 20 per cent of shares were to be auctioned, just as had been done, for example, during the privatization of Nippon Telegraph and

Telephone. This would act as a reference-point for the reduced price of the next 70 per cent, *i.e.* the shares sold to the general public.[5] This second sale was to seek to strike balance between satisfying two demands: that of making the purchase profitable for individual investors, and that of not unnecessarily diminishing the revenues gained by the government. These shares were to be bought by as many individuals as possible. Following the British example, employees were to get preferential treatment: indeed the remaining 10 per cent would be sold to them at half price. *The pace of PFA should be such that at least two-thirds of the assets of the presently operating state-owned companies should become private over a period of 15 to 25 years* (p. 248).

Of course shares had to be paid for, and it was precisely the scarcity of capital in Poland which Kawalec's opponents saw as constituting one of the most significant difficulties with it. This problem has been discussed at length by two other Polish economists, Fedorowicz and Glikman. *Fedorowicz points out that all funds at the disposal of the population and private firms at the end of 1986 accounted for less than 1 per cent[6] of the book value of the productive assets in the socialized sector. Hence, he estimates that the complete purchase of these assets by the population would take over a hundred years (...). Estimates by Glikman based on the same kind of reasoning suggest that the purchase of these assets by the employees would take several hundred years* (p. 249). Against this, Kawalec argued that these authors' estimates of both available and needed resources were based on wrong assumptions, and therefore incorrect. According to Kawalec, the problem of scarcity of capital did exist, but was easier to solve than was at first apparent.

The implementation of these proposals should bring about the following benefits:

- *better economic performance in privatized companies and also in those expecting privatization;*
- *more competition in the economy;*
- *important additional budget income providing opportunities to combat inflation and to finance public expenditure;*
- *creation of a relatively broad base of individual shareholders, offering political guarantees of the durability of the newly introduced market principles and economic freedoms* (p. 244).

---

[5] This procedure must not be confused with selling shares in two or more trenches, as in the case of BP or NTT. The first part is auctioned only to help price the rest, and the sale of the remaining shares proceeds as quickly as possible.
[6] In the Polish text it is 11 per cent, which is what Fedorowicz in fact wrote in his article.

Kawalec ended by considering the prospects for the Polish economy after the successful implementation of so radical a reform. The author suggested that, in the long run, Poland should join the European Community, and that the removal of various import and export restrictions could be an important step towards this goal. A prosperous future for Poland and her people could be ensured only through the integration of her economy with that of the rest of Europe.

According to Lewandowski and Szomburg, the proponents of the alternative model, both the failures of the previous reforms and the depth of the current economic crisis in Poland necessitated a really radical reform programme based on a change in the property structure. *A breakthrough reform must therefore satisfy the following criteria:*
- to bring new actors into the centre, not merely the periphery of the economic scene. These actors would have to represent the interest of ownership, that is, to exercise the full range of property rights in order to maximize their long-run income from capital;
- to create a mechanism of capital allocation, which would be set in motion by the interests of ownership and would ensure the market pricing of assets (Lewandowski and Szomburg, p. 258).

We have already seen that property relationships can be transformed in a variety of ways and some of them were analyzed in the second part of the paper by Lewandowski and Szomburg.[7] The authors dismissed attempts to streamline state property as insufficient. They also rejected laissez-faire reforms (PFB: privatization from below) and group ownership, in that *they fail to guarantee efficiency* (p. 262). *The interests of ownership cannot be simulated by some artificial body, nor can such nominal owners operate in the capital market* (p. 262). What was needed, therefore, was the expropriation of the state, and that in such a way as to *bring the economy as near as possible to the private capitalist model of economic efficiency* (p. 260).

Lewandowski and Szomburg thus proposed a much more radical solution for the Polish economy's problems, namely privatization. The core of their proposals lied in *a real and radical transfer of property rights from the state administration to the broad masses of society* (p. 263). State-owned means of production are to be socialized by reprivatization, by which they mean free

---

[7] Lewandowski and Szomburg, unlike Gruszecki distinguish four possibilities:
- the streamlining of state ownership;
- a laissez-faire programme of lifting all barriers to the growth of the private sector;
- the quest for an original model of a non-state and non-private economy;
- the scenarios of active privatization (p. 260-262).

distribution of shares in previously state-owned companies. This kind of measure has so far been tried out only once. In 1979 a portion of the shares in the British Columbian Resources and Investment Corporation were given away free of charge to all voting adults of the province who applied for them. The experiment was, however, on a very limited scale and not fully successful.[8] In the UK, this kind of measure was advocated by Samuel Brittan (*Financial Times*, 17 November 1983 and 20 September 1984).

Two arguments grounded Lewandowski and Szomburg's proposals. First, in any case, there was the question, supposedly a rhetorical one, why people should buy what already belonged to them. Secondly, it allegedly met the problem raised by the lack of domestic capital in Poland, already discussed at length by Kawalec.

In view of this latter problem, Lewandowski and Szomburg suggested that the changes implied in their proposals should be implemented as quickly as possible. So radical a proposal needed wide public support. The lengthy process of selling shares would involve a phenomenon already observable in Poland: a quite unhealthy symbiosis between the public and private sectors. This effect had to be minimized. It thus seemed preferable to curtail as far as possible the period of 15 to 25 years which, according to Kawalec's optimistic estimate, was necessary for the privatization of two thirds of what was ultimately to be taken away from the public sector. Therefore a different solution to the problem of the scarcity of capital was proposed, a solution which also satisfied the *self-management aspirations of employees* (pp. 264).

At the beginning of the process, the government was to issue some kind of vouchers. The value of each voucher was to be equal to the book value of all state owned firms to be privatized divided by the number of *all Polish citizens aged 18 plus* (pp. 264-265). These vouchers were then to be equally distributed among the adult population. They might then use these vouchers to apply personally for the shares in state-owned enterprises as these were successively offered to the public. Stockbrokers and different consulting firms were to provide all necessary help. Regional stock exchanges were to be created, and the timetable of the whole process was to be public knowledge from the outset. At the same time, it was to be also possible to purchase some shares with money. A further kind of share was to be issued for employees. Like all other adult citizens, the employees were to receive their vouchers; but, if they decided to apply for the shares of the firm in which they work, their vouchers

---

8 *Cfr.* World Bank (1988), vol. 2 and Letwin (1988), pp. 8-9.

would be worth more, *i.e.* the shares would be distributed among the employees at a cheaper rate. Moreover, share-owning employees, unlike other shareholders, would have voting rights at the beginning of the process: a measure allegedly satisfying the workers' aspirations towards self-management. This arrangement was meant to smooth the process of transition from the public sector to the private one. For Lewandowski and Szomburg, it was the employees who were best able initially to control the newly privatized enterprise. Only later would other shareholders be competent to exercise their property rights.

This *property reform must be assisted by a number of ancillary operations and calls for some prerequisites to be met* (p. 266). What was needed first of all was the demonopolization and breaking up of some of the existing structures in the Polish economy, *e.g.* branch unions of enterprises. Further, economic freedom was an absolute necessity. The Polish economy had to be an open one, and the currency convertible, first internally and then externally also. Another reason why this convertibility was necessary was the need to attract foreign capital, capital which, among other things, would enable joint-ventures, and would participate in the auctions of some state-owned enterprises' physical assets. The infrastructure of the capital market would have to begin from scratch, in a situation in which there were no institutional patterns and no previous experience. New institutional investors would have to be established. The fiscal system would have to be reformed, in order to encourage savings and the reinvestment of profits. Finally, since the public sector would not be dismantled completely, what was left of it was to be subject to the newly created institution, *e.g.* the State Treasury, but it was to be run as some kind of a holding. Its management's performance was to be evaluated and rewarded according to economic results.

Soon after the answers to the question: How to privatize Soviet-type economies? were published, first in Polish and then also in English, they were critically evaluated in the light of some Western theoretical writings as well as confronted with the British experience of privatization (Jasinski, 1990a). The upshot of this analysis was as follows: Viewed strictly in terms of economics the principal objective of privatization is an increase in economic efficiency, both for privatized companies (productive efficiency) and for the economy as a whole (allocative efficiency). This objective therefore constitutes the most important criterion for evaluating any privatization proposals. Other objectives may be pursued only insofar as they are not incompatible with the main one. Great care should be taken to avoid ideology assuming a dominating role.

Privatization aims to increase economic efficiency by transferring ownership. In general, this goal may well be achieved. However, a successful privatization demands carefully designed pro-competitive policies and appropriate regulations. Moreover, the chances of success will be improved if a variety of techniques are used. The creation of capital markets together with some degree of their development should precede privatization by a public offer of shares. In other words, PFB is a *conditio sine qua non* of PFA. As to monetary and fiscal consequences of privatization, much care has to be taken to ensure that the proceeds of privatization are used optimally. Privatization may not legitimately be seen as a primary means of solving the budget deficit or inflation problems. Privatization must be understood as part of a broader reform programme, and the other elements in such a programme, their mutual relationships, and their timetabling require detailed planning.

It followed that both models stood in need of serious reconstruction, both with regard to the general ideas presupposed, and the scenarios envisaged. Nevertheless, if one were to choose between the two programmes, Kawalec's proposals offered a better starting point for such reconsideration. The property reform, advocated by Lewandowski and Szomburg, seemed to solve the problem of scarcity of domestic capital, and might result in a faster process of transformation. But the authors underestimated the complexity and scale of such an operation. On the one hand, the number of unresolved issues and the degree of unpredictability were far too high. On the other, given that we were talking about a pioneer enterprise, the programme was not nearly flexible enough. Its rules could not be changed during the process of implementation without risking disaster. The ideological background of their programme (socialization of ownership, self-management aspirations and *Entproletarisierung*) seemed also rather suspect; it prevented the authors' drawing on the solutions that elsewhere had proved at least partially successful. In short, failure was far too realistic a prognosis and the Polish public was unlikely to support yet another grandiose experiment.

How could Kawalec's proposals be completed or improved? Two considerations were of key importance here. On the one hand, this version of PFA, whereby state-owned companies gradually became joint stock companies, would be drawing on the same limited resources of domestic capital as PFB. On the other, this technique of PFA was neither the only technique possible, nor the most desirable. Therefore, Jasinski (1990a) suggested that the whole process should be divided into two stages.

In the first stage economic freedom should be guaranteed in law as well as whatever was needed for market mechanisms to be reestablished. PFB in general should be encouraged, and, in particular, it should be made possible to establish new joint stock companies with freely tradeable shares, which in turn would help to create a stock exchange. Other techniques of PFA, such as trade sales, contracting out, leasing *etc.* could begin then. Given that an important aspect of this stage of reforming the Polish economy was the participation of foreign capital, foreigners and institutions from abroad should be enabled to invest in Poland by establishing new companies, creating joint-ventures and buying state-owned enterprises. Debt-for-equity swap should also be encouraged as far as possible.[9] These measures would have the effect of enlarging the private sector. Other important tasks would be the reduction of the budget deficit and of the rate of inflation, and the introduction of a fully convertible currency.

Those enterprises which would be still in state ownership at the end of Stage 1 should be given maximal autonomy. Radical pro-competitive policies should be introduced, and all monopolistic structures broken up. Particular stress should be placed on developing the banking system, which is absolutely crucial for proper functioning of an economy based on private property. Stage 1 would end once a satisfactory capital market has been developed.

In Stage 2, shares should be issued and sold in those enterprises still under public ownership that were judged suitable for becoming joint stock companies. The price of shares should be determined by the Treasury. They should be offered first, at a discount, to the employees, and then to people and institutions from outside the privatized companies, both domestic and foreign. There should be no limitation on the number of shares available to one buyer. In some cases loans to buy shares should be made available; they would only delay the point at which the Treasury receives the proceeds. Any unsold shares would remain generally available at the initial price. In the meantime, the Treasury would retain them, receiving dividends on them, but having no voting rights. This sequence of measures should be carried out as quickly as possible, and would finally put an end to the state's administrative control over individual enterprises. The whole economy would enjoy efficiency gains even before the transfer of ownership rights was fully completed. Secondary trading should

---

[9] In the case of debt-for-equity swap, the given company should be turned into a joint stock company, and all shares should be controlled by the new owner. Secondary trading should be possible from the start.

begin, and continue freely. Stage 2 should begin on the same day for all companies, the only possible exception being public utilities.

Clearly, the proposals, reminded above, went much further then Kawalec's programme. Indeed, they modified it substantially, and might well seem unduly *laissez-faire*. But was not it the case that only a reform of this kind of radicality would meets the depth of the then structural crisis of the Polish economy?. There was no point in replacing one artificial economic system with another. These suggestions, although brief and sketchy, proceeded also from a conviction that it will not do for Polish economists simply to take over the political rhetoric and ideology of privatization from the West. They were to look hard at what had actually happened in the West and learn from both its successes and its failures. Finally, these suggestions were also to express the author's conviction that privatization, if understood correctly, and pursued in conjunction with other radically market-orientated reforms, will constitute the solution to the present problems of the Polish economy.

2.2 Theoretical Developments and Policy Options

The summary of the "prehistoric" stage of the debate on how to privatize Soviet-type economies, presented above, shows clearly that despite the avalanche of alternative programmes, to which we turn now and the advocacy of which followed the Autumn of the Peoples, the fundamental alternative whether the assets belonging to the state should be sold or distributed free of charge seems to remain valid. However, three *caveats* have to be pointed out immediately. Firstly, selling everything or giving it away appear after almost four years of discussion to be two polar cases which nobody advocates any longer. In other words, these two proposals no longer exclude each other and there seem to be a continuum of theoretical proposals and programmes already being implemented which mix the two in various proportions.

Secondly, since everybody tried to justify his or her proposals, every new proposal was build on rejecting or at least undermining its more or less direct competitors. One result of this is some kind of consensus that there is no best procedure able to solve once and for all the problem of privatizing the post-STEs. More generally, this suggest that many routes and methods not only can but also have to be used at the same time. Such strategy can be seen not only as a damage limiting exercise but also as the only viable way of speeding up the process of redefinition of the property rights structure of Central and East European economies.

Third, the discussion that followed, metaphorically speaking, the change of guard in this part of Europe as well as first practical experiences, broadened the context in which privatization could and had to be seen and discussed. The concepts of transformational privatization (see Chapter C) and of the political economy of privatization (Winiecki, 1992) well illustrate this broadening of the perspective. In other words, one could not consider improving economic efficiency as the only - and perhaps not even the most important, at least not in the short run - objective of privatization. Nor could one's approach be a purely technocratic one. That is, it was not enough to find a solution to the given problem; this solution had to be able to survive the political process of its acceptance and implementation.

2.2.1 Spontaneous Privatization

In this Section we shall present the three main kinds of proposals for transferring property rights. Apart from selling shares, stocks, and/or assets and free distribution we have to take account of so-called spontaneous privatization. Although nobody was advocating it seriously, and despite its comparative neglect by those involved in designing sophisticated procedures, it was simply happening, especially in Poland and Hungary and politicians had to react to it in order to prevent the whole idea of privatization becoming discredited.

2.2.1.1 Pre-transition Developments in Poland and Hungary

Concepts like "spontaneous privatization", "wild privatization", "nomenklatura joint-stock companies", *uwl aszczenie nomenklatury* ("propertization of nomenklatura"), or auto-appropriation (in Polish *samouwl aszczenie*) became part of the rhetoric used to describe processes directly preceding the demise of communist rule in Central and Eastern Europe and present in the first period of the process of systemic transformation of these economies. But to get a better idea of the phenomena described in these value-loaded terms one has go back in time.

Changes in the ownership structure of the economies of Central and Eastern Europe, as measured by the share of the GDP produced by the public sector, had in fact started long before the imminent end of real socialism became evident. That share peaked in the mid-1970s, and later developments in that respect may now rightly be seen as "privatization from below", although nobody could then interpret it in this way. In terms of political economy, this phenomenon was rightly described by Staniszkis as de-articulation of the socialist mode of production (see Chapter C), and there is no doubt that it was a sign of deepening economic and political crisis. At the same time it played an important role in accelerating the train of events which more or less directly led to the changes of 1989.

Admittedly, no communist government is noted for its respect for the law. But this relaxation of ideological constraints was accompanied in Poland and Hungary by two kinds of changes within the legal framework of economic activities. First, public ownership of and control over the means of production was decentralized. The method used in both countries was much the same. In Poland in 1981 (see Chapter C)[10] and in Hungary in 1985 some property rights were transferred from the state to workers' councils and/or assemblies (Sajko, 1987; Gruszecki, 1987).[11]

Despite superficial structural similarities, the situation in both countries was quite different, with obvious implications for future developments. In Poland it was the Solidarity trade union which initiated the changes. After the martial law was imposed, which resulted in banning the trade unions, workers' councils became an important platform for Solidarity activists, despite their rights also having been limited in the process. In consequence, the price to be paid for the autonomy of enterprises was industrial democracy. In Hungary, enterprise councils (or assemblies of workers' delegates) were introduced in two thirds of all enterprises (covering half the employees and capital stock) and had the power to appoint the director, to determine the company structure, to decide about mergers and de-mergers, and to establish new organizations (Grosfeld and Hare, 1991). It was managers who profited most from the moves towards this form of self-managerial socialism. At the end of 1985, the first year in which those councils functioned, managers, economists, administrative workers or employees with technical backgrounds comprised four-fifths of council membership (Crane, 1991). This may not in fact fully reflect the power

---

10 The Law on State Enterprises and the Law on Self-Management of State Enterprises' Employees, 13 September 1981.
11 Such a transfer did not, of course, create new effective owners of assets previously controlled by politicians. It rather increased the degree to which property rights were insufficiently defined and instead of strengthening incentives to increase economic efficiency it simply created new rents to be exploited.

structure of these organs, but it is universally acknowledged that the managers succeeded in gaining an almost total control over their enterprises, becoming their *de facto* owners (Winiecki, 1992). At the same time one must not forget that managers in Hungary were becoming ever more professional and that the role played by political criteria in their appointment began to diminish (Lawrence, 1991).

Secondly, the private sector - in Poland: the non-agricultural private sector - was allowed to grow. This occurred in two ways: the creation of new private firms became, despite frequent vacillation, on the whole easier, and the conditions for foreign direct investment in general, and for creating joint ventures with foreign partners in particular, were liberalized. In Poland the most famous form in which this happened were the so-called *spólki polonijne*, i.e. Polonia joint-stock companies, the capital of which came from people of Polish origin living abroad. In Hungary, the development started with the so-called intra-company working association (ICWA), which made it possible to form a contract relationship between voluntarily established groups operating within a state enterprise and the enterprise itself. Closer to being a truly private new business form was the so-called economic working association (ECWA). This was also a voluntary form but outside the state organization (Mizsei, 1992).

These changes were at the time heralded as ground breaking and could have appeared so, but their direct economic effects were probably small. Though Kornai (1990a) praised the strength of the private sector, the latter was very vulnerable to changes in political climate, locally and nationwide. It could also appear as parasitic on the public sector, in that connections were often more important than entrepreneurial skills and sound investment decisions.

However, as the crisis deepened, further new concessions to the private sector - both domestic and foreign - were needed, and it became necessary to revise the rules according to which enterprises from both sectors could cooperate with each other. In Poland, the 1934 commercial code was revived in 1985 and the Act on Foreign Investment, since then changed many times, was passed by the parliament. These changes were supplemented by the decree about "experiments" issued by the Rakowski government in late 1988. Not surprisingly an eruption of new commercial law companies with participation of state enterprises resulted. In June 1989 there were 2,139 of them (the main business of 60 per cent of them consisted in acting simply as middlemen) and by the end of September of that year their number increased to 12,600 thousand (Gruszecki, 1990). Many of them were later called "nomenklatura joint-stock companies" or "nomenklatura partnerships" and thus the problem of *uwlaszczenie nomenklatury* appeared.

2.2.1.2 Nomenclatura Privatization

In principle there is nothing wrong with trading links between public and private companies. Even intersectoral joint ventures, despite their being more open to fraud structure, could prove effective vehicles to exploit gains from trade. Everything depends on the legal framework within which such cooperation is supposed to evolve as well as on the enforcement of the law and the quality of monitoring. In Poland this framework was largely flawed. The question remains as to whether or not these flaws were deliberately created in order to transform political power of the old ruling elite into economic power.

What is more, even the most frequently used concepts, like that of a "nomenklatura company", are extremely vague. Gruszecki (1990), for example, defines such a company as a commercial law company (limited liability or joint stock), in which a so-called socialized institution (or institutions) (state enterprise, cooperative, association, administrative agency acting on behalf of the Treasury) establishes connections with the manager of such an entity, the manager having the status of a partner in the company. These persons - managers, presidents, directors, etc. - must, of course, be members of the nomenklatura. There were also, according to the same author, "weaker" forms of nomenklatura companies, in which the president, manager or director do not become formally partners, but are members of the supervisory board or are additionally employed in the company's management, deriving various benefits from such an arrangement (Gruszecki, 1990). One consequence of this arrangement was that some nomenklatura members dealt in fact with themselves: they sat on one side of the negotiating table as managers of SOEs and at the same time on the other side as stakeholders and/or directors of private companies. There were cases in which the same person signed a contract for both sides. No wonder that abuses resulted.

Two kinds of actions seemed to be most popular. The first had to do with joint ventures. According to Gruszecki (1990) there is a common knowledge of the existence of actually outrageous cases of such injustice, e.g. extremely low valuation of assets contributed by the enterprise and extremely overvalued contributions in kind made by the partners. When the partner was a foreign investor, this kind of sweetheart deal would involve giving the foreign partner a highly favourable stake in the enterprise and in return the manager would be appointed to an attractive position in the new venture (Lipton and Sachs, 1990).

The second route of *uwłaszczenie nomenklatury* was based on contractual relationships with newly established private firms in which the state managers had a personal stake, i.e. with a "nomenklatura joint-stock company". The manager might then lease the plant and machinery of the state enterprise at highly favourable terms to the private firm, allowing high rates of return (Lipton and Sachs, 1990).[12] The profits of the state enterprise could be very easily transferred to the private firm having exclusive rights on selling the SOE's output. The best way to bias such a contract in favour of the private firm was to use highly favourable transfer prices, the importance of which was increased by persistent shortages (Winiecki, 1992).

Soon after the Mazowiecki government had taken over, the law was changed and the most obvious legal gaps were closed, but very few deals were declared null and void. That was so not only because what appeared fraudulent was in fact legal but also because trading state property for personal gains (Lipton and Sachs, 1990) was only one aspect of what "nomenklatura companies" were all about. They were not only an attempt to exploit the opportunities created by the process of disintegration of the old system but also a response to the excessively stringent conditions in which SOEs had to operate. As it happened, many such companies were established for tax reasons, i.e. to get round restrictions of tax-based income policies, which at that time only worked in the socialized sector. Frequently too, such a company was established in order to bind the most valuable people with the enterprise through employment in the apparently nomenklatura company (Gruszecki, 1990). This in turn explains the seemingly strange behaviour of workers' councils. Certainly, many deals reflected their apathy, but in other cases it was not only nomenklatura members who profited but many workers as well.

The phenomenon described in Poland as *uwłaszczenie nomenklatury* was denounced vehemently in the media, apparently enjoying their newly acquired freedom, and was met also with grass-roots protests. Some Western writers followed that track and pronounced an outright condemnation of that practice: *There is no conceivable justification for condoning these practices, which are equivalent to the worst cases of insider trading in western markets* (Nuti, 1990,

---

[12] Berg (1992) gives an example of how a wholesale distribution enterprise, with several hundred employees, was largely dismantled and operated in private hands, probably without any transaction registered as "privatization". The petrol station had been leased to employees; the trucks had been sold. A private company was using the car park and some of the office space. Polish economic weeklies, such as *Zycie Gospodarcze* or *Gazeta Bankowa*, were at the time full of similar stories.

p. 59). Were these kinds of processes merely examples of asset stripping (Lipton and Sachs, 1990), of a corporate racket (Winiecki, 1992), of a parasitic life inside or on the fringes of the state sector (Ciechocinska, 1992) or even of "legalized parasitism" (Swiatkowski and Cannon, 1992)?

The vehement social protests and public outrage, the public's revulsion etc. mentioned by many authors would suggest that even these expressions are an understatement. Our description suggests, however, that one should be very careful before jumping to unequivocal judgements. Two things seem to be of great importance. First, one has to answer the question about the legal status of the deals. Were they legal, semi-legal, or illegal? As a corollary, there is moral issue: if essential gaps in legal regulations made it possible to establish openly parasitic "nomenklatura companies" without any breach of the law, as seems to be the case in the light of Gruszecki (1990), was it right to make use of those gaps? And was not perhaps the public outcry ultimately caused not by the nature of the deals themselves but rather by the fact that *access to such profits was restricted to a rather narrow circle of inner management and the former party activists who had power, information and contacts that made it easier to take over shares in the new companies step by step* (Ciechocinska, 1992)? Was not this effect strengthened by the fact that, as a result of years of indoctrination, a large part of society tended to regard any manifestation of private economic activity as profiteering? And how instrumental were the media in this process?

Secondly, the issue on which one also has to concentrate one's attention is that of identifying precisely what the main problem of *uwlaszczenie nomenklatury* was? Both the examples reported above and many others show that there were two fundamental problems with this kind of spontaneous privatization: valuation of assets and conflict of interest. Although the later could be relatively easily taken care of even if the managers of SOEs were to be represented in "nomenklatura companies" by their relatives or friends, there is so far no satisfactory solution, not to mention fraud-proof one, to the problem of reckoning the assets of SOEs or of whole enterprises are worth.

Having rejected, rightly, the possibility of using book value to decide the price of what was to be privatized, both for historical reasons and because of the high level of uncertainty involved, one of the authors writing about Hungary claimed that spontaneous privatization resulted in the state getting much less than it would have received if the assets (or whole firms) had been auctioned off (Crane, 1991).[13] Most likely he is right, but it is still far from clear how one

---

[13] On using auctions in the process of privatization, see Section 2.2.2.

should have acted to achieve better results. To translate Crane's statement into a policy recommendation one would have to answer a series of questions: Should enterprises be auctioned off all at the same time, or one by one? Should any restrictions on participation by foreigners, whether individuals or companies, be imposed? Should deals be made only in cash, or should other forms of payment be accepted too? The answers given to each of these questions will doubtless have a substantial effect on the balance sheet of such an operation, but the experience of the *Treuhandanstalt* with privatization in the former East Germany, discussed in more detail later in this Chapter, shows that estimates of the value of national patrimony - and therefore any accusations that assets were sold at too low a price - are likely to be highly exaggerated.

This is not to deny that an important aspect of the problem of valuation was that at that stage nobody effectively represented the state (and the society which the state purported to represent) in order to make sure that the enterprises' assets were not undervalued and given away cheaply to third parties (Kiss, 1991). The experience of both Poland and Hungary shows, however, that closing gaps in the law, laudable as this is, can slow down the process of privatization considerably. There is a trade off between speed and fairness. On the other hand, the fundamental asymmetry present in intersectoral deals, in which "nobody's property" is sold to those who pay for it with their own money, cannot be really eliminated, especially in the absence of developed capital markets. The damaging effects of this asymmetry are rather difficult to control in periods in which political and economic systems are undergoing far reaching transformations.

That is why, despite the fact that the very term *uwlaszczenie nomenklatury* suggests a negative moral judgement on the phenomena so designated, one should not be afraid of indicating some positive consequences of the processes occurring in the final period of communist rule in Poland. In particular one should mention, following Ciechocinska (1992, p. 220), that *in the broad sense of capital formation and the learning process, that activity might be advantageous to society as a whole.*

By accelerating the process of structural reform in general and of privatization in particular - although not of the kind one would perhaps prefer - *uwlaszczenie nomenklatury* was also one of the first important steps toward establishing a market economy in Poland. That was so, firstly, because it increased the share of private property in the economy and, secondly, because it speeded up the process of disintegration of the old systems, thereby indeed weakening the resistance of precisely the nomenklatura. At the same time, regardless of whether the reaction of the public was right or not, *uwlaszczenie nomenklatury* did in fact have also a negative affect on the process of systemic transformation. The political effects of these forms of privatization created a certain amount of fear of privatization in general and in some cases even discredited the whole idea. It even turned into severe criticism of joint stock companies as such (Gruszecki, 1990), which was additionally helped by general ignorance about what a market economy is all about.

2.2.1.3 Spontaneous Privatization in Hungary

One of the differences between Poland and Hungary was that in Hungary the legal framework within which property transformation was started was much better defined and it is changes in the law that mark turning points. First, from 1 January 1989 the new enterprise law extended the right to establish new organizations so as to include establishing partnerships including some state property (Grosfeld and Hare, 1991).[14] This was the legal basis for the early so called "wild" privatization, although in the absence of strong political control and in face of a growing threat of bankruptcy, several big state enterprises began to make use of this legal framework and became converted into different forms of shareholders' companies even earlier (Kiss, 1991).[15]

The transformation law of July 1989 sought to regulate the conversion of state property into partnership form (commercialization) by recognizing the rights of the councils but putting some constraints on the process. These concerned the raising of capital, the entry of external owners, and the requirement that 80 per cent of the shares and securities were due to the State

---

[14] It may be of interest to note that in Poland the Messner-Sadowski team inserted, as soon as in the autumn of 1987, into the Law on state-owned enterprises the following clause: *in economically justified cases the employees' council and the director of the enterprise may apply to the founding organ for transforming the enterprise into a partnership* (Article 29, as quoted in Gruszecki, 1990, p. 3). *However* - comments Gruszecki (1990, p. 3) - *at that time nobody knew how to it, and the government had no intention to follow this idea into practice.* The provision itself was strengthened by the Rakowski government as part of its Law on selected terms and conditions for consolidating of the national economy of February 1989 and it was only then that one actually started to make any use of it. So amended Article 29 of the Law on state-owned enterprises constituted also the first legal foundation for privatization.

[15] The same author - Kiss (1991) - points also out that the term "spontaneous privatization" is often used to describe cases which were neither privatization not spontaneous: *because the changes remain within the borders of state property. The attribute "spontaneous" is also only proper in the sense of "uncontrolled" because (...) the transformation were a rather conscious effort of the state managers to preserve their companies or their personal power through the companies* (p. 2).

Property Agency as owner (or as representative, in law, of the state's ownership interest) (Grosfeld and Hare, 1991).

Unfortunately, this law was easily evaded since it only applied to fully transforming companies, whereas most chose to retain a small state enterprise as a "property administration centre", a unit which held nothing but shares in the newly created spin-off companies, perhaps with a small administrative staff. Other shares would be held by other state firms (e.g. major customers or suppliers; and the banks, often converting some of the firm's debt into equity). *The Economist* (14.04.1990) described it at the time as follows: *state enterprises divided themselves into subsidiary joint-stock companies, which sold equity to each other and to other companies, leaving the parent company with an office, a telephone and a lot of debt.*

The reforms established, in the words of Mizsei (1992), a *status quo* according to which managers had some "rights" to "their" enterprises, which he calls, on the basis primarily of the two laws mentioned, "quasi-ownership" rights. The process of spontaneous privatization therefore started on a larger scale at the beginning of 1989. The combination of decentralized decision-making rights with the advent of modern company structures other than state enterprise gave a strong impetus to self-privatization efforts by enterprise managers (Mizsei, 1992). Two examples described in detail in Lawrence (1991): Apisz (the stationary distribution company), and Tungsram help to give a better picture of mechanisms involved, but one has to remember that both the number of cases and the value of the assets involved were relatively small. According to State Property Agency data, by the end of 1990 the process had affected only Ft100 bn worth of state property, less then 0.5 per cent of the total assets (Kiss, 1992).

Nevertheless, many cases - rightly or not - led, just as in Poland, to public outcry and resulted in changes in the legal framework of property transformation. In March 1990 the State Property Agency (SPA) was formed to regulate enterprise transformation and to provide for the representation of the interests of the state as owner during privatization (Crane, 1991).[16] Enterprises could decide whether they wanted to organize open bidding for the assets to be privatized (in this case the Agency had no right to intervene) or arrange a deal themselves (in which case the SPA could intervene if the deal was found to be unfair or for some other reason unsatisfactory) (Mizsei, 1992). An important

---

[16] What is worth noting is that the legislation was introduced by the old "communist" parliament and that spontaneous privatization was not stopped by the new regime in Hungary.

modification consisted in that it became mandatory to appraise property independently before sale (Crane, 1991).

Any assessment of spontaneous privatization has to start with answering the question regarding the legal status of realized deals. From what some Hungarian economists write about it, it appears that claims suggesting the illegal character of those deals cannot be easily substantiated. Leaving aside the problem of valuation, briefly discussed in the previous Section, there are also authors, like Lawrence (1991), who say that it was not clear who owned the enterprise and therefore question whether the state was legally entitled to the receipts.[17] As a result of the 1984 legislation on enterprise autonomy, ownership seemed to be vested in the Enterprise Council in 85 per cent of enterprises. Therefore, legally, the enterprise owned itself and could presumably dispose of itself (Lawrence, 1991).

Property transformation processes followed different dynamics of in Poland and in Hungary and this had influence on the perceived benefits of spontaneous privatization. To capital formation and learning processes, stressed by Ciechocinska (1992), one may, following Mizsei (1992), add two things. Firstly, this kind of privatization was instrumental in attracting foreign capital; in this respect Hungary was initially far more successful than any other economy of Central and Eastern Europe, especially in per capita terms. Secondly, despite the fact that most of the spontaneous privatization had been limited to partial corporatization of state firms, many large SOEs restructured themselves into conglomerates of corporatized, and partly privatized, firms, usually with a state "holding" unit remaining in the place of the ex-headquarters of the one-time state enterprise. *The organizational decentralization is an undoubted virtue of the Hungarian process* (Mizsei, 1992, p. 293). Furthermore, although changes in the law had some of the intended effects and spontaneous privatization (or at least its acceleration) slowed down somewhat, it still remained, besides establishment of new businesses, the main forum of private enterprise expansion (Mizsei, 1992).

What was the price of these achievements? The most often mentioned loser is the state budget. It is certainly true that, since most of the spontaneous privatizations occurred in the form of joint ventures with foreign capital investment, budget revenue from the process was relatively low (Mizsei,

---

[17] Despite considerable differences in the Law of the two countries, a similar claim with respect to Polish SOEs was advanced by Levitas (1992).

1992).[18] But this is not to say that it could have been higher, for two reasons. Firstly, the real market value of the assets (or whole enterprises) was and still is very uncertain. Secondly, pursuing the objective of maximizing revenue from privatization would have certainly slowed down the whole process and most likely reduced the value of assets in the meantime.

According to Crane (1991), Hungarian lawmakers were also concerned that Hungary's reputation was suffering among serious investors because companies were being sold on the basis of personal contacts, rather than openly, i.e. on the basis of competitive bidding.[19] From this point of view, the desire to make the process of privatization transparent, socially acceptable and controlled, and to give Parliament a greater say is quite understandable. But one has also to remember the paradox noticed by Weitzman (1991), that many efforts made by those in charge of Eastern and Central European economies can be described as attempts to be fair when building capitalism, which is in principle an unfair system.

2.2.2 Selling State-Owned Enterprises

Looking at pre-1989 world experiences with privatization of SOEs, selling them seems to be the most obvious option for post-communist economies. Free distribution of shares was advocated in the West (Friedman, 1976; Brittan, 1983, 1984) and even tried once or twice (Letwin, 1988), but by and large those attempts were to be considered as exceptions confirming the rule. It is therefore no surprise that early suggestions on how post-STEs should be privatized tried to answer the question how to sell SOEs or their assets in post-STEs, as testified by the papers discussed above.[20] Kornai (1990a and b) is also strongly in favour not only of private ownership of the means of production but also of selling assets. It is with his contribution that we shall start this overview.

---

[18] Apart from revenue from the sale, the budgetary gains and losses should include also a loss in revenue from profit taxes because of concessions to foreign investors. But should it really count as a loss, if foreign investors were going to need some incentives in any case? On the other hand, there were gains from higher profits in the future, especially when concessions expired, as well as from putting an end to subsidisation which was rather widespread and which in the case of privatization could be easily discontinued.

[19] Invitations for competitive bidding were rare and competitors offering a higher price were often excluded from the bidding.

[20] See Kawalec (1989) and Jasinski (1990), the most important difference between the two being the answer to the question whether SOEs in post-STEs should be privatized all at once or on one by one basis.

Kornai (1990a, p. 80) considers *it desirable to increase the proportion of the private sector as fast as possible to a point where this sector accounts for the larger part of the country's GDP*, but the main goal of privatization is not to hand out property, but rather to place it in the hands of a better owner. Such an approach has some far reaching consequences for the envisaged speed of the process of transferring property rights, but the main problem with this approach - and, simultaneously, the main difference between Kornai and other advocates of privatization of (SOEs in) post-STEs - is that his attitude toward the state and its agencies is much more positive, not to say full of trust. He writes explicitly that *the state is alive and well. Its apparatus is obliged to handle the wealth it was entrusted with carefully until a new owner appears who can guarantee a safer and more efficient guardianship* (p. 82).[21] At the same time he seems to have taken very seriously the alleged negative consequences of separation between ownership and control, as discussed by economic literature originated with Berle and Means (1933), and that is why he stresses very strongly *the need for visible, "tangible" owners whose private investments (...) give them a strong interest in the firm's success. This dominant group of shareholders could be Hungarian or foreign; the essential requirement is for an effective, direct ownership interest to form* (p. 91). And this is also why he prefers selling SOEs and/or their assets to giving them away as well as why issuing and selling shares plays a secondary role in his recommendations. In other words, privatization of assets takes precedence over privatization of claims.[22]

Since Kornai's book is supposed to be an overall blueprint for turning the Hungarian economy into a market one, his eventual recommendations are also influenced by some more general considerations. The most important factors which have to be taken into account and which further strengthen the case for privatization by selling and not giving away, are the following:
- the sale of state assets is bound to become a major source of income for the state budget and sale receipts will diminish the necessity faced by the

---

[21] Trust that the state is capable not only of managing the passage towards a market economy but also of taking proper care of SOEs in the transition period answers, in the last analysis, the worries about the negative consequences of prolonging the period of the existence of an economy which is neither reformed nor transformed. But what Kornai (1990b) writes on self-perpetuating bureaucracy and indirect bureaucratic control as well as on the problem of "reform/transformation constituency" seems to question this kind of optimism.

[22] This, in turn, seems to play down the possible role of capital markets in post-STEs, especially in the transition period.

Hungarian citizens to contribute the same amount either through taxation or inflation;[23]

- the sale of state property is also one way to pump out the unspent money, the so-called "monetary overhang",[24] which, in turn, highlights the importance of cash-credit ratio.

Apart from being against allowing people to become stockholders "for a song" and in favour of limiting various discounts to a minimum, Kornai is also opposed - as one could expect - to "spontaneous privatization" and, unlike Mizsei (1992), very sceptical with respect to gains from any restructuring (e.g. conversion of SOEs into joint stock companies) which is not a real privatization. In particular, for him *it is inadmissible for the previous managers themselves to choose who the new owners should be or promote themselves to the top of the list of new owners* (p. 89).

As far as foreign owners are concerned, part of Hungary's state wealth can be sold to them but *only to the extent compatible with the nation's interest* (p. 86). It means that it may be worth placing an upper limit on the proportion of Hungarian SOEs' property that foreigners may buy, even though no such restrictions should be imposed on foreign direct investment.

The prime purpose of privatization is to nurture the incentive force private ownership provides (p. 93). In order to achieve it, the members of the private sector should be given a chance to buy the wealth of the state sector in suitably separated parts, paying real market prices, although Kornai adds immediately that a credit construction related to such a sale must be established[25] and that leasing, already widespread in Hungary, should be further encouraged. The potential buyer should always be notified of the public sale, i.e. the whole process of marketing state wealth should be fully public.

Methods used should take into account the branch of the economy and the size of firm concerned but writing about how in practice assets and/or whole enterprises should be sold, Kornai (1990a) does not really go into the details of such an operation and limits himself to point out that auctions should be used as much as possible. Papers by Maskin (1992) and Bolton and Roland (1992), to

---

[23] But at the same time, such sources of income may weaken the pressure to reduce subsidies and restructure public finances.

[24] Of course, everything depends on what the state does with the money received - see Section 1 of this Chapter.

[25] This arrangements should be governed by two principles: *First, that the upper limit on sales to private parties is not determined by the current total of private wealth. (...) Second, this credit should be granted to real flesh-and-blood persons instead of distributing it through an intangible stock market* (p. 85).

which we turn below, show that this simple recommendation has far reaching consequences and involves finding a solution to a multitude of practical issues.

Maskin (1992) is an application of the theory of auctions to the problem of selling assets in post-STEs. Such an application is more than appropriate because auctions, which provide a familiar and simple method for reallocating resources, are very suitable for situations in which a seller is uncertain how much each buyer values what is being sold.[26] *By inducing buyers to compete against each other, auctions tend to fulfil these two objectives better than do the most common alternatives to auctions: price-setting by the seller, negotiation between the seller and individual buyers, and, as has sometimes been proposed for the countries of EE, simply giving the assets away* (p. 115).

Maskin (1992) discusses three main types of auctions: the high-bid auction (each bidder submits one bid, in ignorance of the other bids), the second-bid auction (each bidder submits one bid, in ignorance of the other bids; the bids are opened, and the highest bidder pays the amount of the second-highest bid and wins the object) and the English auction (each bidder is free to revise his bid upwards and when no bidder wishes to revise his bid further, the highest bidder wins the object and pays his bid).[27] Apart from the aforementioned procedures, one further important distinction is that between private and common values: in a private-value auction, each player knows his value with certainty, although he may still have to estimate the values of other players; in a common-value auction the players have identical values, but each player forms his own valuation by estimating with his private information (Rasmusen, 1989, pp. 246-249).

If we conceive "efficiency" as pertaining to the control of resources, as Maskin (1992) does, and if for the purpose of measuring it we assume that *the social value of a unit of capital is equal to the maximum of the potential buyers' private valuation of the item* (p. 116),[28] then one of the most important propositions established in this paper is that *in the case of private values, the second-bid and English auctions are efficient* (Proposition 1, p. 121). Efficiency of the high-bid auction depends on additional, strong symmetry and.

---

26 When we are selling capital goods, the buyer's valuation corresponds to how productive he expects them to be is in his hands, which is important when our attention is focused not only on maximising seller's revenue but also on matching assets with productive and entrepreneurial skills of their purchasers. Some types of auctions, as we shall see, are able to assure that both goals are achieved simultaneously.

27 The procedure not discussed by Maskin (1992) is the so-called Dutch auction in which the seller announces a bid, which he continuously lowers until some buyer stops him and takes the object at that price, which is strategically equivalent to the high-bid auction (Rasmusen, 1989, p. 249).

28 This means that all relevant markets are perfectly competitive and ignores risk-aversion.

informational assumptions (Proposition 2, p. 121). The English auction (but not the other two) remains efficient under common values, provided that each buyer's information can be represented by a one-dimensional parameter (Proposition 4, p. 126). When information is multidimensional, i.e. when the seller wants not only to receive payments for the assets but also to preserve jobs, as is often the case in Central and Eastern Europe,[29] no auction can be fully efficient (Proposition 6, p. 128), but the second-bid and English auctions tend to be more efficient than the high-bid auction (Proposition 8, p. 130).[30]

From the point of view of having to derive from these propositions practical conclusions, the assumptions of Maskin (1992) with respect to financial constraints are of crucial importance. For the most part of the argument it is assumed that there are no financial constraints. The author seems to be aware of the problems following from relaxing this assumption and points out two related issues: first, the buyer with the highest valuation may not be able to pay the winning bid, i.e. the ability to use the assets may not coincide with the ability to pay for them[31] and if the seller himself lends the money to be repaid out of the buyer's return on capital, one faces a moral hazard problem (Aghion, 1992); secondly, the return may be insufficient to repay the loan and the buyer may simply go bankrupt. As far as their solutions are concerned, however, the only indication to be found in Maskin (1992) is that using vouchers, distributed free of charge, to bid for assets is not a solution because what is being sacrificed is efficiency: *it may be efficient for a given investor to own all the capital, but if he is allocated only a fraction of the vouchers this cannot happen* (p. 132).

These difficult problems became, in a sense, the starting point of Bolton and Roland (1992). Unlike Maskin (1992), this paper argues from the very

---

[29] See also Winiecki, Jan, *Mity polskiej prywatyzacji*, *Rzeczpospolita*, 9.12.1992.

[30] The very problem of different outcomes - and of various degrees of efficiency - of various types of auctions follows from the fact that capital markets are not perfectly efficient and therefore unable to correct all misallocations.

[31] It is in this context that one of the arguments in favour of free distribution is sometimes formulated: in post-STEs it is only former black marketeers and old nomenklatura, allegedly managerially inefficient, that have money to buy what is being privatized. It would unjust, so the argument goes, to let the wealth accumulated under the old regime to put them in a advantaged position. It may be so, but the following two quotations contain important *caveats*:
The winners in the new systems of EE are likely to be correlated with the winners in the old systems of EE, because there is a statistically significant, if not perfect, correlation between aggressive opportunists on both cases, and in the end there is not a whole lot that can be done about it (Weitzman, 1991, p. 252).
If the ex-socialist countries really wanted to keep former black-marketeers and members of the discredited nomenklatura out of the privatization process, the wealth of these people would have to be confiscated outright. It would be rather useless to restrict their portfolio choices (Schmieding, 1992, p. 105).

beginning that bids for state-owned assets and firms should make use of various securities, which is a very important development.[32] This innovation helps to distinguish between two phases in the privatisation of SOEs in post-STEs: *the phase of transfer of control (which can be achieved by auctioning state assets in exchange for non-cash bids) and the phase of transfer of claims (which can take place in stages)* (p. 292).

In order to overcome the stock-flow constraint, caused by the assumed shortage of capital, they consider three types of non-cash bids: standard debt, voting shares (or common stock) and non-voting shares (or preferred stock).[33] Such bids would allow many (potential) buyers with little current wealth, e.g. a team of managers and/or workers, to *bid for state assets by committing either to sharing future revenues with the state or to fixed future debt repayments to the state* (p. 292).

Bolton and Roland (1992) suggest the following scenario: Firms should first be commercialized; in a second stage a set of firms to be auctioned off should be advertised. A deadline should be specified for the submission of sealed bids to the privatization agency in charge of the auction. The rules of the auction should be clearly spelled out and basic information about what exactly is being privatized should be made available to the bidders (p. 294).

Such a procedure should, in principle, be able to reconcile several desirable objectives: speed of privatization, higher efficiency, introduction of capital markets and balanced budgets. What is more, apart from arguments in favour of using auctions put forward by Maskin (1992), they point out that these procedures not only reduce the informational rent of the winner, but also are able to reveal useful information about the underlying common value of firms, not to be underestimated in view of the necessity to develop capital markets in post-STEs. But there are also some problems with their proposals.

One of them is how to exclude frivolous bids. To overcome this difficulty Bolton and Roland (1992) suggest that the government imposes either minimum cash payments, determined on a case-by-case basis by the

---

[32] The main shortcoming of their analysis is that they assign too much importance to the revenue received by the Treasury. They seem to have assumed that the whole surplus of SOEs becomes automatically a source of budget revenue. This was so under what Kornai calls "classical socialism" (Kornai, 1992, pp. 71-75), but is not no longer the case. For example in Poland, *ceteris paribus*, for the state to preserve the cash flow from SOEs at an unchanged level, it would be enough to retain this fraction of equity - with or without voting rights, it does not really matter - corresponding to the so-called "founding fund" (as distinguished from "enterprise fund"), on which SOEs pay "dividends" (some kind of a capital tax) since 1988.

[33] A more complete list of non-cash bids should also include leasing contracts and managements buy-outs, which, at least in Poland, in fact proved to be the most popular privatization procedures.

privatization agency, or severe penal sanctions on the new managers if they fail to make the promised payments. Further, part of the non-cash bid should be debt so that when the firm does not meet its obligations, the government could force it into bankruptcy. But does it really cover all the possibilities of dysfunctional - from the point of view of the seller - behaviour by prospective bidders?

Another problem is that of how to preserve the incentives of the winner. The solution proposed by Bolton and Roland (1992) contains two measures: a ceiling of say 80-85 per cent (depending on the size of the firm) of non-voting shares that can be pledged may be imposed and, similarly, a maximum debt-equity ratio may be specified so as to reduce the risk of default.

These kinds of precautions reveal what is the main problem with using auctions in privatization. It is not whether enough bidders take part in auctioning off the assets to be privatized but how not to reduce abnormal profits to zero. That is so because, if the values of both precautionary measures are known in advance, as they should be, then, if the seller wants to maximize his revenue, it will be irrational to submit bids below these border values. Then either the cash part of the bid is given the leading role, which would sacrifice the matching aspect of Bolton and Roland (1992) proposal, or multidimensionality of the bids, warned against by Maskin (1992) as inefficient, has to be introduced. When Bolton and Roland (1992) write that the role of the selection committee is basically that of an investment bank in that it has to rank business plans[34] and can disagree with the estimates provided by the bidder who in turn should be given the right to appeal against the committee's decision it implies that assets will have to be sold on grounds other than the maximization of the proceeds from the sale. But is not then all of this equivalent to - and cannot it be simplified to take a form of - a managerial contract, as suggested by standard solutions to the agency problem? If this is true, than perhaps those who advocate free, direct or indirect, distribution of shares may be right. But it may also be the case that there is no simple and universal solution to the problem of how to privatize post-STEs.

---

[34] An additional problem how binding such business plans should be in the future: should the winner ask the selection committee for permission whenever he or she wants to take into account any change in his or her business environment?

2.2.3 Free Distribution

Theoretical and practical difficulties with organizing sales of the public sector assets notwithstanding, authors advocating free distribution stress some other advantages of this approach to privatization of post-STEs. For example, this method should speed up the process of privatization and therefore the allegedly damaging effects of plundering the firms would be minimized. Political considerations as well as arguments making use of the concepts of fairness and justice usually take the central stage. Proposing free distribution promises help in developing capital markets and gets round the thorny issue of the extent to which foreigners should participate in making the best possible use of what the communists left behind them.[35]

Specific proposals reflect, to some extent, priorities of their authors, which, in turn, makes these proposals much easier to criticize. But a much more satisfactory basis for a taxonomy of free distribution procedures is provided by answers to the following questions: (1) to whom is the ownership being given away? (2) are the shares to be distributed directly or through some intermediaries, or will the beneficiaries receive some form of currency (vouchers) with which they can choose which shares to acquire? and (3) are the beneficiaries to become active or passive owners, and if they are to be passive, who will supervise management? In other words, various proposals can be classified according to the group of beneficiaries, the mode of distribution and the role played by the beneficiaries in the governance of privatized companies (Frydman and Rapaczynski, 1991, p. 260).

As far as the first criterion is concerned, most proposals envisage that it will be all citizens - or at least those who will want to participate - to whom the assets will be given. For this reason Weitzman (1991) deserves special attention because in this paper it is argued that the principle of squatter sovereignty: *Let those who work the land and the machines own them, at least initially* (p. 254). In the context of self managerial elements in various reforms attempted in STEs, such an idea does not seem very original[36] and is certain to attract a lot of criticism ranging from alleged inefficiency of workers' ownership and impossibility of a "third way" to unfairness of such a method. But Weitzman seems to have answers to all of them and the most important thing about his

---

[35] Another often repeated argument against sales and in favour of free distribution is usually formulated in terms of insufficient domestic capital. But the real problem behind this kind of rhetoric is rather the desire to get high prices for what is being sold. Of course, available resources determine possible prices, but this is no argument against using sales in East and Central European privatizations.

[36] A similar solution was advocated in Poland by Krawczyk (1990).

proposal is that the role he envisages for worker ownership *is not an attempt to find a "third way", but a practical means of getting to the "first way" faster and more reliably, I will argue, than the standard alternatives* (p. 259).

In practice things should be organized as follows:

1) enterprises are corporatized. The enterprise is given a legal structure that resembles state owned enterprises in market economies. Accommodation of debts, typically by cancellation, is accomplished to enable firms to begin with a relatively clean balance sheet;

2) the concept of "share ownership" of enterprises is given operational meaning. A legal and administrative framework is created that defines the rights and obligations of share ownership, and that determines how shares can be sold or otherwise transferred. Legitimate and illegitimate operations with shares are defines and enforcement mechanisms are specified and put into place; special attention is paid to the problems of beginning with worker owned firms;

3) shares are given to workers in the enterprise. Shareholders decide on governance structures, market strategies, work standards, whom to fire and hire, and so forth. Workers are legally entitled to sell share or buy shares from outsiders or each other;

4) wages *per se* are no longer paid by the government. Workers can pay themselves dividends, etc., as they see fit within the constraints of the budget;

5) the enterprise is put on a hard budget constraint. No state subsidies are paid, or, at a minimum, state subsidies are phased out by a rigid time schedule (Weitzman, 1991, p. 265 - 267).

Why should this really lead to a full-blooded capitalism? The main reason is that *except in the rare case having probability measure zero that the cooperative dividend happens to equal exactly the going wage rate, forces are set in motion that dissolve the cooperative. The worker-owned cooperative is thus an unstable or transient organizational form* (p. 261). In other words, worker ownership should be used in Central and Eastern Europe precisely because *it is a fair generalization to say that worker ownership has not served as a long-term driving force in any successful real economy* (p. 258). And this is not the only paradox implied by Weitzman (1991). Capitalism is not a fair system and capitalists are not nice guys, he says. Why then so much attention is paid to create an unfair economic system in a fair way? Or do East Europeans - and their numerous Western advisers - expect their capitalism to be different? Scarce bureaucratic, managerial, and credibility resources should not be wasted on fine tuning a distribution process which in any event is rapidly going to get out of control and take on a life of its own. *Instead, effort should be put into a well designed system of ownership, defining exactly what title means, how people can buy, sell, and otherwise transfer property rights; and into a tight, well-managed progressive tax system* (p. 254). It is taxes that should be used to correct the apparent injustice of applying the principle of squatter sovereignty.

The second line of defence is built around the idea that *the privatization process should follow the historical analogy of how private property actually developed in the West* (p. 255). This requirement implies, on the one hand, that transfer of property rights in post-STEs should be designed along simple, basic lines. It should also be as quick as possible and *the last market to worry about and pay attention to is the capital market* (p. 256). On the other hand, the high-tech instruments of financial markets that are appropriate to advanced stages of capitalism should be rejected and their use postponed, not least because of the highly risky nature of *the ahistorical, artificial holding company/mutual fund type schemes* (p. 256). As the remainder of this section shows, this kind of criticism has fallen on deaf ears.

The most specific feature of Weitzman (1991) consists in making workers the only beneficiaries of free distribution of all the public sector assets. Yet one does not have to go as far to achieve apparently similar results. For example, Beksiak *et al.* (1990) argued in their programme prepared at the request of the parliamentary club of "Solidarnosc" (OKP) that the process of privatization might gain enough momentum if 20 per cent of shares were given to employees. They would constitute a clearly identifiable group of shareholders and would be best placed to control the management. The state would retain the remaining 80 per cent but without voting rights. These shares could be later either sold or distributed free of charge or both, which in principle seems to be a very flexible solution, allowing for various responses to future political and economic developments (Winiecki, 1992).

Since nobody seriously argued in favour of giving enterprises for example to their managers or, for that matter to any other chosen group,[37] the

---

[37] Such a gift would not be, from the economic point of view, as irrational as it at first appears. If we accepted that, for example, the main goal of privatization it to maximize the investment potential, which is obviously of great importance for the future growth of post-STEs, *firms should be given for free to those potential owners who have the most money, that is to the nomenklatura and the erstwhile black marketeers* (Schmieding, 1992, p. 102). Taking this line of argument to the extreme, it could even be argued that the state firms should be given away to foreigners with well-established links to the world capital market, even though the East German experience suggests that there could be difficulties with having all such gifts accepted. This also shows that drawing extreme conclusions from one dimensional approaches may produce paradoxical and difficult to accept recommendations.

only alternative is that all (adult) citizens should become beneficiaries of privatizing post-STEs. This conclusion was taken most literally by Feige (1990), in one of the first schemes for privatization in the then USSR. He proposed that each citizen would receive shares in an aggregate of industrial enterprises, some 46,000 in all. A bundle of equity share would comprise an equal fractional ownership share in each and every state enterprise. This bundle is termed a "citizen share". Of the citizen shares, 50 per cent would be divided equally among all citizens, and the rest would be distributed among the central government (10 per cent), the individual republics (20 per cent), and private investors (20 per cent). Some shares are given to - or retained by - various levels of government mainly for fiscal reasons: budgetary problems are bound to appear sooner or later and owning shares is probably the least distortionary way for the government to obtain revenue (Borensztein and Kumar, 1991). The 20 per cent of shares to be auctioned off separately for each firm constitutes a response to the problem of monitoring, based on the idea of the so-called core investor.

Two things have to be noticed about Feige's proposals. First, no scheme envisaging free distribution, however sophisticated, will be complete without suggesting realistic solutions to the agency problem and trying to find a private, domestic or foreign core investor is only one possible solution. Secondly, citizens may benefit from free distribution either directly or indirectly, i.e. they may either be given shares in individual companies or in institutions - call them financial intermediaries - which in turn have shares in privatized firms.[38]

Once it is decided to use financial intermediaries, the list of questions which have to be answered in this way or another by each plan becomes quite long. In consequence various proposals can be classified according to the following relations: between the intermediaries and the state, between the intermediaries and the small investors, between the intermediaries and the companies in which they are invested, between the intermediaries and other kinds of financial institutions as well as between the intermediaries and foreign and international financial institutions (Frydman and Rapaczynski, 1991, p. 262).

Since these relations are to a large extent independent of each other, one can in principle imagine an almost infinite number of schemes. What follows presents only some examples. We shall start with distinguishing two main types

---

[38] As the voucher scheme put into practice in Czecho-Slovakia shows, these two possibilities do not exclude each other. What is more, combining them makes the organizational issues more complicated but at the same time increases flexibility of the privatization process.

of financial intermediaries. Even though very often the word "holding" is used to describe the newly introduced institutions, what is actually meant is either a privatization agency or a mutual fund. The former is a transition device and its role is to restructure, divest, and sell.[39] The latter is supposed to become part of a new, emerging ownership structure, i.e. an institutional investor playing an active role on the capital markets. How active this role is going to be with respect to firms' management and business strategies varies from proposal to proposal.

The plan presented in Frydman and Rapaczynski (1991) is supposed to fulfil four main requirements: speed, social acceptability, effective control over the management of privatized enterprises, and assured access to foreign capital and expertise. Financial intermediaries are important not only because they solve the legitimacy problems associated with selective giveaways but also because of help that they offer in overcoming the *status quo* and solving the problem of control over management of privatized companies. In other words, financial intermediaries will take on the role of core investors, so crucial for Feige (1990) and Lipton and Sachs (1990). Unlike Kornai (1990) and Weitzman (1991), whose distrust of the separation between ownership and control was all too evident, Frydman and Rapaczynski (1991) claim that it is precisely this kind of separation that will help to solve the problem of control.

In practice it all should proceed as follows:

The enterprises to be privatized should be divided into several groups, each comprising no more than 150-200 companies. Each of these groups should be auctioned off separately. After the first group is sold, there would be an intervening period during which the new shareholders would elect the boards of directors of the enterprises and the policy-makers and the public would be able to assess the initial consequences of the chosen strategy of privatization. (...) the vouchers for each privatization phase would be issued separately, and the validity of the vouchers would expire at the end of a given phase (p. 265).

Obviously, the most tricky issue is that of proper design of auctions. Frydman and Rapaczynski (1991) envisage several stages in which the agents are asked to rebid several times. The actual sale would take place according to a rule that facilitates convergence and limits the agents' strategic manipulation. A key

---

[39] In Poland they were first proposed by Swiescicki (1988) and after the election of 4 June 1989 by Gomulka (1989, [1992]), who called his intermediaries "investment banks", but in general one has to distinguish between holdings which are only a new institutional arrangement to reorganize the public sector without changing its ownership status and holdings which are to be used in the process of privatization.

feature of the proposed auction is that the enterprises *would not be auctioned off seriatim*; all would be bid for *simultaneously* at every stage.

In fact, there would be two separate auctions. In the first, the agents would be able to bid for, say, three large blocks of shares in each company - one of 20 per cent and two of 15 per cent.[40] In the second one, the remainder of the shares would be sold through a different procedure: the agents would apportion their remaining vouchers among the companies of their choice and would receive a number of shares determined by the level at which the prices would clear (p. 266).

The plans proposed and described in Blanchard *et al.* (1991) go in a different direction because privatization agencies are preferred to mutual funds. According to these authors, the governments of Central and Eastern Europe should proceed as follows:

1. The government creates a small number of holding companies, each holding and having full control over a portfolio of individual firms. Each holding company is headed by a manager who is assisted by a management team composed of foreign and domestic experts. The manager is appointed and can be replaced by the government.

2. Shares in the holding companies are distributed equally to all. They are then traded in the stock market, perhaps after some phase-in period.

3. The purpose of the holding companies is to restructure and divest. Each is subject to an explicit termination date, by which time any firms still held by the holding companies are closed or sold on the stock market. Proceeds from sales of firms by the holding companies are returned to shareholders through dividends, and holding companies are prevented from either borrowing or issuing additional equity.

4. Subject to those constraints - and obviously within the confines of the law, including antitrust legislation - holding company managers are free to strike deals as they see fit. They may close firms, wait for offers, ask for bids and sell through auctions, sell shares in individual firms on the stock market, or engineer more complex deals and combinations. They may sell to foreigners, to financial institutions, to individuals, and to workers if the prospective buyer have or can borrow required funds (p. 43).

There are some obvious problem with relying so heavily on holdings playing the role of privatization agencies. Mismanagement and reluctance to divest themselves of power are only two such examples. But Blanchard *et al.* (1991) hope to solve them by appropriate compensation mechanisms.

---

[40] In this way the problem of finding a private core investor is replaced by searching for a dominant shareholder, which only underlines the problem of *quid custodiet ipsos custodes* and leaves it without any satisfactory solution.

Development of financial markets is high on the agenda of Tirole (1991, 1992)[41] but at the same time he is aware of difficulties in getting them started. The second very important element of his plans is competition-oriented restructuring,[42] almost completely neglected by other proposals. His scenario, in which he pays a lot of attention to the issues of market structure and regulation and which uses holdings as vehicles of free distribution, is worth being reported extensively and can be summarized in the following way:

I. Noisy phase
1. Definition period
1.1. A divestiture commission is created with independent representatives of government and representatives of international institutions on its board, assisted by domestic and foreign experts. The commission will perform the most obvious cases of competition-oriented restructuring.
1.2. Firms are renationalized, and then divided into three groups by the divestiture commission. The first group consists of the firms in naturally competitive sectors or in sectors in which foreign competition will not substantially hinder the growth of firms. These firms will be allocated to holding companies as soon as possible. The second group consists of firms that will need to be broken up by the divestiture commission before being handed to the holding companies at the end of the definition period. The third group is composed of natural monopolies and will either remain under public ownership, or else be transferred to the holding companies and remain regulated in the long term.
1.3. A safety net is created to protect workers from the hardships created by the forthcoming private restructuring period
1.4. The main elements of property, contract, bankruptcy, and antitrust laws are enunciated and put into operation
1.5. Holding companies are created and incorporated.
The number of holding companies depends on country size and available expertise. (...) The shares of a holding company are distributed freely and equally to all citizens but will not be traded before the mature phase. (...) The board of directors selects the holding companies' managers and puts them on an incentive scheme. During the noisy period, managers of the holding companies receive a salary. (...) Low-powered incentive schemes, i.e. small stock options, seem appropriate. The main incentives for the holding companies' managers during the noisy phase, besides relative performance, evaluation, are career concerns and monitoring by the directors. (...) The holding companies are endowed with the shares of the firms to be privatized. (...) There are two variants: (1) each firm is allocated to a single holding company; (2) each firm is shared among several holding companies. (...) Firms are allocated randomly to the holding companies to avoid capture as well as to roughly equalize the initial quality of portfolios.
1.5.1. the managers of the firms are given employment contracts

---

[41] The two papers are almost identical and the differences between them are of secondary importance. In what follows it is Tirole (1991) that will be quoted.
[42] Whether this task is easier when assets are sold then when they - or claims on them - are distributed free of charge is a separate issue. Tirole (1991) simply assumes free distribution.

1.5.2. regulation of public enterprises and private regulated firms is as in the private restructuring

1.5.3. a merger commission is created (possibly the divestiture commission becomes the merger commission after having broken up firms)

2. Private restructuring

2.1. Holding companies restructure firms

2.2. The government completes the legal system

2.3. The government sets up agencies to regulate the banking sector and the stock market

2.4. The government sets a timetable for trade liberalization and defines foreign exchange guarantees for the capital inflows.

2.5. Firms put modern accounting structure in place

2.6. Borrowing

2.6.1. each company hires or trains domestic and foreign analysts who start studying the potential of the firms (not only the holding company's) that the holding company will be allowed to bid on

2.6.2. regulated private firms are subject to cost-of-service regulation

2.6.3. state-owned enterprises are also subject to some form of cost-of-service regulation

II. Mature phase

3. Inception of the stock market

Holding companies, newly created firms, and institutional investor, and possibly foreigners bid on each firm. (...) a mechanism is set up to prevent interlocking directorates in tightly oligopolistic industries. (...) to induce trade among holding companies and therefore to create incentives to collect during the noisy phase information about the firm's value, a fraction of each firm can be earmarked for holding companies that did not own this firm before

4. Market period

4.1. Immediately after the inception period the markets for the firms' and the holding companies' stocks are open to all (...) The holding companies' assets are thus now liquid.

4.2. The government and the (nonequity holding) foreigners lose their voting rights in the boards of directors of the holding companies

4.3. Firms can issue equity and bonds and can borrow from (newly created) domestic banks

4.4. The managers of firms and holding companies are presumably put on incentive schemes that are more powerful than those during the noisy phase

4.5. Trade liberalization is completed according to the predetermined timetable

4.6. Regulated firms are given more innovative and more powerful incentive schemes than cost-of-service regulation ("incentive regulation") (pp. 247-253).

Using holdings, i.e. either mutual funds like in Frydman and Rapaczynski (1991) or privatization agencies like in Blanchard *et al.* (1991) or Tirole (1991) leads to a situation in which all (participating) citizens benefit from privatization by free distribution in an indirect way, unlike in Feige (1990). But there are other possibilities which can be described in similar terms. If shares are used, for example, to provide funds for pension schemes or to capitalize banks, citizens will still remain beneficiaries, even though perhaps in a slightly more indirect way. This is precisely what one can find in Lipton and Sachs (1990).

Compared with the schemes, which have already been briefly presented in this Section, the proposals of Lipton and Sachs (1990), although among the first from the chronological point of view, seem to be most eclectic. For them *the economic challenge is to combine the redefinition of property rights with the creation of vital financial market institutions* (p. 294). That is why these two economists proposed the following:

At the outset, we recommend that hundreds of the largest enterprises be converted into Treasury-owned joint-stock companies. (...) Right from the start, some firms could be managed on a case-by-case basis (for instance, where a private bidder comes forward). Most firms, however, would follow a special track emphasizing the rapid distribution of shares. A portion of shares would be given at a low price or at no charge to workers, and another portion of shares would be transferred rapidly and free of charge to various financial intermediaries (such as mutual funds, pension funds, and commercial banks). Shares in these intermediaries will in turn be distributed or sold to households. Finally, the government would retain a portion of the shares of each enterprises and would gradually sell them off as a block to "core investors" who are to take a key role in management of the enterprise. In this way, we hope to combine rapid privatization through free distribution with the advantages of case-by-case sales (p. 299).[43]

As one can see, the proposals of Lipton and Sachs (1990) are supposed to achieve many goals at the same time, but their implementation will have to be accompanied by creating a completely new legal and institutional environment. Apart from the necessity of creating mutual funds this involves opting for the so-called universal banking, like in Germany and Japan and unlike in the Anglo-Saxon countries.

---

[43] More specifically, Lipton and Sachs (1990) suggest that, in addition to the 10 per cent distributed to the workers, around 5 per cent of the shares would be reserved for compensation for the managers and the corporate board. The second tranche of shares, around 20 per cent of the total, would be used to capitalize a new private pension system. The third tranche would consist of 10 per cent of the shares and would be used to capitalize the existing state-owned commercial banks (60 per cent of this tranche) and the insurance sector. The fourth tranche will consist of 20 per cent of the shares of the enterprises that will be distributed generally to the adult population of Poland. The shares of the enterprises would be distributed to several private investment trusts (which are closed-end mutual funds), whose shares in turn would be freely distributed to the adult citizens of Poland. After the initial distribution of the shares, the investment trusts would be free to actively manage their portfolios. Each individual would receive one share in one of the investment trusts. After this phase is completed, the government will retain roughly 35 per cent ownership in the partially privatized companies. Following the free distribution of shares, any number of methods might be used to dispose of the remaining government holdings, including public offerings, private placements of shares, and further free distribution (p. 329 - 331).

2.2.4 Either Selling or Giving Away?

The discussion, reported briefly above, in which so many distinguished economists took part[44] could suggest that privatizing post-STEs is an either/or issue: either the assets, which are at present controlled by the state to a larger or smaller extent, are sold or they are given away free of charge, regardless of the method used. However, such an exclusive alternative is definitely false. Firstly, the assets under conside.ation are by no means a homogeneous group and they include not only large enterprises but also land, flats and shops. It would be, therefore, presumptuous to assume that all of them should be privatized in the same way, which is what is ultimately suggested by this alternative. In other words, with respect to the assets as a whole using different methods is much recommended, even if the results of trying to match methods of privatization with various types of assets may be sometimes arbitrary and in consequence questionable.

Secondly, the either/or alternative does not hold even with respect to any individual set of assets. If, for example, an enterprise is transformed into a joint stock company, there is nothing inconsistent in giving away some shares and selling the rest. What is more, neither various groups of beneficiaries (e.g. workers and all citizens) nor different methods of distribution (e.g. either directly or through some kind of mutual funds) do not exclude each other in most cases, although trying to combine too many procedures at the same time may unnecessarily complicate the whole process.

The issue of whether to sell or to give away the assets goes much deeper, however, than only the recommendation of using a pluralistic approach to the problem of privatizing post-STEs. If these assets, according to the universally accepted legal doctrine, are owned by the nations represented by their respective governments, is selling them really a sale? Is giving them away really free of charge? In other words, to comprehend what this process really amounts to and what its nature is, one has to look at it from the point of view of its redistributive consequences.

Those who buy what belongs to all, buy it from the rest of the population. Those who receive it in form of giveaways, if all are free to participate in the distribution process, simply receive their share of what all owned together. The budgetary balance sheet changes but *ceteris paribus*, i.e. at

---

[44] See also, for example, Vickers (1991), Stiglitz (1991, 1992), Fischer (1992), Aslund (1991), and Bornstein (1992). For one of the most extensive bibliographies on privatization in Eastern and Central Europe, see Brabant (1992).

given levels of state expenditures and assuming that receipts from sales are treated as part of budget revenue, *the population would reap the financial benefits of privatization either via a direct distribution of proceeds or via correspondingly lower taxes* (Schmieding, 1992, p. 101). If no foreigners take part in the process and if transferring assets from the public sector to the private one brings about no efficiency gains, the net wealth of any economy changes only if the state wastes some of the revenue from privatization. In consequence, one can, following Schmieding (1992) state it very bluntly: *Whether the domestic citizens can afford to buy ownership titles in firms and how their net wealth may change are not matters of sales versus give-away schemes. These methods are mainly different devices for distributing the same amount of wealth* (p. 102).

Does it follow from this that in the last analysis there is no difference between the two methods of privatizing post-STEs, or, for that matter, anything else anywhere else? Not necessarily. On the one hand, giveaways *make the financial gains from privatization much more visible - and more directly identifiable with privatization - than in the case of property-sales-cum-tax-reductions* (p. 102), the more so as people in many countries are usually in favour of higher state expenditures but against higher taxes, at least for themselves. On the other hand, even if the net wealth of the population as a whole does not change, some people can gain and others lose. That is why Schmieding conjectures that *the core of the complaint about a lack of domestic financial assets is not that this genuinely impedes the privatization of state-owned assets. Instead, those who use this argument are really saying that they do not like the distributional consequences which a public offering of ownership titles would entail under these circumstance* (p. 102).

Apart from this political considerations, criteria that can be used to choose one of the two - or their combination - include operational simplicity and ability to achieve at the same time other objectives, e.g. those already discussed in this Section. Minimizing transaction costs is also an important consideration (Vaubel, 1992). But since it seems that political and economic objectives will always have to be to some extent reconciled, Schmieding (1992) comes out with his own proposals. He writes that *if the political support argument for giveaways is serious, I would prefer the way which is most visible and interferes least with efficiency, namely the regular distribution of at least part of the privatization proceeds* (p. 107). Among many advantages, as compared with various schemes based on vouchers, Schmieding stresses in particular the following:

In the case of sales with a distribution of revenues, ownership titles would at least be acquired by those who want to hold them and perhaps even exercise corporate control; the short-term hazard of an excessive spread of ownership would be minimized. Most importantly, the distribution of proceeds could help to weaken opposition against the participation of foreign capital. The more foreigners are allowed to bid for ownership titles in state firms, the higher the price will be - and hence the privatization proceeds to be distributed to the citizens. The citizens would thus experience a direct and positive link between foreign capital and their own material well-being (p. 105).

Whether greed is going to be more powerful than xenophobia, or whether self-interest can be identified with the national interest is debatable. But looking at privatization from the point of view of its redistributive effect and of its effect on net wealth of the population once more confirms the importance and central character of the main theme of this book, i.e. of the relationship between privatization and foreign direct investment.

3. Privatization in Perspective

In Western Europe privatization has occurred in Germany, Spain, and France as episodes of liberal economic policies, but massive privatization occurred in Western Europe under the Thatcher government, where a few dozen firms were privatized over a decade - with some emphasis on broad ownership ("mass capitalism") which the government perceived as a guarantee against looming attempts of future Labour governments to reverse the process. The Know-how fund set up for the support of the Eastern European transition and the expertise of banks and investment firms involved in British privatization plays a considerable role in central and eastern Europe. A second major West European force is the German government which takes advantage of its experience with rapid privatization of East German companies via the Treuhandanstalt (THA; State Trusteeship Agency), and representatives of a subsidiary of the THA as well as high level civil servants and many agents from the business community are active in central and eastern Europe, including Russia. In Russia some German advisors, including Mr. Kartte, the former head of the Kartellamt - the Berlin-based Agency Against Unfair Competition - are supporting regional privatization schemes. The third major West European influence in the transformation process is through the PHARE program which actually is an OECD program administered by the EC. The London based EBRD (in which the US has no controlling stake) is the fourth basically European institution active in the support of transforming socialist economies, but until 1993 it financed only very limited privatization and restructuring projects because it was so difficult to find a niche between domestic capital sources and foreign commercial banking sources available in ex-CMEA countries.

Privatization means finding investors for acquiring existing firms, but also creating new business establishments. The creation of new small business establishments has been important for innovation and economic growth in many OECD countries (Acs and Audretsch, 1991), but has been neglected in Eastern Europe almost completely for many years. The number of self-employed and supporting family members has increased in some OECD countries in the 1980s and has not only spurred growth but also reduced unemployment to the extent that unemployed have set up private enterprises and the new firms have created new jobs. The share of the self-employed (outside agriculture) in total employment reached in the UK, Italy, Spain, the Netherlands, France, Germany, the US and Japan in 1990 11.6, 22.3, 17.1, 7.8, 10.3, 7.7, 7.6 and 11.5 per cent, respectively, while the share in ex-CMEA countries was not higher than 3 per cent.

Adjustments on the supply side in former CMEA countries are critical to a successful transformation process since a rising standard of living, full employment and the ability to service the foreign debt depend on modernizing and reorganizing firms, creating new business establishments and finally raising exports.

Taking into account the experience from West European privatization programmes in the 1980s - especially in the UK - one may expect significant improvements in factor productivity only if privatization takes place in industries with a high intensity of competition (Bishop and Kay, 1990). This points to the need to link privatization programmes with active competition policy in the nontradables sector and competition policy and import liberalization in the tradables sector. To join privatization and competition is important for stimulating economic growth.

Privatization should make the economy more flexible and responsive to relative price signals. However, private investors will also be very sensitive to political uncertainties and instabilities created by unstable and inconsistent economic policy. If, for instance, the capitalization horizon of private investors is shortening because of high and volatile inflation rates many productivity-augmenting investment and innovation projects might no longer be feasible and government would record lower tax revenues than in an economy with a high rate of investment and innovation and hence a high economic growth rate. This points to the importance of linking privatization programs with the introduction of an adequate political system design and consistent macroeconomic policies. Privatization deprives the bureaucracy of the command over resources and privileges, while politicians lose options for alternative careers in management or board positions. The political economy suggests that few in the political system are well motivated to proceed with privatization.

3.1 Privatization Procedures and Privatization Activities in Former CMEA Countries

Privatization takes a long time as all privatization experiences in central and eastern Europe show - with the exception of the former GDR, where industry will be almost fully privatized within five years. In late 1992 about 40 per cent of value-added in Poland and Hungary, and in the CSFR about 20 per cent of GNP were from the private sector. The Polish figure is somewhat an overstatement because about 10 percentage points are accounted for by private Polish agriculture. The share of employment in the private sector was close to 50 per cent in Poland and Hungary in early 1993.

Taking into account value-added in the emerging capitalist shadow economy figures for private sector output may be somewhat higher than indicated. However, there is no doubt that privatization is a very information intensive and time-consuming process. Moreover, with each chunk of state firms privatized the external environment of the remaining would-be privatized firms is changing. In contrast to privatization in Western Europe one cannot argue that privatization leaves input prices, output prices and technologies used unaffected. Indeed one often cannot apply marginal economics because the scope of change is so radical.

The transforming countries have organized privatization in different ways. One may organize privatization mainly in the form of a state-organized privatization process "from above"; or one could privatize the privatization process in the sense that government would entrust consulting firms and banks with finding new owners for existing firms; or one could seek to establish an international bureaucratic approach in which international organizations such as the World Bank group and the EBRD would play a major role.

There are some strategic questions in privatization (Welfens, 1992b):

- Should small firms or big firms be privatized first? Privatizing small firms entails the problem that smaller firms, often suppliers of big inefficient state firms, will become more efficient so that big firms improve profitability - possibly without much of their own efforts. However, concentrating on small firms first has the advantage of creating privatization momentum which is crucial for a sustaining privatization process.

- Should privatization focus on a few dozen big firms which typically represent 1/3 of value-added in former CMEA countries or should one adopt sectoral privatization programs which will expose only a smaller fraction to market allocation each time a subprogramme is realized? One should clearly focus on sectoral privatization programmes because competition is a horizontal phenomenon in the first place; and privatization needs competition as an additional ingredient if efficiency gains are to be reaped.

- Should emphasis be primarily on privatizing existing firms? The answer is clearly no. Labour productivity in ex-CMEA countries is inferior relative to even poor countries in the EC, and hence privatization (as well as structural change that will reduce the share of industry in GNP) is bound to create mass unemployment unless policy would focus on the task of supporting the creation of new business establishments early on. Many new establishments will fail in the course of competition, but competition is indeed a process with unknown ex-ante winners and survivors, so that the efficiency gains from competition cannot be obtained for society without accepting bankruptcy of non-viable firms. Competition is a dynamic discovery process (Hayek, 1968) which should re-generate variety (of products, process innovations, organizational patterns etc.).[45]

3.1.1 Eastern Germany

The most comprehensive and fastest approach to privatization is the German Treuhandanstalt (THA; under the supervision of the Ministry of Finance and the Ministry of Economics) model of transferring ownership rights to private investors. The Berlin headquarters and its 15 regional offices, responsible for most of the smaller companies to be privatized, massively employed its own

---

[45] The promotion of new firms seems to be of particular importance in the transforming economies. However, this can be only a long term approach since - referring to West German figures - only 50 per cent of newly established firms survive the first five years and then on average do not have more than 5.5 employees. The failure rate in Eastern Europe is likely to be even higher.

resources and outside consulting firms in order to organize a swift privatization process.[46]

By the end of January 1993 2,442 firms were still owned by the THA which started in 1990 with some 8,000 firms whose number increased by dismemberment of major firms. A total of 12,672 firms was on the books of the THA in the period 1990-92. Beginning 1 July, 1990 - the date of German Economic, Monetary and Social Union - investment budgets of DM 173.2 bill. were assured to the THA which typically requires investors to guarantee a certain amount of investments and workplaces.

Labor market aspects were important: 1.4 million workplaces were assured by private investors and gross sales proceeds amounted to DM 40.6 billion (roughly $ 25 billion which should be compared to the GDR's GNP of $ 120 billion in 1990) 1958 management buy-outs occurred of which 214 were accounted for by the THA Berlin office and 1,744 by the regional THA offices. Foreign investors bought 556 firms and made investment commitments of DM 17.4 billion and commitments for 122,501 workplaces. Seven thousand and forty one firms - compared to 13,183 claims for restitution filed with the THA - had been reprivatized by January 1, 1993, that is returned to the previous owners. This mainly concerns former GDR citizens which left the GDR until June 1952 and GDR citizens whose firms had been nationalized in 1972. Two hundred and sixty-two firms and 6,227 assets (mainly buildings) were transferred to local authorities which play a strong role in the German federal system and which often can be expected to use assets more efficiently than federal or regional authorities; 2,340 firms had been closed by the end of January, 1993, and this represented almost 20 per cent of all firms on the books for the THA. Overall, 11,234 firms or enterprise sub-entities, 28,694 hectares of agricultural land and 13,788 real estate objects had been privatized by January 31, 1993; 2442 firms were still to be privatized, and many of them certainly represented problem cases of the THA.[47] Some 6,000 people working on the staff of the THA have thus organized an impressive privatisation, although one certainly can criticize certain aspects of THA activities. With the West German economy facing a recession in 1993 it turned out that commitments for investment and jobs were often not kept even by major West German companies, and that penalty fees - stipulated in contracts - were not collected. Moreover, the rapid privatization procedure in Eastern Germany resulted in negative zero net revenues from privatization and left no significant

---

[46] For some organizational aspects of the THA see SCHIPKE (1992).
[47] All figures are from the monthly THA bulletin Monatsinformation, 1/1993, February, 1993, Berlin.

mechanism for government to participate in future capital gains.[48] In late 1992 the Bonn government decided to save "industrial cores" in THA firms which basically means that a greater amount of subsidies would be allocated to big industrial firms deemed to have a chance of long term restructuring and survival.

Foreign Investment

Foreign investors could have been expected to play an important role in the East German privatization process if unit labour costs in Eastern Germany had not exploded. The advantage that Eastern Germany's political framework is identical with that of Western Germany and that East German firms provide direct access to EC markets probably was overcompensated in many cases of would-be investors by cost disadvantages in Eastern Germany, where nominal wages were allowed to increase much faster than productivity could be improved. Foreign investors could have raised sales proceeds of the THA strongly if massive investment inflows had forced West German firms to launch counter-bids to prevent pressure from new competitors. Eastern Germany could have become a spring-board for renewed competition in Germany, but excessive wage rates and the application of the principle of restitution before compensation - creating a myriad of property right uncertainties - effectively killed this opportunity. Property rights uncertainties certainly were more critical for foreign investors than for West German investors which often not only enjoyed the advantage of knowing the legal domestic system in full detail but of being well connected to the Bonn government or the governments of the five new states (Länder) in Eastern Germany.

Foreign investors have indeed played only a minor role in privatizations of the THA. About 5 per cent of all privatizations involved foreign investors, where firms from France, the UK, the US, Switzerland, Austria, Canada, the Netherlands and Italy dominated (see Table D1).

---

[48] Sinn and Sinn (1991) argued that government should keep a minority equity stake in THA privatized firms in order to benefit from future capital gains. Welfens (1991, 1992b) suggested a capital gains tax for privatization procedures in central and eastern Europe. For a broader analysis of German unification issues see Welfens (1992a) and Sinn and Sinn (1991).

Table D1: Top Ten of Foreign Investors in Eastern Germany
(ranking based on weighting all categories A, B, C)

Source Country	Investments Commitments (A in DM Mio.)	B: Workplace Commitments	C: Number of Privatizations
France	4,800	21,024	60
U.K.	1,556	15,390	74
USA	2,786	12,530	56
Switzerl.	901	13,626	87
Austria	634	13,019	83
Canada	1,820	16,555	6
Netherl.	1,000	7,227	46
Italy	522	3,583	25
Denmark	409	2,707	24
Sweden	107	3,500	23
Other	2,823	13,340	72
TOTAL	17,358	122,501	556

Source: THA, Monatsinformation der THA, 01/93, p.16.

It is surprising that French investors are the leading FDI investors in Eastern Germany; in Western Germany French firms are not among the top three source countries of FDI. Interestingly some state-owned French firms are among the leading investors in Eastern Germany. It might be that political considerations have played a role on both the side of the THA and on the French side in some cases. However, for French investors - as for other foreign investors - access to local markets and to the overall market are likely to have played the decisive role for investment projects. It is surprising that Japanese investors have been quite reluctant to invest in Eastern Germany; given the hostility of part of the East German population against foreigners and Asian people in particular one might find a partial explanation in anti-foreign sentiments of the former GDR population. Despite all GDR ideology of internationalism it turned out that people in the former GDR were not very open-minded *vis-à-vis* foreigners. Indeed lack of international tourism and the lack of positive experiences with the valuable contributions of FDI to employment, technology and GNP might explain some facets of the anti-foreign sentiments in Eastern Germany. However, one should not overlook that German unification reinforced nationalism in Germany in general and the rising immigration in combination with economic difficulties faced in the course of unification caused anti-foreign sentiments among a minority of West Germans, too.

The number of employees in Treuhandanstalt firms was reduced from 2.9 million to 1.6 million by the end of 1991. A first Treuhandanstalt estimate of the value of assets in 1990 amounted to DM 200 billion, but later estimates put the net value of assets at only DM 30 billion (BMF, 1991, 26-27); the final count may well show a negative net worth of the GDR's industrial assets evaluated under the conditions and rule of capitalism. From a theoretical perspective the Treuhandanstalt has adopted an adequate strategy in the sense that sectoral privatization schemes were developed so that privatization and competition were combined; this might have lowered sales prices but competition-induced efficiency gains should finally result in higher economic growth and higher tax revenues which could outweigh the effect of reduced sales proceeds for the German Ministry of Finance.

Assessment

Many firms had no chance to survive because of the sharp revaluation of the East German currency in the context of German Monetary Union of July 1, 1990. The east German industry's export ratio was about 20 per cent and an effective revaluation by more than 100 per cent made it difficult for many firms to survive the leap to capitalism. Moreover, wage pressure - driven at first by fear of rising intra-German migration in the case of a persistent 4:1 West-East wage gap - created additional problems; even after reaching 2/3 of West German real wage levels in late 1992 unions pressed for full wage parity, despite the fact that the productivity gap had on average remained at the 3:1 ratio of 1990.

Wage pressure of unions, often led by West German representatives, is easily explained by the desire of unions to attract new members from firms in the former GDR. Overgenerous wage concessions which effectively destroyed between 500,000 and 1 million jobs in Eastern Germany in the period 1990-92 are largely explained by the federal government's overestimation of expected short term productivity gains from introducing the market economy in Eastern Germany and insufficient recognition that producer prices in the former GDR and hence marginal value products of labour were bound to fall steeply once the GDR industry was fully exposed to West German, EC and world competition (GDR producer prices fell by 40 per cent after unification). Moreover, some representatives of the employers' organizations in Eastern Germany were from Western Germany and may have allowed excessive nominal wage increases because the implied cost advantage of East German industrial locations would be a guarantee against rising potential competition from East German firms. It is quite difficult to understand why collective bargaining did not result in provisions that would have encouraged workers to invest into either their own company or in investment funds which in turn could have been linked to the firm or the industry where workers are employed. Creating a broader wealth-owning stratum could have been a major task in Eastern German economic reconstruction, but it was not really recognized as such by government or the labour union.

The net revenue expected from all privatization activities, including measures for restructuring and liquidation, is expected to be negative in Eastern Germany. This is not surprising given the fact that German unification rendered a considerable part of the GDR's capital stock obsolete.[49] Integrating the GDR into Western Germany and thereby fully exposing the GDR industry to the shock of world market competition and the strict requirements of the West German legal framework, including environmental laws, sent asset prices down; this was reinforced by the Treuhandanstalt's procedure to attach many strings to asset sales: typically the investor would have to guarantee a minimum amount of investment over a certain period and not to reduce the labour force below a specific level. However, one may assume that in the long term there will be considerable capital gains in Eastern Germany, most of which will be tax free, despite the fact that massive public investments and publicly financed retraining programmes will strongly contribute to making assets of surviving firms more valuable. A modest, possibly even regressive capital gains tax could have been imposed in order to obtain some indirect return on investment from those who will enjoy windfall profits from successful East German economic restructuring. However, with an average tax-income ratio of roughly 0.24 every saved firm brings a capitalized future tax revenue of 6 per unit of output if one assumes for simplicity infinitely lived firms and a real interest rate of 4 per cent. If the private capital-output ratio is 3 and public investment relative to private investment is 1:4 (typical of Western Germany; however, with so little private investment in Eastern Germany in the first transformation stage the ratio for the

---

[49] The Rybczynski theorem would suggest that Eastern Germany would intensify the export of goods in which labour - relatively abundant after the exogenous obsolescence of part of the capital stock - is used intensively. This, however, is impossible because the factor price ratio is sharply changing in favour of labour: with a unified labour market east German wages are soon to reach West German wage levels (and in West Germany capital is relatively abundant!). Thus the stagnation of East German exports can be explained, and, indeed, without state subsidies for exports to eastern Europe East German exports had sharply reduced.

former GDR was instead 4:1 at first) one has to take into account that public investment per unit of output is 1/4 so that the capitalized net revenue effect is smaller than indicated, and this would be further reinforced if government subsidized private investment over longer time periods.

A major problem in Eastern Germany is the sluggish inflow of foreign direct investment, which to some extent is not surprising given the high degree of political and economic uncertainties faced already by West German investors. These investors who typically are well connected in the political scene in Bonn/Berlin enjoy a strategic advantage over foreign rivals because they could hope to get firm-specific or sector-specific financial assistance and subsidies if investment projects turned out to become nonprofitable and hence unemployment increases would seem unavoidable - the federal government would step in to avoid unemployment rates from rising above a critical threshold so the investors' contract with the Treuhandanstalt is effectively renegotiated in case the firm gets additional favours from government. Foreign investors are less well positioned in Germany's political arena - except for the case that they already own major subsidiaries in Western Germany - and might therefore be extremely hesitant with investments in Eastern Germany. The xenophobic reactions of part of the East German population observed in 1992 have further reduced prospects to attract foreign direct investment.

Berlin as a traditionally international city (this concerns both West Berlin and East Berlin) will, however, attract some additional FDI inflows in both the service industry and in the manufacturing industry; the latter will often be headquarter services and not so much industrial activities. The biggest problem for private investors in Eastern Germany so far has been that real wage increases have far outpaced productivity growth. Productivity has slightly increased in absolute terms between the second quarter of 1989 - when economic and monetary union occurred - and the first quarter of 1992. But relative to Western Germany there was no increase, so that productivity stayed at 1/3 of the West Germany level, while unit labour costs jumped from about 40 per cent of the West German level to 2/3 in mid-1992. Productivity growth which is reported to be faster in privatized firms than in those firms still held by the Treuhandanstalt will catch-up with Western Germany only after a lengthy adjustment period and under the condition that sufficient private capital formation allows East German workers to catch up with West German productivity levels. The enormous West German resource transfer of some DM 160 billion to Eastern Germany will not be available in any other ex-CMEA country. However, this favourable element is largely offset by aspiration levels of East Germans which have leapfrogged after economic unification and by the fact that devaluation of the currency was no longer a policy instrument of Eastern Germany once monetary unification had been completed. For this and many other reasons even the East German case of privatization and foreign investment is at best the basis for a small economic miracle.[50]

Structural change in Eastern Germany in the four years 1989-92 is considerable, but the main problem remains that unit labour costs in Eastern Germany were raised to a level twice as high as in Western Germany; (West) German unions pushed for wage parity with the argument that otherwise westward migration from Eastern Germany would continue on a massive scale (as it was in 1990); however, it is often overlooked that for people to stay in their favoured places it suffices that wage disparities - evaluated at local purchasing power parities - are not too big, and indeed even within Western Germany there are divergences of some 20 per cent. Unions have not taken into account that high unemployment rates, partly caused by excessive wage claims, could be equally important as a factor encouraging people to move westwards. The basic pitfall of unification was to allow trade unions and employers' organizations to agree in 1990/91 on pre-determined trajectories for achieving wage parity in Eastern Germany by 1994/95; that is to fix terms for wage parity before industry had been fully privatized. Private investors and private owners would have been much more reluctant to adopt a fast track approach to wage parity than employers' organizations and trade unions were under the protection of the THA (or the non-existence of private business organizations). Employer's organizations in Eastern Germany were often dominated by West German industrialists which, of course, were not eager to allow Eastern Germany to become a springboard for low-wage newcomers in the all-German or the EC market. The West German taxpayer was footing the bill by allocating increasing subsidies to East German firms and by massive tax breaks for mainly West German investors willing to invest in the former GDR. In many oligopolistic markets West German firms acquired East German firms not so much because of expected profits but because of fear of falling market shares in case competitors would acquire the respective firms. Among the few positive developments in Eastern Germany is the fact that the households' savings rate has increased - from 4 per cent in the first half of 1990 to 10.3 per cent in the

---

[50] See on further aspects of German unification Welfens (1992a).

second half of 1991 which is only three percentage points lower than in Western Germany.[51]

3.1.2 Poland

A multi-track approach is typical of the Polish privatization programme in which the Ministry of Ownership Changes is the main authority in the programme. Privatization can take the form of transformation or "liquidation". The latter means that the company is dissolved and the firm's assets are sold or leased to the owners of a new distinct company. Transformation means that the state company remains an entity in the course of the privatization process, where the company initially is transformed into a joint stock company owned by the Polish Treasury (intermediate stage of privatization: "commercialization"). In the intermediate commercialization stage a board of directors is appointed by the owner, the State Treasury, and eventually new private shareholders. In the stage of commercialization the workers' council is dissolved, and instead workers are given 1/3 of the seats at the supervisory council. Commercialised firms are then sold either by (a) public offering, (b) trade sale - a single investor acquires the company through competitive bidding - or (c) mass privatization; the latter means that vouchers are issued so that adult citizens get a stake in the privatization process. Vouchers can be exchanged for shares in the newly created investment groups, so that effective corporate governance can be assured and hence capital gains be realised. In the mass privatization programme some 400 firms will be restructured and certificates of participation in investment funds will be distributed; shares in the funds will be traded after first year results (OECD, 1992, pp. 35-26).

The Law of Privatization was passed in July 1990. Privatization in Poland has focused on big firms across various industries in a first stage,[52] and only after it was recognized that resistance by these big firms was so strong that the programme never developed momentum were sectoral privatization

---

[51] Savings rates had fallen to 0 and 1.2 per cent in the 2nd half of 1990 and the first half of 1991, respectively; see DIW (1992), Wochenberichte, Nov. 26, p.8.

[52] By the end of 1991 transformation privatization had realized only 30 privatization of big and medium sized firms; 16 direct sales, 8 public offerings and two leveraged buy-outs were accomplished. The Warsaw Stock Exchange offered in early 1993 a very limited listing with only 20 stocks, similar to the Budapest Stock Exchange which, however, seems to be more dynamic. Trading in government securities is likely to be the more profitable and expanding business in the medium term.

programmes envisaged. Thirty-four sectoral studies have been prepared with the help of foreign consulting firms.

By mid-1992 90 per cent of Poland's small privatization programme had been completed. Only a dozen former state firms could be transformed into joint stock companies, quoted on the new Warsaw stock exchange. There was some success with the "liquidation privatization" which has created more than 1,000 private enterprises. This form of privatization means that certain plants of a former state firm - or the whole firm - are sold to the private sector, mostly the employees of the former state firms; the employees often benefit from leasing arrangements or arrangements that effectively allow a purchase of assets in several installments. More than a dozen big firms were sold to foreign investors which paid about $ 1 billion However, in general FDI inflows were slow, much concentrated on small- and medium-sized firms and rarely in the form of greenfield investment which would immediately add to the capital stock of the host country. The mass privatization programme finally brought into being in 1993 is intended to privatize some 600 joint stock companies in a two-stop approach via vouchers. Citizens will get vouchers and have to allocate these to several investment funds. This will concern 60 per cent of the capital of these firms; 10 per cent will be offered to employees at preferential prices and 30 per cent will be held by the Treasury.

While one could justify the preference prices for employees with arguments related to the efficiency wage literature it is difficult to find an economic argument for the government to maintain a controlling equity stake. If the government's equity stake would consist of preferred stock without voting rights one could argue that government wanted to make sure that future capital gains at least partly will accrue to the government and the citizens, respectively, but the Polish case is obviously more characterized by the idea that government should keep some direct control over enterprises. This will create additional uncertainty since one cannot predict how governments in the future will make use of their discretionary power and their influence via stock ownership. The Ministry of Ownership Change will become integrated - together with the Ministry for Industry and Trade and the Ministry for Construction - into the Ministry for Planning which thereby effectively will become an Economics Ministry. Output in the Polish private sector is in the range of 30-40 per cent, where some uncertainty is due to the thriving black market activities and the underreporting of income fuelled by the desire to save taxes. To privatize the more than 3,300 firms in state industry and to establish a deeper stock exchange market with several dozens firms will certainly take longer than initially envisaged by post-1989 Polish governments. Sales proceeds from privatization have been disappointing, but it should not be overlooked that hyperinflation reduced both real wages and real wealth of most Polish citizens sharply so that the marginal willingness to pay was reduced. The savings rate of private households is some 7 per cent, but this low value is not really surprising in view of annual dollar incomes close to $ 2,500.

A considerable shortcoming in Poland has been that privatization from above has been strongly favoured over the creation of new business establishments. From a theoretical perspective emphasis should be put on both avenues of privatization (Jasinski, 1990c). The Polish case is also characterized by considerable reluctance to fully entrust the private sector with the task of running firms (Sadowski, 1991). The initial focus of privatization policy on big firms may not have been adequate since targeting the biggest 200 or 300 companies first in the privatization process also means facing the most entrenched and well-organized resistance against privatization programmes.

Privatization plans were delayed several times in Poland and in 1991 hardly more than 1/3 of value-added (outside agriculture) was in private firms. FDI inflows have been very sluggish and reached only some $ 600 million in 1991 and are expected to exceed $ 1 billion in 1992/93. Almost all big investments made between 1986 (Marriott Hotel) and 1991 were of American origin. While big MNCs were reluctant to invest in Poland, joint ventures which typically are small firms mushroomed. Between 1989 and the end of 1991 some 5,000 joint ventures were allowed, of which some 1,700 were firms with German capital totaling about $ 170 million; firms from the US, France and Sweden followed with 80, 70 and 55 million committed. Dutch, US, Norwegian and British investors increased their investments strongly - while German joint venture activities stagnated - in 1991/92, and this may be the result of the liberalized joint venture law of July 1991; the Polish government also authorized some 50 joint ventures with companies from the CIS in 1991/92.[53] This law has removed restrictions on profit repatriation and abolished the minimum investment of $ 50,000 (in 1989-91 the average amount of capital reached $ 140,000); special tax relief is offered if investments are made in high technology fields and in industries with high unemployment, if stocks of more than $ 2 million are acquired and if at least 20 per cent of sales is from exports. However, high technology investment can hardly be expected

---

[53] See IWD-Mitteilungen, August 20, 1992, No. 34, p.6, Cologne. On some problems of Polish privatization see Fallenbuchl (1991).

to be made within a joint venture arrangement. Technology-oriented firms will normally seek 100 per cent ownership.

The Polish State Foreign Investment Agency (SFIA) began its operation in 1991, but has not been very active outside the country in its efforts to attract foreign investors. Interestingly, the SFIA is a joint stock company fully owned by the Treasury which is represented by the Minister of Privatization; this suggests that the implicit link between privatization and FDI is taken into account in the political sphere. Only about 20-30 per cent of all joint ventures - except for Hungary, this holds for most other ex-CMEA countries, too - are operational. Despite small amounts of capital committed and the focus on the service industry and labour-intensive activities the wave of joint ventures could be valuable for achieving economic restructuring and increasing trade intensity.

3.1.3 CSFR

The Ex-CSFR has almost completed the whole small privatization process which started in January 1991. Some big companies were sold to foreign investors, but after the elections of June 1992 foreign investment inflows slowed down as it became clear the country would split. The first "coupon" privatization scheme, which included some 1,500 firms out of more than 4,000 in May 1992, paradoxically could lead to considerable foreign investment, in the sense that Slovakians either directly or through the more than 400 investment funds (2/3 of all investment points were allocated to these fonds each of which may not hold more than 20 per cent of a firm's equity, but must invest in at least ten different firms) could acquire Czech firms, and in turn Czechs may have bought firms in Slovakia; an open question is how ownership of the 60 federal firms will be divided up between the two new states.

A computer system was installed to determine the market-clearing prices of privatized companies. The second wave of voucher privatization which should include another 2,000 state firms in 1993 will be difficult to organize. The first two auction rounds in 1992 were successful since 122 state firms could be fully privatized and several hundred have at least sold considerable amounts of shares. The 8.5 million voucher holders - each endowed with 1,000 investment points obtained for a nominal fee of 1,035 koruna - have bid for the shares of some 1,500 state companies valued at 299 billion korunas ($11.2 billion), where stocks were priced in terms of shares per 100 investment points. One thousand three hundred and sixty-nine firms of the 1,500 former state firms have some shares to sell in the third round. The innovative voucher approach conducted in the CSFR has created, at least in the first two rounds, a broad stratum of stock owners which, however, over time could boil down to the 20 per cent margin of the population which is holding shares in the US and the UK. A major problem occurred with the disintegration of the CSFR. The Czech Republic had attracted more than 80 per cent per cent of all FDI inflows in the ex-CSFR. It remains doubtful whether the Slovak Republic can significantly improve its attractiveness as a host country for FDI after it has introduced its own legislation and currency.

In mid-1992 the percentage shares for various methods in large-scale privatizations were dominated by joint stock company establishments and free transfers in the CSFR (see Table 2). Free transfers accounted for a share of 26.8 per cent, while joint stock companies represented 38 per cent.

Table D2: Transformation Methods in Large-Scale Privatization in the CSFR
(for 1 044 projects approved, mid-June 1992)

	number	percentage
A. Public auction	172	7.8
B. Public tender	103	4.7
C. Direct sale to a designated owner	336	15.2
D. Joint stock company	839	38.0
E. Privatization of state property in the business of other Juristic persons	168	7.6
F. Free transfers	592	26.8
TOTAL	2 210	100.0

Source: Czech Ministry of Privatization as quoted in OECD (1993), Trends and Policies in Privatization, p.43.

Table D3: Structure of Transformation in the CSFR, Methods D and E

	capital stock (in Kcs bill.)	percentage (in per cent)
Vouchers	200.8	62.1
Free transfer	38.1	11.8
Direct sale to a designated owner	9.0	2.8
broker (bank or stock exchange)	4.8	1.5
National proper- ty fund	56.5	17.5
Additional pur- chase of assets by restituents	1.0	0.3
Other	13.0	4.0

Source: OECD (1993), Trends and Policies in Privatization, p. 43

Where supply exceeded demand (1,022 cases) only 33 per cent of the available shares were sold, while in cases where supply roughly equalled demand 100 per cent of available shares were sold (48 firms in the first privatization round); equilibrium was reached - if necessary and feasible - by cutting back investment fund shares by the amount of excess demand, where such demand was less than 25 per cent higher than share supply (OECD, 1993, p. 44). Demand exceeded supply in 421 cases.

In the second half of 1993 trading in about 1,500 companies formerly owned by the CSFR state will be organized. There will be a jump start of stock trading, but it is uncertain that the voucher experiment will be successful. Banks and investment funds which own or administer most of the privatized firms are expected to exert effective corporate governance if incentives are right and market conditions are orderly. Four hundred and thirty-seven investment funds attracted almost 3/4 of the coupons that entitled Slovak and Czech citizens to bid for state companies. The twelve biggest funds snatched up 40 per cent of the vouchers distributed for the first wave of privatization. They did so by promising hefty capital gains, i.e. they would redeem privatization vouchers at 10-50 times their costs; Harvard Capital made the boldest promises and concentrated its holdings on 51 of the former CSFR's best companies. Since funds are restricted to holding no more than 20 per cent of a company's equity, funds cannot easily exercise effective control of firms in a way that would lead to rapid increases in productivity and profitability. Harvard Capital under its founder Viktor Kozeny is reported to have allied with various other groups and sometimes foreign investors to establish effective corporate governance (Economist, 1993a, p.88). The ex-CSFR's voucher privatization scheme certainly is the most innovative procedure developed so far in central and eastern Europe. It could guide and influence privatization procedures in other ex-CMEA countries to a large extent if this holistic approach to systemic change turns out to be successful. Due to the split of the country in 1993 it will not be fully clear to which extent success and failure have been influenced by the political disintegration.

3.1.4 Hungary

Hungary enjoys the advantage of having started the move towards market elements in allocation already in 1968 and of having partially removed the foreign trading monopoly already in the first half of the 1980s. However, the real switch to capitalism occurred only in 1990. The small privatization process started in Hungary with considerable momentum but then slowed down for various reasons. In 1992 only about 50 per cent of all small firms had been privatized, and many firms' premises had only been leased on a long term basis. Leasing privatization lets one expect that investments in these firms will be smaller than in the case of full private ownership. In the field of big privatization Hungary has adopted a gradual privatization process whose slow speed may be in line with the long Hungarian record of piecemeal reforms since 1968, but which actually reflects politico-economic impediments in the privatization process. By end 1991 only a dozen of some 2,000 firms to be privatized had been sold to private investors. The more than 100 firms whose assets had been evaluated by mid-1992 could find private investors more quickly.

The number of approved conversions has increased quickly in Hungary as Table D4 shows. Thirty-four cases of self-privatization - often considered to be not fully controlled and consistent with the law - were recorded before January 1992. Privatizations initiated by the company or by an investor increased from 27 at end-1990 to 190 at the beginning of 1992. The number of state initiated privatizations reached only 18 in early 1992.

Table D4: Approved Conversions of State Companies into Business Partnerships in Hungary

	Dec. 31, 1990	Dec. 31, '91	Jan. 31, '92
Self-privatization			
NUMBER OF FIRMS	0	20	34
Company and/or			
investor-initiated			
NUMBER OF FIRMS	27	180	190
BOOK VALUE (bn HUF)	26	193	198
TRANSACTION VALUE	42	281	288
State-initiated			
NUMBER OF FIRMS	0	18	18
BOOK VALUE (bn HUF)	0	150	150
TRANSACTION VALUE	0	182	182
Total			
NUMBER OF FIRMS	27	218	241
BOOK VALUE (bn HUF)	26	345	351
TRANSACTION VALUE	42	465	473

Source: OECD (1993), p. 49

The fact that transaction values did not systematically fall short of book values testifies to a gradually improving accounting system and relatively realistic perceptions of asset prices. Hungary's new bankruptcy code which makes company managers liable for delaying declaration of illiquidity could bring an additional element of financial truth into Hungary's economic life.

Since projects for privatizing utilities and for setting up private ventures for infrastructure developments were discussed in 1992 a rising number of state initiated privatizations can be expected from 1993 onwards. For the government it seems important to maintain privatization momentum to widening the scope of privatizations in two ways as compared to the initial state of privatization: (a) foreign investment which accounted for 80 per cent of privatization revenues in 1992 will be allowed to focus on a greater range of assets, including some utilities; and (b) Hungarian residents will be encouraged - probably also in the context of some voucher scheme - to participate more actively in the privatization process.

The State Privatization Agency had envisaged several branch privatization schemes (e.g. construction industry), but slow progress encouraged new forms of privatization which has returned to - now modified - forms of spontaneous privatization. Both would-be investors and existing firms can launch an initiative for privatization, and the government expects to privatize more than 1,000 firms within two years. Employee buy-outs, management-buy outs and public auctions were also encouraged. A new bankruptcy law which came into force on 1 January, 1992, is expected to facilitate the liquidation of firms than cannot be restructured successfully.

The Hungarian subsidiaries of 15 multinational firms created the Hungarian Association of International Companies in September 1992 in order to lobby more effectively for foreign investors' interests which will represent by end-1992 some $ 4.5 billion The Hungarian per capita stock of more than $ 400 foreign investment accumulated within 4 years is impressive and might well double within the 1990s. By contrast Poland's per capita FDI stock is less than one-tenth of the Hungarian value and only the Czech republic seems likely to reach per capita figures that could come close to Hungarian figures.

In the Hungarian privatization process small firms have played a considerable role (Szirmai, 1991). Many new firms have targeted both the domestic and foreign markets and have thereby contributed to Hungary's rapid export growth in the early 1990s. Private firms can be expected to be more flexible and responsive to price signals than big state firms and thereby could contribute overproportionately to export growth. Hungary has tried to maintain momentum in the privatization process by offering the telecom industry and some infrastructure projects to private bidders in 1993. However, in Hungary one can also hear increasing criticism that the country is sold out to foreign investors or that foreign investors and banks first acquire assets at discount prices and then sell them to other foreign investors with considerable profits.

3.1.5 Bulgaria

Small privatization slowly progressed in 1991. The whole privatization legislation was complicated by the considerable Turkish minority and fear of high potential Turkish investment inflows. The last communist government had laid down in the constitution that foreigners could not own land. Bulgaria has embarked upon an international privatization approach in the sense that World Bank experts were closely involved in the privatization laws adopted in late April (in his capacity as an academic the present author, P.W., was also involved in providing advice to Bulgarian officials active in the privatization process). A state privatization agency controlled by members of the government and of parliament will organize auctions and sales to private investors.

Employee ownership at preferential prices will be allowed up to a share of 20 per cent of capital. Twenty per cent of firms' capital will be allocated to a special social fund and be used for paying indemnities to former owners. Foreign investors can acquire an equity stake in privatized firms. Since owner-occupied housing plays a considerable role in Bulgaria most families are protected against rapid increases in the market-clearing level of housing prices and rents.

3.1.6 Romania

The small privatization process started at a slow pace in 1991, while big privatization is proceeding within a comprehensive approach. The Romanian way to privatization is straightforward in the sense that in a first stage some 7000 firms (limited liability companies or stock companies) will be created from the 6,200 medium-sized and big state firms. Some 300 firms will be maintained as state firms, namely in a form that is similar to the French régie autonomes - mining, the arms industry and the energy sector are concerned. In the second round of privatization the public receives via vouchers 30 per cent of the book value of the 6200 state-run enterprises; vouchers issued by the National Privatization Agency operating since June 1992 can be traded freely among domestic residents. Some 5,500 small and medium-sized state firms have been allocated to five SOFs (State Ownership Funds) into which private and foreign investors can buy and sell. The other 70 per cent of all commercialized companies will be assigned to a state ownership fund which will sell over time assets to private owners. In the first and second round foreigners are not allowed to acquire privatized firms. Foreign consulting firms and banks will play a limited role in the separately organized privatization of some 25 medium-sized state enterprises.

There are 6,280 firms envisaged for a mass privatization programme (OECD, 1993, p. 53), where 483 are large firms (asset value more than Lei 500 million), while 2568 are small firms (asset value less than Lei 50 million). Since Romania is directly exposed to ethnic unrest in the former USSR and the former Yugoslavia conditions for political stability are unfavourable. Internal stability could be endangered by various problems, where the revival of nationalism and in this context problems in integrating the Hungarian minority are crucial.

3.1.7 Ex-USSR

The Ex-USSR represents an extremely complex case because of the political, economic and monetary disintegration process that is underway in the CIS which is also facing ethnical unrest in many regions. Given the flux of political and economic events it seems reasonable to refrain from an assessment of the privatization process except for a few remarks on crucial problems. Russia and the Ukraine face the most difficult privatization tasks because of the more than 70 years of Communist rule that have to be neutralized in all fields of political and economic life if a market economy is to be achieved. In Russia two privatization waves in 1992/93 are expected to lead to the privatization of about 20 per cent of state firms. Small privatization will make considerable progress in 1992, but often with the shortcoming that government competition policies are absent and that hyperinflation distorts the relative price signals and hence weakens the efficiency of market allocation. Big privatization will start in 1994: firms will be converted into stock companies and 25 per cent of equity capital will be freely transferred to employees and another 5 per cent to management. The remaining 70 per cent is available for outside investors.[54] A major problem in both the Ukraine and Russia is the very important role of former armaments firms which face difficult problems for economic conversion. Know-how of military personnel could indeed become the basis of a number of successful new firms, *e.g.* in the telecom business which could become an expanding industry (Welfens, 1992b, ch. E) important for both a market economy with its decentralized decision-making (and hence the need for widespread communication networks) and at the same time for absorbing part of the unrest that characteristics the former Soviet military.

Foreign investors still face major restrictions, and discretionary power of political authorities plays a considerable role in Russia. The conflict between the Russian President and the Parliament as well as political conflicts between Russia and the Ukraine could severely undermine privatization programmes and even more so foreign direct investment inflows. Russia is the only ex-CMEA country - besides Hungary and Poland - where Japanese firms have launched major foreign investment projects. However, for political reasons (the conflict over the Kurile islands) Japan is not eager to support Russia's transformation programme.

---

[54] This information is based on Deutsche Bank Research (1992).

3.2 Medium Term Prospects for the Privatization Programmes

The general impression from this short survey of privatization programmes is that very different avenues to privatization have been adopted in the ex-CMEA countries. If raising exports were the prime goals of privatization Hungary's performance is favourable if raising the share of output produced in the private sector is the criterion, the former GDR would rank first; one is, of course, hesitant to pretend that the ex-GDR case is comparable to the other transforming economies.

Foreign participation in privatization has been limited in all countries except for Hungary where 80 per cent of privatization proceeds came from foreign sources. For various reasons Hungarians find it easier to accept FDI than other transforming economies. One reason for this could be that many Hungarian firms anticipate that they have options to become foreign investors themselves in the long term. Ethnic Hungarian minorities as well as the early foreign trade reforms - dating back to the 1980s - could stimulate enough Schumpeterian talents in Hungary and allow sufficient development of owner-specific advantages that in the late 1990s Hungarian firms could join the new group of MNCs from the newly industrializing countries.

Small privatization is the least difficult task to achieve although it is not a priori clear that the present use of certain premises would also be the best use under private competition. Therefore one should encourage employees who have bought the so far state-owned shops or small firms to swap assets with other new entrepreneurs and even to sell part of the real assets obtained in the first round. A modest capital gains tax would not discourage such economically beneficial activities, but still allow society to get a share of the positive sum game of privatization. Foreigners could well face higher capital gains tax rates than domestic residents. Since many private production and services activities depend on the provision of local public infrastructure an incentive system that would encourage local government to readily provide land, information, services and specific infrastructure would be most useful. A regional sales tax as well as property taxes that partly accrue to local authorities and partly to regional authorities could be means to support pro-market and pro-business attitudes of local and regional governments.

Big privatization should be embedded in a long term programme of growth policies because removing obstacles to economic growth and actively encouraging economic actors to take a long term view in investment and savings is success-promising. An outward-oriented strategy that helps to properly focus decisions concerning investment and human capital formation would be the natural complementary element in such a strategy. Without rapid economic growth there are neither prospects to attract considerable FDI inflows nor a chance to catch up with Western Europe. Privatization from below, that is the active promotion of new business establishments, is a much neglected element in most privatization programmes in Eastern Europe. The move to a dominantly private business sector will bring greater income inequalities and a greater need for adjustment at the micro level; this characteristic of capitalism will not be easily accepted in the formerly socialist economies where people often associate market economies simply with a higher standard of living. Privatization cannot be organized without regard to the development of unemployment. Transitory unemployment cannot be avoided; however, market-clearing mechanisms can be improved in various ways. To reduce housing shortages and to provide tax incentives for greater mobility are just two possible steps. There are many more aspects of privatization that require a more comprehensive analysis.

The fact that sales proceeds from privatization have been less than initially expected by the Treasury in various transforming countries is a budget problem only in a short-term perspective. If privatization means rising output and rising exports the rise of future wages and profits should be of greater interest than short term impacts. Another disappointment has been - at least in some countries with high expectations - the small and hesitant inflow of foreign investment. Hungary has been a notable exception in the ex-CMEA area. For countries which can be expected to join the EC the anticipation of reduced political risk could quickly increase the inflow of capital; the case of Spain and Portugal in the 1980s is interesting here.[55]

The development of stock exchanges is quite important for eastern and central Europe. Real benefits from this require considerable time and a certain size of the market which in turn requires that at least several dozen firms are quoted at the stock exchange. Trade in stock futures could be particularly interesting because it would indicate the market assessment of the transformation process and thereby generate and dissipate valuable information.

---

[55] Spain recorded FDI inflows of some $ 50 billion in the period 1982-91.

4. Selected Policy Issues

Privatization raises a host of theoretical issues - many of which were addressed in previous chapters and sections. Here selected aspects related to privatization policies will be raised. Privatization requires that well-defined ownership rights are transferred to private owners. Moreover, the question arises whether efficiency gains at the microeconomic level - at the level of the firm - can be gained without considering industry problems and macroeconomic problems at the same time. Subsequently we will briefly focus on the issues of sequencing, uncertainty, the role of capital markets, some welfare effects of privatization and macroeconomic effects of privatization and FDI.

4.1 Sequencing Issues - A New View on External versus Internal Liberalization

To organise the privatization process in a way that economic catching-up is achieved is essential for central and eastern European economies. Privatization itself will solve many problems of allocation inefficiency, but it will also create new problems for societies in transition. Firms can be privatized faster and to a broader extent if some selective (transitory) protection is accorded to privatized industries. Bold foreign liberalization moves are not very useful if they have to be reversed soon and if they sharply reduce the scope of industries that can be privatized under given political constraints. Poland in 1990/91 was a typical case of an overambitious external liberalization: in January 1989 the average import tariff was reduced from 17.2 per cent to 4 per cent, but by the end of 1991 import tariffs had been raised again to 26.2 per cent;[56] the only reasonable change was the change in the tariff structure which became more even across industries and which more closely followed Western patterns of tariff escalation (low tariffs for raw materials and high tariffs for final products).

Internal or External Liberalization First
Liberalization in the context of systemic transformation means first the liberalization of output prices. Output prices will reach market clearing levels, and to the extent that this happens in a monopolistic situation prices and profits

---
[56] Figures are from GATT (1992).

will be higher in the short run than in the medium term. As soon as privatization is unfolding progressively and import competition allowed, prices and profits will reduce, and in many cases this will make privatization almost impossible at positive prices - unless quick reconstruction is feasible. Hence there is a clear link between output prices and asset prices. Moreover, prices of formerly preferred stores of values - say used cars, alcohol and even foreign exchange - could fall to the extent that shortages in goods markets are eliminated via price liberalization, privatization and competition. The price of foreign exchange is, however, likely to increase in real terms because import liberalization is likely to depress output prices of import-competing goods; moreover, in countries with high inflation rates foreign exchange will become an increasingly preferred asset, and a higher real exchange rate would simply reflect the relatively increasing demand for foreign real money balances. Poland embarked upon a Big Bang external liberalization under the Finance Minister Balcerowicz, but this strategy was not sustainable as it quickly turned out. The many benefits hoped to be achieved from rapid external liberalization were not realised in reality, and it seems that economic theory could explain this. Internal liberalization in the sense of privatizing firms was much delayed and in Poland the initial state aim of the first transformation government under Premier Mazowiecki turned out to be absolutely illusory: by the end of 1993 50 per cent of industry was to be privatized. In reality less than 25 per cent of industry will be privatized in Poland and expected privatization proceeds have turned out to be totally unrealistic.

The rapid import liberalization reduced domestic output prices and profits of firms and hence reduced government revenues from dividends and taxes on capital income. The value-added tax - with a standard rate of 20 per cent - was only introduced in 1993, along with a new (first-time) income tax on wage income. Hence after a transitory rise of profits and state receipts in the stage of monopoly prices government revenues reduced sharply and inter-enterprise debts started to increase. These debts reflect to a wide extent a hidden liability of government because privatizing firms will require taking debt out of the companies' books to an extent that leaves firms as viable competitors. Sharp external competition also created the problem that firms to be privatized refused to accept dismemberment which often had been necessary if optimum plant sizes were to be realized and excessive wage pressure to be avoided in the long term. Many firms in Poland became unable and unwilling to meet financial obligations when confronted with excessive import pressure and increasing domestic competition. Of the 1,700 enterprises supervised by the Polish

Ministry of Industry and Trade more than 750 state-owned firms were behind in their payment obligations (tax and social security) in July 1991; this was twice as much as in January 1991; also in July more than 450 firms were not paying the obligatory dividends to the Treasury, compared with 165 in December 1990; according to bank evaluations more than 170 industrial enterprises had lost their creditworthiness as of May 1991 and were behind schedule in paying obligations to other firms, and about 250 industrial enterprises were operating at a loss in April 1991, compared to only 65 at the end of 1990 (OECD, 1992, p. 77). The OECD report notes that as a result of liquidity and profitability problems in Poland the consequent restrictions on working capital have the following effects:

- purchases of inputs are artificially reduced and this will depress industrial output and sometimes reduce product quality;
- routine maintenance will be deferred, thereby raising future production costs and the risk of production interruptions;
- product diversification and sales expansion cannot be financed;
- "capital consumption" is stimulated; equipment is sold for very low prices and even valuable equipment is scrapped.
- One may add: R&D expenditures important for viability in competitive markets are reduced and resistance to competition is raised and the reduction of state subsidies is stifled.

Major problems with liquidity and profitability of firms in transforming economies cannot be avoided in any case. However, it seems clear that an overambitious external liberalization drive reinforced many problems. For theoretical reasons it seems indeed clear that one may well consider proceeding with internal liberalization and privatization first and only later accelerating the external liberalization process. Too rapid an external liberalization will create serious macroeconomic problems and raise strong resistance against effective internal liberalization; if macroeconomic problems exceed a critical threshold level external liberalization could indeed be revoked and the economy would be stuck with incomplete internal and external liberalization at the same time. The order of economic liberalization is not exchangeable here. If internal liberalization has made considerable progress the improved resilience on the supply side of the economy could indeed be conducive to a sustaining external liberalization process.

In a market economy private competitors have to find out in a dynamic discovery process where comparative advantages are and where investment and innovation projects should focus on. If import protection allows quickly proceeding with privatization the dynamics of market forces are much more prevalent than in the case of continued state-ownership in a free trade environment. This is so because free trade (or relatively free trade) in the rest of the world solves the information problem about international relative prices, while the domestic information problem of adjustment costs can only be efficiently solved by private market allocation - under restricted external competition the adjustment trajectories are certainly different than in a free trade regime, but most important is the full transition to a private market economy. The move to free trade can be achieved later in a gradual and pre-announced fashion. Even present investment decisions need not be misguided by only gradual external liberalization as long as a progressive external liberalization scheme is credible and widely known in advance. One should ensure that external liberalization will be implemented in the long run.

4.2 Role of Uncertainty and Risk

Ownership rights typically are not well-defined in former CMEA countries because workers, management, the state and other enterprises - which allocated credits to the respective firm - all have certain rights in the use of the firms' assets and the appropriation of income accruing from the use of these assets.[57] Uncertainty about the amount of future profits and the impediments of appropriability both reduce the value of firms to be privatized. Imitating complex Western legal codes and imposing additional complex rules to cope with the legacy of the command economy create unnecessary uncertainties and risks for entrepreneurship. A simplified legal code and a simple and enforceable tax code could be two important ingredients of successful transformation policies.

Without clear liability rules and without government basically accepting liability for all off-site damages under socialist production private investors will be very reluctant to invest in industrial firms with contaminated sites and heavy-polluting production.

Financial risk is another problem in the privatization process, where we refer to inter-enterprise credits and the type of negative externality that might be

---

[57] A particular problem is that land in many CMEA countries was not the property of firms, but remained property of the socialist state so that as a first step the Treasury must sell or somehow transfer the land on which the factory or firm is operating. For a comparative perspective of privatization problems in socialist industrialized countries and developing countries see UNIDO (1992).

created by a few firms becoming illiquid; other firms which extended credits to these illiquid firms could face illiquidity and bankruptcy even if they were viable firms under normal (post-transformation) market conditions. Inter-enterprise credit relations constitute a very grave problem, especially because inter-enterprise credits reached high values in 1991. Relative to bank credits inter-enterprise credits amounted to 25.2, 27.6 and 166.3 per cent in the CSFR, Hungary and Poland, respectively (UNCE, 1992, p. 100). The Polish case as well as the Russian case of extremely high inter-enterprise debt poses particular obstacles to privatization because failure to remedy the debt problem before privatisation creates the risk that several bankruptcies could trigger a whole chain of illiquid firms which are unable to collect trade credits; banks which gave credit without collateral are also facing grave risks in such circumstances such that the whole banking system faces special illiquidity risks. That many firms will go bankrupt in the first transition stage can hardly be avoided because human capital and real capital are partly and suddenly rendered obsolete by the switch to market-clearing prices and foreign economic liberalization. The debt overhang problem was emphasized by Aliber (1992) who also notices the problem that - similar to problems in the US in the 1980s - many indebted firms face the risk of going bankrupt as soon as cash flows are insufficient to meet interest payments. Internally or internationally caused adverse price shocks or interest rate shocks could lead to such problems in Eastern Europe. This holds most notably for those countries with high external indebtedness and small Western net export potential. If official debt service comes under strain, government will have to raise additional taxes or to reduce expenditures and both moves are a threat to the profitability of a privatized industrial sector where firms already face financial risks from within the private sector.

Hence one should reduce the book value of firms' assets down to the market value and somehow solve the problem of inter-enterprise debt. One solution could be to set up a special government agency which would buy up firms' claims to other firms and issue in turn marketable bonds which could offer both a fixed rate and a variable "hat rate" on top which would depend on the performance of those firms against which the agency holds financial claims. Domestic state debt would not be raised critically by such an operation since state debt relative to GNP reached low values of 19.2, 7.0, 1.1 and 11.7 per cent in Bulgaria, the CSFR, Poland and Romania respectively in late 1991; only in Hungary was the percentage rate with 62.7 per cent almost as high as in many West European countries (UNCE, 1992, p. 100). Privatization of firms will in many cases only be possible if government takes socialist enterprise debt into its books, so that the ratio of public debt to GNP - low in ex-CMEA countries, except for Hungary - will quickly rise. A high debt burden of privatized companies would leave private firms vulnerable to interest rate shocks and certainly would impede prospects for expansion at the microeconomic level, but also at the macroeconomic level.

4.3 Decisive Role of Capital Markets and Banks

To some extent the transforming economies face similar problems to industrial latecomers Germany and Italy in the 19th century, when a strong role of banks and R&D policies as well as import protection contributed to economic catching-up. While firms in the UK and the US built their expansion on anonymous capital markets German firms and Italian firms strongly relied on bank financing and retained earnings. The different role of banks in development was emphasized by many authors (e.g. Gerschenkron, 1962; Tilly, 1989). The economic catching-up of Asian NICs in the 1960s and 1970s also does not reflect a pure strategy of marketization and liberalization; for technologically backwards countries some reliance on import protection and export promotion as well as a strong role of banks might indeed be useful. This holds - as in the historical context of European late-industrializing economies - because firms from latecoming countries would in an environment of free competition and free trade be unable to generate high profits which in turn are required for financing technological catching-up.

Clearly, firms from leading industrializing countries will benefit from Schumpeterian innovation rents that bolster their normal profits. Equally important, established firms (in industrialized economies) with an established technology, marketing and profit record will find it easier to raise equity capital for profitable investment projects even if there is not always a short-term return on investment - but long term profitability could be very high. New firms in industrial latecomer countries have no comparable reputation and would be unable to raise similar amounts of equity capital; with banks stepping in as a major source of capital and enjoying the advantage of directly monitoring the technological and economic performance of companies, the reputation problem of new firms can be overcome. There is, of course, the risk that a tendency to high retentions of profits reduces the efficiency of the capital market and the average marginal product of capital. However, monitoring clearly gives an information advantage that could overcompensate the disadvantage of high retentions (with respect to EC countries: Hellwig, 1991). High rent-seeking activities are another risk associated with a limited use of capital markets. Restructuring existing firms quickly and efficiently is quite important for successful transformation and economic growth. From this perspective it seems obvious that actual privatization policies made a pitfall: the privatization of banks and regulations that would allow an easier monitoring of firms were neglected. One cannot rule out that encouraging cross-ownership - typical in post-1945 Japan - might also have been an interesting strategy to allow firms a better monitoring of other companies' restructuring so that a firm's own restructuring strategy could be adjusted in an adequate manner.

The capital market necessarily plays an important role in achieving economic efficiency in the transforming economies. Investment GNP ratios of socialist economies were much above those of West European economies. The economic stagnation of the 1980s suggests that the marginal product of capital must have been close to zero so that the investment selection process under the (reforming) planned economy was very inefficient. Total inventories also exceeded the inventory turnover ratio of Western market economies.[58] A competitive banking system and a viable stock exchange are needed as an effective means of pricing investment decisions and valuing firms.

Without a functional capital market there is also no market for corporate control which is all the more important in Eastern Europe since family-businesses in industry are relatively unimportant in the transforming economies, so that principal-agent problems need to be checked by competition in goods markets and capital markets.

Certain problems, however, cannot be avoided in any case; for instance stock markets might be subject to volatile speculation waves; and prices in stock markets and foreign exchange markets could exhibit "overshooting effects" (short term price reactions are greater than those warranted by long term equilibrium solutions). Overshooting occurs in Dornbusch-type exchange rate models (Dornbusch, 1976) because prices are not perfectly flexible in the short run so that very strong exchange rate changes and temporary real exchange rate changes absorb e.g. monetary policy impulses. In an inflationary environment

---

[58] Total inventories in months of turnover were 1.81 in Polish manufacturing, compared to 1.48 and 1.52 in the U.S. and Canada, respectively. See Berg and Sachs (1992). In Poland and Russia the effective ratio of inventoring hoarding to sales was, however, indeed higher than indicated by Berg and Sachs because market prices of output under competitive conditions in Poland (Russia, Romania and other socialist economies) could be much lower in the long term than in the command economy - with its lack of import competition.

there could be a second type of overshooting effect which, following Bilson (1979), may be dubbed the magnification effect which occurs even under fully flexible prices in the short term.

As long as most banks are still state-owned and competition is limited in the financial services industry and banking one cannot assume that the pricing of investment projects and investment risks will be optimal. Indeed, it will be distorted in favour of state firms, and many projects by privatized firms as well as by would-be newcomers will be crowded out by investment credits that are biased in favour of state industries. Therefore the privatization of the banking industry under competitive conditions would be quite important. Finally, it is important that macroeconomic policies allow a positive real interest rate to hold (which might not be the case in countries with very high inflation); otherwise firms would be stimulated to realize investments whose marginal product of capital is negative and whose long term economic profitability is quite dubious.

Taking into account the experience of Korea (Collins, 1990) and other NICs growth-oriented investment policies require that real interest rates be positive; the East-Asian experience of positive real interest rates is much in contrast to Latin America's negative real interest rates coupled with slow growth. The yardstick for evaluating competing investment projects in East Asian countries has been positive real interest rates and relative world market prices to which firms were encouraged within an outward-oriented policy to respond quickly. A case study of Korea suggests that promoting exports amounts to a quasi-support of Harrod neutral technological progress (Sengupta, 1992).

Capital markets will be much affected by the degree of convertibility established and the degree of capital account liberalization; the convertibility problem itself is quite complex (e.g. Williamson, 1991, Welfens, 1992b). Restricting capital outflows is a likely policy adopted by governments in the transforming economies. With high public deficits there is a considerable probability that capital outflows will be restricted in order to hold down real interest rates. Capital imports are less likely to be widely restricted, although in most ex-CMEA countries the first transformation period is characterized by some restrictions: foreigners may not acquire certain assets or exceed threshold stakes in investment funds etc. Restrictions on capital flows mostly serve the purpose to keep interest rates down and to avoid adverse exchange rate effects. The latter is often considered important in countries with a high external debt.

4.4 Welfare Effects of Privatization

Applying some general considerations of Tirole (1988, ch. 2) to the case of socialist economies in transition one can provide a strong argument as to why privatization and competition policy should play an important role in an early stage of the reform process. While the long term benefits can primarily be expected in the form of an improved innovativeness, including a higher speed of diffusion, the short term benefits of competition mainly concern the fact that consumer rent will, of course, be higher under competition than in a monopoly. Governments might be interested in maintaining ownership in monopolistic state firms for quite some time in order to reduce the budget deficit via high profit transfers. However, in reality there is a great risk that insufficient monitoring would lead to gradually falling profits as stated in the official accounts of state firms; managers and employees could appropriate most of the windfall profits that might accrue to at least some state monopolies in the new environment with price liberalization.

Our basic argument here is the following. There is a risk that economic distortions increase over time, namely as the elasticity of demand is increasing in many markets; there is also the risk that foreign investors which acquire a monopolistic producer will appropriate a gradually increasing share of the potential consumer rent under competition. The reasoning is straightforward. If we assume (for simplicity) constant marginal costs c and an isoelastic demand function of the type $q = p^{-\epsilon}$ ($\epsilon > 1$), one can show (Tirole, 1988) that the welfare loss from a monopoly is the difference between welfare under competition (W^C) and welfare in the monopoly case (W^m), namely such that the welfare loss L is a positive function of the elasticity ϵ.

$$L = W^C - W^m = [c^{1-\epsilon}/\epsilon - 1] \left[1 - \frac{(2\epsilon-1)}{(\epsilon-1)} \frac{(\epsilon)^{-\epsilon}}{(\epsilon-1)^{-\epsilon}} \right] > 0$$

For our analysis a particularly relevant case is that of a relatively high elasticity of demand. In the transition to a market economy, a more diversified assortment of products will become available so that over time the increasing availability of substitutes will raise the demand elasticity; a more varied supply could ultimately erode monopoly positions unless the original monopoly itself engages in product differentiation. Furthermore, one may assume that - at least in many cases - the elasticity of demand will increase with higher real income so that the switch to a market economy and greater prosperity brings about more elastic demand in markets for standard products. Technically, in the following analysis we will treat demand elasticity as given, but we are interested in the question as to which way consumer surplus or social welfare (as the sum of consumer and producer surplus) behaves as ϵ changes.

In a socialist economy the switch to more producers typically will go along with an increasing product variety and hence a move towards monopolistic competition. In consumer markets one may assume as a long term result an increasing variety such that for each commodity there will be a rising number of close substitutes which makes individual demand curves increasingly elastic.

With a switch from competition to monopoly the relative welfare transfer that occurs between consumers and producers is given by $Z^m/W^c = \epsilon^{-\epsilon}/(\epsilon-1)^{-\epsilon}$ so that the right-hand side is an increasing function of ϵ. The share of the potential consumer rent that is appropriated by a domestic monopoly - possibly acquired by a foreign investor - is an increasing function of the elasticity of demand.[59] It is clear that with heavy FDI in monopolistic industries there could be an international welfare transfer to the disadvantage of the host country. This negative wealth effect could be compensated by the positive welfare effect that is expected from trade liberalization (unless there is a case of immiserizing growth).

If privatization is not feasible in the medium term for political reasons one could strictly expose the respective firms to import competition or even expose them strongly to world market competition by a policy of active export promotion. It should be clear that certain barriers to imports - e.g. concerning inputs - will be an effective barrier to export. In the nontradables sector one could actively nurture the establishment of new firms.

4.5 Allocative Efficiency and Distributive Disequilibria

Allocative Efficiency
From a pure economic perspective almost all firms and industries can be privatized. Fershtman (1990) argued that even in the case of natural monopolies

---

[59] With $\epsilon=2$ the monopoly gain in the sense of increased profits from switching from competition to monopoly is about 2/3 of consumer welfare W^c. This is particularly important for savings and investment.

private ownership could indeed be a preferable option with respect to allocation aspects, mainly because private owners will adopt a different maximization strategy than managers in a state monopoly.

There are many theoretical arguments that let one assume that private firms' performance is superior to that of state-owned firms, so that privatizing some state-owned firms can often be expected to generate economy-wide benefits. In contrast to the case of privatizing individual firms the case of privatizing a whole economy may yield ambiguous results for the economy at large because macroeconomic effects cannot be overlooked. While the privatization of some individual firms will not strongly affect the exchange rate or the interest rate, massive privatizations will have an impact on these variables; the fiscal deficit, the unemployment rate as well as other macroeconomic variables could be affected as well, and the microeconomic repercussions from such macroeconomic changes should not be overlooked for the issue of privatization.

In transforming socialist economies privatization will entail a considerable rise of the unemployment rate since socialist firms used to hoard labour and were reluctant to introduce advanced (labour-saving) technologies. Moreover, the economic opening up of the economy and the sharp change in relative prices (e.g. energy prices) renders part of the capital stock obsolete so that profit-maximizing firms will have to reduce employment. However, hyperinflation which was characteristic for Poland and Yugoslavia in the late 1980s considerably reduced real wages such that the pressure for redundancies was not as high as it otherwise might have been. Real money balances and hence households' wealth fell sharply in the process of high inflation and this could encourage a rising savings rate necessary to restore the initial wealth position over time. Higher savings imply a reduced domestic demand which should also fall as formerly high socialist investment outlays reduce until firms can recognize new profitable investment opportunities. Falling domestic absorption implies an improving current account position which is exactly what was observed in Poland, the CSFR and Hungary in the period 1989-92. The current account surplus is transitorily reinforced by a transitory "monopolistic export boom" (Welfens, 1992b) which will occur as a result of removing export quotas and introducing profit maximization incentives in the whole economy.

Distributive Disequilibria

A major effect of privatization will be an explicit redistribution of wealth. Ownership of real capital, real estate, domestic bonds, foreign exchange and domestic money will bring about asset-specific risks and - with functional capital markets - positively correlated rates of return for each type of assets. If privatization is organized in a way that only a small minority of the population will enjoy wealth while the majority of the population is paying taxes for the state supplying infrastructure and for the state paying interest on debts that emerged from the former financial restructuring of state-owned and later privatized companies, the result will be strong inequalities in wealth and income. In open capitalist societies these inequalities will become much more visible than the socialist system's silent and probably less extreme inequalities in income, wealth and access to imported goods and foreign exchange. Conflicts over the distribution of income and wealth could indeed destabilize the emerging market economies of Eastern Europe and thereby prevent productivity increases related to improved static and dynamic efficiency from being fully mobilized. Slow economic growth, however, will prevent the East-West income gap in Europe from narrowing so that Western Europe will face sustaining immigration pressure which in turn could destabilize societies and reduce growth prospects in the whole of Europe. A special problem could result if privatization is organised in a way which would cause a substantial currency depreciation so that the burden of the foreign debt would increase.

4.6 Privatization Cycles?

An open question in Eastern Europe is whether privatization programmes will yield stable demarcation lines between the private sector and the public sector. From a theoretical point of view the few arguments which could justify state-run firms are such that no major swings between privatization and nationalization can be justified. If such swings would occur - and they have occurred in EC countries in the past - one will look for ideological reasons and politico-economic impulses (state bureaucracy/election cycles).

Western Experiences: The UK and France

British privatization experience under the Thatcher government can be considered valuable in many respects. Not more than a few dozen companies were privatized over a decade and despite all the expertise available in the city of London the programme was not an easy success story. However, British Steel and British Airways are certainly two impressive examples of how an industry can be turned around; the transformation of a state monopoly, British

Telecom, into an almost full-fledged private monopoly (facing the challenge of its small competitor Mercury) was not very impressive, but it is nevertheless interesting because it points to the importance of embedding privatization in a pro-competitive strategy if static and dynamic efficiency gains are to be fully mobilized. Not surprisingly, privatization meant rising unemployment rates (this held even in Japan's privatization of the national railway system in the 1980s). However, the conclusion to be drawn from this is unclear. In a Schumpeterian-neoclassical synthesis one could argue that improving market-clearing mechanisms in the labour market is important to help privatization from translating into rapidly rising unemployment.

To this neoclassical ingredient one could add the Schumpeterian proposal that the creation of new firms has to be much encouraged by government, so that privatization from below should be joined with privatization from above. Finally, one could try to organize privatization in a way that labour supply declines endogenously, namely via increasing per capita wealth of workers which is assumed to reduce labour supply. The latter, however, will be difficult to achieve since it would require organizing privatization in a way that (i) the majority of the population obtains a free share in the ownership of real capital and (ii) that privatization and other policy strategies are organized in way which leads to considerable and sustaining capital gains. Whether these possible elements of an anti-unemployment policy are politically feasible is an open question.

The British privatization showed that many new share-owners decided to sell their shares within the first year; only 57 per cent of those who bought shares within the privatization programme had not sold their shares after one year (Schnabel, 1990). Whatever privatization avenue is chosen, it will be difficult to avoid a strong concentration of industrial property rights over time. At least tax policies could systematically encourage people to buy shares.

The share of output generated in nationalized or state-dominated firms has been unstable in some West European countries, most notably in the UK and France (Guski, 1988). In 1936 government nationalized the arms industry in France and created from several private railway companies the state-owned SNCF. After World War II Air France, Renault, mining, several banks, public utilities and most insurance firms were nationalized. In 1982 five industrial firms and 39 banks were among the companies nationalized, and in the case of the high tech firms MATRA and DASSAULT government acquired a minority equity position. The level of government control had thereby reached 3500 firms. In manufacturing industry 16 per cent of employment, 28 per cent of value-added and 36 per cent of investment were controlled by government whose influence was reinforced by the dominance of state banks in the allocation of credits. In the mid-1980s a major privatization programme was launched. Forty per cent of state firms were reprivatized and the considerable surplus between indemnifications awarded in earlier nationalizations and the proceeds from placements at the stock exchange was used both to reduce government debt and to infuse additional capital into remaining state enterprises. The successful French privatization in the 1980s was built upon three principles: (i) The French government chose favourable emission prices and thus rewarded investors with capital gains; (ii) 10 per cent of equity capital of privatized firms was offered at a 50 per cent discount to employees; (iii) controlling groups of investors were actively sought, mainly by offering 25 to 30 per cent of equity capital to banks, holding companies, and insurance companies.

The French privatization experience is no less valuable for drawing some conclusions with respect to Eastern Europe than the widely discussed experiences in the UK. British nationalization and privatization experiences also point to an unstable demarcation between private industry and state-owned firms. In the Eastern European case there is a similar potential problem, namely that privatization might proceed over many years, but later government might roll back part of the privatization progress; this might occur, for instance, for outright ideological reasons or as a result of arguments in favour of reducing unemployment by a greater role of state firms or arguments derived from the theory of strategic trade policy. The basic phenomenon of such long term ambiguities in privatization can be captured in a LOTKA-VOLTERRA model.[60] Developing a very simple approach, we will denote the number of private firms as X and that of state firms as Z, while Y is real gross national product and J is the level of technological know-how; alternatively X and Z could denote the share of value-added in the private sector and the state industry sector, respectively. Small x, y, z and j denote the logarithms of X, Y, Z and J, respectively.

Equation (A1') suggests that there will be real output cycles in such a mixed economy with politico-economic determined expansions and contractions of the private and the public sector in certain time intervals.

(A1) $y = f(x,z,j)$ and

---

[60] An introduction into LOTKA-VOLTERA type cycles is provided by Gandolfo (1980) and Berck and Sydsaeter (1992).

(A1') $dy/dt = f_x \, dx/dt + f_z \, dz/dt + f_j dj/dt$

Economic theory suggests that the output elasticity of private firms is greater than in the case of state firms or, alternatively, the marginal product of factors in the state industry is lower than in the private sector where firms will realize the marginal product rule and hence have to strive for a competitive return on investment in real capital and human capital formation.

The change in the number of private firms which consists of privatized firms and newly created firms is assumed to be given by equation (A2); the change in the number of private firms is given by (A3):[61]

(A2) $dX/dt = kX - aXZ$

(A3) $dZ/dt = -hZ + bXZ$

The parameters a,b,h and k are positive and may be assumed to represent politico-economic influences. Equation (A2) states that the number of private firms increases with the number of existing private firms (this is the anti-thesis to MARX's concentration prophecy and implicitly assumes that many new firms can be created in an open economic system), but the expansion created by the existing private sector is counterbalanced by the size of the state sector as represented by the number of state firms; the latter could be explained by the fact that state-owned firms are often not profitable and since the tax burden for the private sector is rising with the number of state-owned firms a growing public sector reduces prospects for the further growth of private firms.

According to equation (A3) the number of state firms is a negative function of the already existing number of state firms Z, but the size of the private sector positively affects the growth of the number of state firms. The latter could reflect the empirical observation that a greater number of profitable private firms generates rising tax revenues which in turn allows the state bureaucracy to allocate capital and subsidies to a greater number of firms than otherwise.

This model has a quasi-equilibrium $X^* = h/b$, $Z^* = k/a$ which can be interpreted as the average values of the number of private firms and state firms over time; there will be cycles characterized by periods in which both the number of private firms and of state firms increase and periods (recessions) in which both will decrease; there will also be periods in which the number of

---

[61] We disregard the size of firms here which in reality reflects a version of GIBRAT's law in the private sector.

private (state) firms is rising, while that of state (private) firms is falling. Such an approach could explain cycles of privatization and nationalization.

A slightly modified LOTKA-VOLTERRA-type model in which the number of private firms grows logistically - hence is closer to reality - if there are no state firms is the following (state firms would vanish according to (A3') if there were no private firms which indirectly fund/justify them):

(A2') $dX/dt = kX - aXZ - eX^2$

(A3') $dZ/dt = - hZ + bXZ - cZ^2$

This model has an asymptotically stable equilibrium

(A4a) $X^* = (ah + kc)/(ab + ec)$;

(A4b) $Z^* = (bk-he)/(ab + ec)$; assumption $bk > he$

The ratio of private firms to state firms is given by

(A5) $X^*/Z^* = (ah + kc)/(bk-he)$.

As regards the parameters it is obvious that the private sector will become the larger the greater a,h, c and e, and the smaller b. Since X^*/Z^* is asymptotically stable the output of the economy would be stagnant without exogenous technological progress. An interesting question which has been often raised in the literature concerns, of course, the question whether in a setting with endogenous technological progress the innovation rate is higher in the case of a greater share of private firms in overall output than in the case of dominating state firms.

4.7 Macroeconomic Effects of Privatization and FDI

Privatization will have significant effects not only in the microeconomic sphere, in the sense that firms will be pushed towards producing at minimal costs, but there will also be considerable macroeconomic effects. These effects concern the increase of supply elasticities, labour market effects and the adjustment speed in markets which can be assumed to clear faster in an environment of private business and competition than in a regime with state-run firms.

Labour Supply-Effects
If hyperinflation and the effective distributive effects of privatization bring about for the majority of the population a fall in real wealth, economic theory suggests two important macroeconomic effects. The savings rate of employed

persons will increase because the gap between the actual wealth position and the long term wealth target has widened; note, however, that at the aggregate level the average savings rate could fall if the unemployment rate rises strongly: unemployed persons typically are dissaving rather than saving. Second, labour supply will be affected (Welfens, 1993e), at least if - as assumed here - per capita wealth is an argument in the labour supply function. Labour supply of most individuals will increase and with a capital shortage being sustained at least in the medium term one would consequently expect rising unemployment rates. A voucher privatization scheme that spreads wealth in a more even way than other privatization schemes in which only those are favoured who already own financial wealth or real assets could create some upward wage pressure; this holds to the extent that per capita wealth enters the labour supply function (certainly with a negative sign). One may not necessarily conclude that international competitiveness will be reduced thereby because wealth ownership is in market economies, often the basis to obtain bank credits at favourable rates so that the formation of human capital and of housing capital might be accelerated, and this should stimulate economic growth. Economic growth in turn is the basis for exploiting dynamic economies of scale - much emphasized in the new growth theory (Romer, 1990) - and thereby could contribute to improve the competitive position in international markets.

Privatization could create a strong counterbalance against unions so that wage negotiations will be strongly influenced by the speed and scope of the privatization process. It might be that in countries with widespread ESOP arrangements one might observe increased wage flexibility over time. To some extent workers could be more interested in long term capital gains and could therefore consider allowing temporary wage concessions to be made in times of economic recession. This could be an important ingredient for ensuring labour market-clearing. Such arrangements could also be part of built-in stabilizers in the new capitalist systems of central and eastern Europe. However, more important probably is the introduction of true insurance principles in unemployment insurance schemes. For regions with high (low) unemployment rates the contribution rates should be higher (lower) than average so that there is an incentive to avoid unemployment - a suggestion that could also be applied in OECD countries (Welfens, 1985; 1992b); workers and firms in regions with a consistent full-employment record could receive reimbursements of contribution payments (similar to the principles governing liability insurance for car drivers in some West European countries).

Current Account Effects

Most economists will share the assumption that private firms will be more responsive to real exchange rate changes than state firms. To the extent that this is true exchange rate policies could become a preferred instrument in the adjustment process of transforming economies. Privatization can contribute to balance of payments problems because the state can no longer directly control imports. An important policy question is which exchange rate regime is to be chosen. By all standard criteria discussed in the optimum currency area literature there is no reason to support fixed exchange rates. However, the policy credibility problem common to the new central banks in the ex-CMEA area might suggest fixed exchange rate regimes after hyperinflation has been erased, namely in order to borrow policy credibility from abroad. However, this would mean that market forces would not be allowed to determine the equilibrium exchange rate in a period of sustaining and thorough real and monetary adjustments. This does not seem to be a prudent policy strategy. With a flexible exchange rate regime establishing current account convertibility and internal convertibility (necessary in countries with currency substitution, but not otherwise as West European convertibility policies in the 1950s showed) is probably easier to achieve and to maintain than with a fixed exchange rate approach; a crawling peg might be an alternative. Import demand in a privatized economy will be quite elastic so that the Marshall-Lerner condition is more likely to be expected than in the case of state-run firms. Of special interest here is the Robinson condition because it contains the supply elasticities and the demand elasticities.

5. Interdependencies Between Privatization and FDI

Privatization is expected to ensure the best use of real assets and to stimulate innovation and diffusion processes under the pressure of profit-maximizing firms. Whether firms will act as profit-maximizers as long as they are still state-dominated or dependent on the Treasury is an open question. In the presence of foreign investors, however, there will be increased pressure on all firms in industry to minimize costs and act as profit maximizers provided that import competition is not restricted; otherwise foreign firms might follow monopolistic pricing of domestic firms. Thus FDI in the nontradables sector is likely to be positively influenced by lack of competition and a sustained role of state firms. Indeed, in the very first stage of price liberalization it is unclear how the commercialized firms will react (Dinopoulos and Lane, 1991), and some could try to adopt both employment and market share goals. But as soon as a critical mass of firms has been privatized and if a sufficient degree of foreign investors is present one may expect that there will be very strong pressure on domestic firms to behave in a way that output and prices in industries will be consistent with profit maximization. In oligopolistic markets there might be deviations from standard results only if price leadership is exerted by state-run firms or if domestic banks or political regulations lead to distortions.

Both privatization and FDI could create some common problems. Clearly, one has to expect a short term increase in unemployment; only with new business establishments by domestic or foreign investors will new jobs be created. In oligopolistic industries FDI flows should normally rapidly contribute to creating new employment because rivalistic firms will stimulate each other not only to serve the host country market - growing slowly at best as long as economic growth is not taking off - but also the world market. Privatization could reduce tax revenues because of shadow economic activities of private entrepreneurs and underreporting of income, while foreign investors typically use transfer pricing to reduce tax payments in host countries. Moreover, privatization and FDI typically mean that government has to cover rising expenses for social security needs, social services (many of which were supplied in socialist economies at the factory level) and unemployment benefits. While both privatization and FDI tend to weaken labour unions which then no longer face politicians but entrepreneurs in wage bargaining, one may anticipate that foreign investors will contribute to upward wage pressure (as a result of high productivity growth and technology transfer, respectively), while privatization will reduce wage pressure. With a uniform labour market and full labour mobility, the nontradables or the tradables sector could determine the pace of wage increases. FDI inflows will certainly stimulate structural change in the tradables sector. There could be positive spill-over effects into the nontradables sector. This holds also with respect to productivity improvements. A privatized firm is likely more quickly to imitate innovative modes of production and organization than state firms.

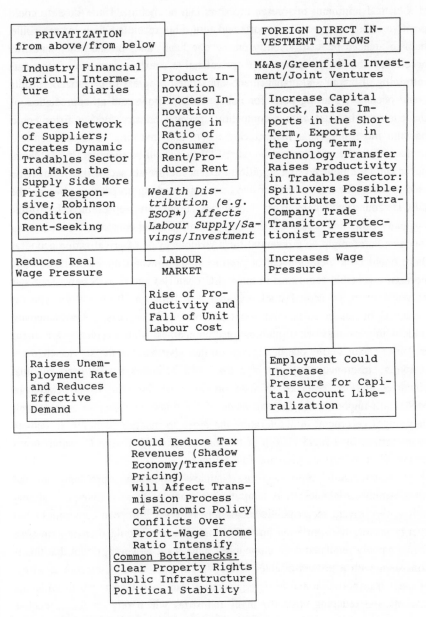

*ESOP=Employee Share Ownership Programme

Figure D1: Effects of Privatization and FDI in Systemic Transformation

If a critical minimum of foreign investors can be mobilized one should expect positive effects for growth, exports and future tax receipts which in turn could help to achieve political stability on the one hand, and, on the other hand, to accelerate the costly process of privatization, restructuring of firms and retraining of labour and management. Substantial progress in privatization itself could become a starting point for rising capital inflows and an appreciation of the currency because with a competitive private industry foreign firms could become more interested in acquiring assets and investing in new greenfield projects. Equally, if privatization fails, FDI flows will be sluggish. If FDI flows never can be mobilized to a significant extent the private sector might never be able to bring about a comprehensive economic catching up process *vis-à-vis* the OECD countries where most technology flows are represented by intra-company flows and cross-licensing among multinational companies (MNCs). As much as there might be a potential for a virtuous cycle of privatization and FDI there could be a vicious cycle of protracted state ownership and lack of FDI. Foreign ownership represents in major EC countries and the US between 2 and 10 per cent of the capital stock and shares of between 10 and 50 per cent in industrial output or sales, and about 1/3 of OECD exports is intra-company trade within the network of multinational companies. MNCs typically are in the tradables sector on the one hand, and, on the other hand in the service industry (banking, insurance etc.) provided that such activities are allowed by host countries and not reserved to state providers or domestic firms. Therefore MNCs are important for the expansion of the tradables sector in general, and they might be crucial in accelerating the move to modern economic structures characterized by a rapid growth of the service industry. Figure D1 summarizes major effects of privatization and FDI inflows.

Privatization represents a complex adjustment problem in the transforming economies. It is tempting for many of these countries to simply imitate the private sector-public sector mix of West European economies. The energy sector, transportation and telecommunications would then remain state firms, namely regulated state monopolies. One may, however, doubt that this is consistent with a growth-oriented strategy. The provision of telecom services, of mass transportation and energy generation can contribute much to widening markets and reducing costs for many industries which rely on the respective inputs, and, of course there could be direct benefits under private competitive provisions. Hungary, Poland and Bulgaria are countries in the ex-CMEA area which want to privatize at least part of the telecom industry and are also considering major private infrastructure projects.

It might be that an optimal privatization strategy would actually start with privatizing telecom and public utilities on a competitive basis; small countries might consider joining neighbouring countries so that market sizes sufficient for competing providers can be created. Even major infrastructure projects - such as building new highways - could be organized within the private sector. If new highways are administered by government one might at least consider a toll system which allows the introduction of a pay-as-you-use financing scheme; France for instance had no widespread highway network in the 1960s, but 30 years later its toll-based highway system is as widespread as the West German system. Toll-based networks also allow differentiation of user costs during rush hours and non-rush hours. Public utilities, railways and airlines as well as telecom services have been set up as state run services in Western Europe only in the last quarter of the 19th century and after the second World War, and in Western Europe entrenched resistances on the side of employees and the state bureaucracy prevent gains from privatization in these fields. In central and eastern Europe, there is a unique opportunity to exploit economic backwardness in these sectors and move ahead of even vague privatization schemes that some liberal minded politicians in Brussels or elsewhere in Europe have envisaged. The demise of the state as an entrepreneur has begun in Western Europe where institutional and economic integration encourage a new kind of handshake between the visible hand of the national or multinational firm and the invisible hand of market forces (Welfens, 1992d).

The diversity of privatization objectives and the difficult initial economic situation make privatization a very difficult process which above all needs momentum to be fully carried out. As soon as private business activities are growing fast - even with double digit rates - the GNP share of the state enterprise sector will decline. In 1992 industrial output increased for the first time in the Polish transformation and other ex-CMEA countries are expected to follow in the mid-1990s. However, high economic growth rates are required for economic catching-up (and some minimum political stability in the CIS is also needed). Without high inflows of FDI high economic growth can hardly be reached.

Chapter E

Foreign Direct Investment: Issues and Policy Approaches

1. International Direct Investment - A Challenge for Central and Eastern Europe

International direct investment is a normal ingredient of capitalism in OECD countries, where investment of multinationals is a two-way phenomenon and often occurs even in the same industry as international cross investment. FDI flows have increased particularly in the 1980s when FDI flows were reoriented towards intra-OECD flows rather than North-South flows. The debt crisis of the 1980s might partly explain unfavourable developments for developing countries, but supply-side policies in the US (Reaganomics), the UK and Germany as well as the EC single market programme certainly also explain the renewed interest in intra-OECD investment opportunities. In the 1980s reduced capital controls, privatization and deregulation contributed to widening the M&A menu for international investors. Since political risk plays no major role in OECD countries one may expect that multinational companies' investment decisions will lead to an equalization of the marginal product of capital (MPC) and real interest rates, respectively, across countries. The economic opening up of central and eastern European countries with their relatively low real wage rates and considerable human capital should hence be conducive to persistent FDI flows in the long term.

Two-way foreign investment has increasingly characterized transatlantic economic relations in the 1980s, while the FDI flows across the Pacific - both from a US and an EC perspective - remained very uneven. Japan became a major and even a leading source country of FDI outflows, but so far plays a minor role as an FDI host country.[1] Eastern European economies are new actors in the global quest for foreign direct investment.

FDI has firm-specific aspects which are related to the fact that ownership-specific advantages are important in overcoming investment barriers in host countries where domestic incumbents enjoy the natural advantage of knowing legal regulations, local preferences and other regional specifics. Industry-specific characteristics are also important; some industries - especially those which have a high R&D intensity and are characterized by high advertising expenditure/sales ratios - are characterized by foreign direct investment activities and multinational firms, respectively. For most firms with products of considerable technology content licensing is a very poor alternative to foreign direct investment because licensing implies appropriability risks and indeed could nurture future rivals not only in export markets but in the home country of the parent company, too. Inward American FDI is related to management intensity, a capital requirement variable and an inverse proxy for product tradability; and similar results hold in empirical studies for other countries (survey: Clegg, 1992). The more sophisticated products are and the more important after-sales services and hence the opportunity for product and price differentiation, the more likely FDI is to be superior to serving foreign markets purely via exports. Finally, locational aspects and hence the locational qualities in potential host countries play a role, where empirical analyses show that political risk and instability play negative roles for foreign investment inflows (e.g. Schneider and Frey, 1985).

The economic opening-up of central and eastern Europe is especially changing the European landscape and European patterns of FDI flows. While Spain and Portugal - attracting more than ECU 70 billion in FDI inflows and portfolio capital inflows in the period 1981-1993 - were the big winners in FDI inflows in Europe (together with the U.K. under the Thatcher government) - the new winners of the 1990s might be in the ex-CMEA area. There are, however,

---

[1] In 1985-87 the US accounted for 35.8 per cent of all FDI outflows in industrialized market economies, followed by Japan with a share of 22.6 per cent and the UK with 18.6, France with 6.3 and the Netherlands and Germany with 4.5 per cent and 3.1 per cent, respectively. See Stehn (1992), p.7.

serious impediments for countries in central and eastern Europe to become major hosts of FDI, except for Hungary which represented about 50 per cent of the region's $ 8 bill. stock of inward FDI (accumulated 1989-92) at the end of 1992. Clearly, political instabilities in the region and the fragile state of the new democracies are not very conducive to stimulating foreign investment inflows. While one prerequisite, namely convertibility is likely to be achieved in all smaller ex-CEMA countries by the mid-1990s, political stability and expanding host country markets will be achieved only under favourable circumstances.

Attracting high FDI inflows could be a crucial accelerating impulse for systemic transformation, trade and economic growth in central and eastern Europe. However, as the experience of developing countries shows (where FDI inflows are heavily concentrated on a few countries) FDI inflows may show a very uneven regional distribution and it will be difficult for the ex-CMEA areas to really mobilize considerable investment inflows. Economic problems and political uncertainties could be major impediments, and other problems could stem from the intensified global quest for mobile investment funds; the ASEAN countries decided in 1992 to set up a free trade area in part because they want to bolster their position in the global quest for foreign investment inflows. At the same time high FDI inflows could be a prerequisite to achieve economic prosperity and political stability. There might indeed be a vicious circle: insufficient FDI inflows - political instability - insufficient FDI inflows. We will analyze the question of what impact FDI could make upon Central and Eastern Europe and which policy options are reasonable to realize in the context of the general task of transformation policies. In reality there will, of course, be country-specific divergences with respect to (normalized) FDI inflows, but we will deal only with two groups of countries: prospective winners and prospective losers.

2. Role of International Direct Investment in Central and Eastern Europe

FDI inflows have been very uneven in the ex-CMEA area as is shown in Table E1. The number of foreign investments registered was highest in Hungary in early 1992 and reached more than 11,000 which is 1/3 of all registered investments in the area. Foreign equity capital in the smaller ex-CMEA countries also concentrated on Hungary. The Commonwealth of Independent States recorded some 6,000 joint ventures, many of which are not operational; the stock of inward FDI reached some $ 6 billion. As is well known, in the

Czarist industrialization attempts 100 years ago foreign investment played an important role, and it might be that FDI could again play a major role in the modernization of Russia and the Ukraine (this time excessive import tariffs should be avoided). Moreover, one could expect that Russia would become a source of outward FDI flows in the long run, in part because at least some Russian firms have an active interest in securing continuous supply of spare parts and intermediate products from firms in the smaller ex-CMEA countries, and an equity stake could be the best way to ensure survival of suppliers and continuous two-way economic ties.

Table E1: FDI Registrations in Central and Eastern Europe, Beginning of 1992

	number	foreign equity (mill. US $)
CSFR	4 000	480
Hungary	11 000	2 089
Poland	5 100	670
Bulgaria	900	300
Romania	8 022	231
CIS	5 400	5 650
TOTAL	34 422	9 420

Source: UN (1992), World Investment Report, Geneva

Since socialist systems considered FDI as exploitation by foreigners and shunned FDI inflows because political control over the economy would partly be weakened by the presence of foreign investors it is not surprising that FDI is not popular in central and eastern Europe. Even in Hungary, which traditionally has been relatively outward oriented, economic nationalism makes FDI an issue of the political debate. In all smaller countries of central and eastern Europe there is fear of German dominance via a dominant share of investment from Germany which already is the most important export country for most transforming economies. In some countries problems with ethnic minorities are juxtaposed with fear of foreign investment influences; in Bulgaria there is fear of strong Turkish foreign investment inflows, while Romania is likely to watch with distrust inflows of Hungarian capital. Clearly, high and regionally diversified investment flows that directly promote the modernization of manufacturing industry would be important for all transforming economies.

A first assessment of international direct investment in central and eastern Europe points to the motive of capturing markets as being dominant in the first stage of transformation (Hunya, 1992, p. 509). In Hungary and the Czech Republic cost advantages of firms from neighbouring Austria and Germany, respectively, certainly also play an important role for foreign investment in projects whose output will go both into domestic markets and export markets. Exporting from one ex-CMEA country to one of the other countries in the region will rarely be an important motive as long as trade relations between the ex-CMEA countries reduce or stagnate and as long as non-tariff barriers as well as tariff barriers play a role in central and eastern Europe. The Visegrad group - which is composed of Hungary, the ex-CSFR and Poland - is the only example of relatively liberal regional trade, although one cannot overlook that the countries involved were unable to agree upon a free trade zone. The association treaties of the EC which were concluded with the three countries mentioned contain local content rules for each country such that there is no incentive for intraregional specialization in the production of export products for EC markets. This also means that foreign investors have no incentive to establish a wider network of subsidiaries, where the network would use locational advantages of all Visegrad countries in an integrated and consistent manner. As regards the size of the host country market in terms of the population of the country only Poland, the Ukraine and Russia are really interesting. Romania with 23 million inhabitants might be included, too. However, in all countries mentioned per capita incomes are below $ 3000 and hence lower than in Greece or Portugal. In contrast to these two countries foreign investors do not gain access to the huge EC market - except for the case of Poland, Hungary and the Ex-CSFR (maybe) in the distant future.

Foreign direct investment can naturally play only a limited role in the restructuring and modernization of East European economies; even very attractive host countries in Western Europe or East Asia had only 10-15 per cent of capital formation undertaken by foreign investors; in Austria the share of industrial assets owned by foreign investors is about 25 per cent and this is a ratio which could be attained by Hungary in the 1990s, too (Hunya, 1992). While it is clear that FDI inflows cannot replace efficient and dynamic domestic capital formation, it seems equally obvious that FDI can make a valuable contribution to modernizing the economy, to linking the host country's industry to world markets - via trade and technology transfer of the MNCs - and to influencing attitudes in ways that increase productivity and economic growth; e.g. Japanese subsidiaries in the US and the UK are certainly not only important in terms of capital formation and trade, but also in changing labour-management relations in industries strongly influenced by Japanese transplants.

The typical focus of MNCs on the tradables industry and sometimes on technology-intensive industries suggests that areas that are most important for economic growth could be particularly promoted by FDI. To the extent that upgrading of export product assortments is promoted by the presence of multinational's subsidiaries one may expect that the terms of trade improve via FDI. Moreover, the terms of trade will effectively improve if the range of exported products is widened to include products of higher technology contents (e.g. most SITC 7 products). By shaping the export sector on the one hand, and, on the other hand by influencing the import sector FDI can decisively influence the structure and size of the tradables sector.

The new growth theory (e.g. Romer, 1990; Grossman and Helpman, 1991) emphasizes positive technology spill-overs from the tradables sector as well as dynamic economies of scale which often can only be realized if firms export to the world market (firms in Russia might be an exception since in some fields firms could rely on a huge domestic market, similar to the case of the US).

FDI inflows will increase the production potential and thereby have effects on the supply side and since with a rising presence of foreign investors the propensity to import or export could change there will be supply-side and demand-side effects on the goods market equilibrium. Privatization will also have macroeconomic effects, where increasing supply elasticities as well as demonopolization effects - influencing the price level - could be important. Privatization and FDI will affect all macro markets of the economy, especially the labour market and the foreign exchange market. Exchange rate movements will influence the net wealth position of countries with high foreign debt, the development of the trade balance, the sectoral mix tradables sector/nontradables sector and foreigners' propensity to invest; if some groups of domestic residents hold foreign exchange there will also be changes in the distribution of wealth within the country. There could indeed be considerable distribution effects that should not be overlooked in a debate which typically is centered on allocation aspects. Besides a look at some basic developments in privatization and FDI we want to take a look at some of these issues in this chapter. We will also raise the question to what extent economic catching-up opportunities in Europe are influenced by asymmetric foreign investment income positions.

3. Foreign Direct Investment as Long-Term Opportunity

FDI has played a very important role in the 1980s as an engine of growth in OECD countries and in some NICs. Capital has become more mobile and modern telecommunication and computer technologies facilitate the spatial organization of international firms whose subsidiaries nevertheless enjoy considerable autonomy in decision-making. In modern capitalism firms have become bigger than ever, but the degree of decentralization has not necessarily reduced if one takes into account the high degree of internal flexibility and autonomy in many modern firms.

Given the shortage of capital and entrepreneurship in formerly socialist countries of the CMEA area it is important to attract foreign capital to a considerable degree. In the course of Russian, Hungarian and Czechoslovakian industrialization foreign capital played an important role, and this historical precedent leads one to expect that for Russia, Hungary and the ex-CSFR it might not be too difficult to accept considerable foreign investment. Compared to the 19th century and the interwar period there is nowadays one additional important source country, namely Japan whose outflows were the highest worldwide in 1990 and 1991. While Japanese investors have been reluctant to invest in central and eastern Europe in the first stage of transformation (whereas Japanese MNCs are active in China) investments from MNCs from some Asian NICs have been more forthcoming so that the traditional source countries from the OECD area are no longer exclusive sources of FDI. Since about 1/3 of OECD trade is organized as intra-company flows within the network of multinational companies and their respective subsidiaries, the expansion of trade both in the former CMEA area and in the east-west context could be stimulated by FDI. As regards balance of payments effects one may note that FDI inflows typically contribute to a trade balance deficit in the medium term because subsidiaries tend to import modern equipment from industrialized western countries in a first expansion stage. In the long term, however, rising output of subsidiaries will increasingly be exported (under an adequate policy framework) to the country of the parent company or to third countries; this at least is the pattern suggested by the Korean example (Inotai, 1991).

An important question concerns potential restrictions for foreign investors in central and eastern Europe, where all countries have made it difficult for foreigners to acquire land. Hungary has had the most liberal FDI laws since early on, while Poland and Bulgaria for example adopted a liberal legislation only reluctantly. Many countries in the former CMEA area are afraid

- for historical reasons - of German dominance in direct investment inflows (share in Poland: about 30 per cent) which raises political concerns in part because the united Germany is also the most important export market. Whether foreign firms should be favoured over domestic firms is an open question, but as long as state firms dominate one must indeed anticipate that a neutral tax and commercial policy would indeed discriminate against foreign investors (Inotai, 1992).

Foreign investors can become important not only for production, exports and employment, but also as a catalyst for political change - both in the host country and in the home country. Trade liberalization in the EC could be achieved more easily in the long term if politically influential parent companies lobby for reducing trade barriers to allow greater imports from foreign subsidiaries. However, in the short term and medium term MNCs' subsidiaries could also impair trade liberalization, namely by lobbying for higher tariffs in host countries in order to raise profitability of local investments made. Fiat's calls for higher tariff rates on imported cars in Poland, and similar cases with Samsung in Hungary and Daimler Benz in the CSFR (lobbying even for tariffs on imported used trucks) are examples of such effects.[2] The presence of MNCs could also reinforce the potential for currency substitution, and this may reduce seigniorage from the expansion of the domestic money supply for the host country. Currency substitution, however, could also reduce the probability of exchange rate overshooting in a Dornbusch-type exchange rate model so that excessive exchange rate volatility can be avoided more easily in the presence of foreign investors;[3] this in turn could reduce the risk premium on portfolio capital inflows.

3.1 Order of Magnitude and Basic Issues in International Investment

Global direct investment rapidly expanded in the 1980s and contributed to the growing international network of multinational production activities. For most

---

[2] The impact of MNCs on host governments and home governments has rarely been addressed. An exception is Panic (1991). On some aspects of FDI in eastern Europe see Svetlicic (1992).

[3] In the Dornbusch (1976) model an expansion of the domestic money supply M leads in the short run to a currency appreciation which is necessary to bring about an anticipated appreciation rate $-dlne/dt$ that allows to fulfill interest parity $i- dlne/dt= i^*$. The domestic nominal interest rate i ($i^* =$ foreign rate) must fall if the demand for money is to match the increased real money supply. While the long term multiplier is $dlne/dlnM = 1$, the short term multiplier is higher by a factor of Z and this factor is reduced under currency substitution since an anticipated appreciation rate raises the (relative) demand for domestic money.

OECD countries FDI flows are a two-way phenomenon, although there are sometimes strong bilateral or regional imbalances (notably in Japan whose outflows to almost all other OECD countries skyrocketed, while inflows stayed almost flat in the 1980s). Cumulative outflows of FDI during the 1970-90 period are estimated to have reached some $ 1,330 billion, where outstanding FDI stocks were $ 421.5 billion for the US, 233.6 for the UK, 201.4 for Japan and 114.5 for Germany in 1990. Outflows were highest in Japan (48 billion), followed by the US, the UK, France, Germany, Sweden, the Netherlands, Italy, Switzerland and Taiwan (33.4, 24.1, 22.3, 20.9, 14.1, 11.8, 7.1, 6.4 and 5.4 billion, respectively). Inflows were dominated by the United States, the UK and Spain with $ 37.2, 33.9 billion and 18.1 billion, respectively, but considerable amounts were also attracted by France, the Netherlands, Italy, Australia, Canada and Switzerland whose inflows were between 8 and 4 billion in 1990 (JETRO, 1992); the highest inflows in Eastern Europe were recorded in Hungary, the CSFR and Poland with $ 1.5 billion, some $600 million and some $500 million, respectively. Figures for 1992/93 will be slightly higher, but so far only Hungary has an impressive FDI inflow, and Hungarian firms - sometimes building on expatriate communities abroad - could also become the first significant source country of long term capital outflows (a position which in central and eastern Europe was held only by the CSSR in the interwar period). $ 1.5 billion of FDI inflows in Hungary implies with 10 million inhabitants that annual per capita inflows are $ 150 in a favourable case; for Poland this would mean FDI inflows of about $ 6 billion, while in reality just 10 per cent of that amount was forthcoming in 1992. For Russia Hungarian per capita figures would imply annual FDI inflows of roughly $ 25 billion, while not even $ 2 billion was reached in 1992.

International investment in telecom, in resource exploration and some joint ventures in manufacturing were attracted by Russia, but no momentum can be built up as long as political uncertainty rules. In such a situation even special trade and investment zones cannot help very much.

Table E2: Global Foreign Direct Investment and Equity Investment (billion US $, annual averages)

	1975-79	1980-84	1985-89	1990	1991
Total					
Outflows	35.3	42.4	134.9	222.4	177.3
USA	15.9	9.6	22.8	33.4	29.5
Japan	2.1	4.3	23.8	48.0	30.7
EC	14.1	20.9	59.4	97.5	80.5
Developing					
Countries	0.6	1.4	6.5	12.9	11.8
Global Inflows	26.9	52.6	117.6	179.6	157.9
Industrial					
Countries (A)	19.9	36.2	98.1	148.7	115.2
USA	6.1	18.6	48.2	37.2	22.2
Japan	0.1	0.3	0.1	1.8	1.4
EC	11.4	14.2	38.4	85.9	67.7
Asia(excl. Japan)	1.9	4.7	10.8	19.9	25.7
Eastern Europe	0.0	0.1	0.1	0.5	2.3
Latin America	3.6	5.4	5.7	7.8	12.0
Portfolio Investment Inflows in Industrial Countries	25.0	57.8	186.0	159.1	388.7
Net Equity Inflows in Industrial Countries(B)	3.7	10.8	31.4	-16.0	90.1
B in % of A:	*18.6%*	*29.8%*	*26.7%*	-	*57.1 %*
USA	1.5	3.4	8.7	-14.5	9.2
Japan	-0.2	3.5	-9.1	-13.3	46.8
EC	2.2	2.1	22.7	11.5	32.1

Source: Bank of International Settlements, 62nd Annual Report, Basel 1992, own calculations.

As the example of China shows, special economic zones can be a valuable ingredient for economic growth, technology transfer and export expansion; however, the maintenance of political stability and an export-oriented economic policy in a favourable environment of open markets abroad (mainly the US and Japan in the case of the People's Republic of China) are prerequisites; finally, the regional economic divergence between special economic zones and other regions of the country cannot be allowed to become excessive because otherwise massive migration will develop and internal trade barriers could be erected. MNCs from Asian newly industrializing countries - Taiwan, Korea and Hong Kong - became major investors in the Asean group; Japan accounted for 15 per cent of investment in the Asean-4 (Asean, excluding Brunei and Singapore) in 1991, compared with 15.4 per cent for Taiwan alone and 29.5 per cent for all four tigers (Economist, 1993c). As exchange rate movements made exports of the four tigers (Taiwan, Republic of Korea, Hong Kong and Singapore) less competitive, costs were also rising because of labour shortages. Firms from the tiger group were facing the choice between moving upmarket or moving offshore; offshore production has become a viable option in many cases. Some emerging MNCs from the Asean group (Thailand, Malaysia, Indonesia, Philippines, Brunei, Singapore) joined foreign investors from traditional source countries in China in the early 1990s.

Foreign direct investment flows reached some $200 billion worldwide in 1990/91, up from average annual values of $42.4 billion in the period 1980-84 and $134.9 billion in the period 1985-89 (BIS, 1992). The group of source countries is highly concentrated and so is the group of recipient countries. Considerable equity inflows - as part of portfolio investment - have reinforced the international flow of risk capital in the industrial countries (see Table E2).

Average annual equity inflow values reached $31.4 billion in the period 1985-90, and in 1991 there was a record flow of 90.1 billion, equivalent to 1/3 of total portfolio outflows. The EC recorded annual inflows of $ 22.7 billion annually in the period 1985-89, up from roughly $ 2 billion annually in 1975-1984. Given the increasing outflow of foreign capital and the amount of equity investments worldwide there is a considerable potential that could in principle be tapped by transforming countries in the former CMEA area. The increasing mobility of real capital, however, is also raising specific problems. Potential host countries face more fierce competition for foreign capital, and Central and Eastern Europe is doing so in a period of high real interest rates in Europe.[4]

---

[4] The surge in real interest rates is partly due to German unification; see on German unification Welfens (1992b).

Empirical evidence and historical experience hold two lessons for countries eager to attract foreign capital inflows: (a) portfolio investment flows are highly mobile and sensitive to nominal and real exchange rate fluctuations which imply a risk premium on investment (Tilly, 1992); but (b) there is little evidence - except for the case of developing countries - that FDI flows are influenced by exchange rate volatility (Bailey and Tavlas, 1991); FDI flows could, of course, be influenced by long term real exchange rate changes that lead to capital gains or losses. A real appreciation of the currency of major source countries will encourage FDI inflows into transforming economies because real assets then become cheaper in terms of the investor's domestic prices. In industrial countries equity inflows amounted to about 1/5 of all portfolio inflows which, of course, are more volatile than FDI flows.

In 1991 equity inflows in industrial countries reached a very high level of almost 60 per cent of FDI inflows, but the more traditional percentage share of some 25 per cent would also be impressive. This suggests that portfolio investment flows could also play a significant role in Eastern Europe. EC countries and the US might support such developments by introducing tax exemptions for investment funds investing in the transforming ex-CMEA countries. The figures in Table E2 shows furthermore that equity flows can vary considerably over time but that such portfolio inflows into the stock market can under favourable circumstances be even higher than foreign direct investment proper.

FDI within the EC is estimated (Yannopoulos, 1992) to have reached some $ 20 billion in the form of intra-EC flows and some $ 40 billion in extra-EC flows in the second half of the 1980s. The intensified competition in the single market environment could have some positive investment spill-over effects in those ex-CMEA countries which it is anticipated will join the Community in the near future. Hungary, the ex-CSFR and Poland are - given the recent association treaties - the most obvious candidates.

In order to assess the possible impact of FDI inflows in Eastern Europe one may analyze the effect of EC FDI inflows. $ 60 billion of total annual FDI inflows into the EC plus another $ 30 billion of equity inflows should generate additional value-added of some $ 150 billion in the EC if one assumes that the capital output ratio is 4:1 and that output is generated over a ten year period. The direct value-adding effect of these capital flows thus reached more than 10 per cent of total EC exports (1988: ECU 907 billion); if one would include technology spill-over effects and take into account that part of EC trade is generated by multinational companies the economic significance of FDI inflows and equity inflows in the EC is even higher. Eastern Europe basically could hope to attract at least part of the worldwide FDI flows and equity inflows. FDI inflows into Eastern Europe jumped from an annual value of $ 0.1 billion (1989) to $ 0.5 and 2.3 in 1990 and 1991, respectively; however, almost half of FDI inflows was recorded by Hungary where the stock of FDI at the end of 1992 will reach some $ 5 billion Foreign investment flows could indeed contribute to some 10 per cent of gross capital formation in the 1990s and would thereby match the high values of Taiwan recorded in the 1960s.

Whereas Asian NICs always enjoyed the advantage of almost unrestricted access to the huge US market East European economies are less well positioned with respect to Western Europe. The EC has been reluctant to fully liberalize imports in the association treaties signed with the CSFR, Poland and Hungary in November 1991. Textiles and agriculture are potential fields for high export growth of transforming economies, but the EC has remained quite protectionist in these areas. Foreign investors will, of course, be quite reluctant to invest much in any of those industries of central and east European countries where EC import barriers are existent or looming. For the smaller ex-CMEA countries it would therefore be important to target not only EC markets but other markets in industrial countries, the NICs and the developing countries as well; establishing free trade within a wider group of transforming economies is also important.

The arguments in some of the smaller countries that local production could serve both a growing domestic market and a huge Soviet market have become invalid and probably never were sound. Foreign investors will often invest directly in the new republics and states of the former USSR territory, and such huge potential markets could also be covered by subsidiaries located in other low-wage countries, e.g. in South-East Asia.

3.2 Some Theoretical Aspects of Direct Investment

In the socialist era socialist countries were not open to foreign investment inflows, except for joint ventures which never reached a significant role for growth and trade, except perhaps in Hungary in the 1980s. When in 1990/91 the former CMEA countries opened up to foreign investment they did so upon recognizing that in the world economy (a) FDI flows had shown higher growth rates in the 1980s than trade, and (b) that foreign investment inflows could help to overcome Eastern Europe's capital shortage and help to promote trade and technological progress.

While many OECD countries and most NICs actively promote inflows of foreign investment (Wells and Wint, 1990), the former CMEA countries are quite hesitant in actively promoting FDI at home, let alone setting up promotion offices abroad. However, investors need information about the new investment opportunities and for the government it might in turn be useful to learn about the preferences of would-be investors from abroad; this can best be achieved if one sets up investment promotion centres abroad which in the long term could also alert East European firms to seize investment and trade opportunities abroad (here lies one strength of the Japanese External Trade Organization). Focusing primarily on foreign exporters which might become willing to substitute exports to Eastern Europe by local production is not sufficient because a considerable group of would-be investors might until then never have had economic relations with the ex-CMEA countries. Indeed, these countries are known to have had very limited trade with capitalist countries. An active search for foreign investors and entrepreneurs could not only raise the amount of FDI inflows but raise the sales proceeds from selling to foreign investors; and it could raise the number of firms in each industry such that pro-competitive effects would be created. To systematically reduce information costs for foreign (and domestic) investors by a simplified economic system design could also be useful because it would reduce information costs and thereby could raise the interest of foreign firms. Moreover, barriers for FDI could also be reduced by an outward-oriented systemic design in at least some areas; if one would opt for "institutional imports" in the sense that legal principles and policy rules of major OECD countries - representing also the most important source countries - would be adopted many would-be investors could be encouraged by the fact that the rules of the game were similar to those known from the home country or countries in which major subsidiaries already are located.

If one takes the experience of EC countries (Molle and Morsink, 1991) into account one may well expect that FDI inflows start only after a minimum level of trade has been established; this may be valid at least for part of the FDI potential of the ex-CMEA area. Hence it would be all the more important to launch a successful foreign economic liberalization (Welfens, 1992b) that would quickly raise the levels of East-West trade. The very high traditional shares of intra-CMEA trade of the CSFR, Bulgaria, Romania and the USSR let us expect that these countries face a disadvantage in attracting FDI inflows - compared to Hungary and Poland. One may presume that those firms which were exporters or importers thereby accumulated information about long term profitable investment opportunities in the potential host countries. This learning from trade can not be a very quick road to indirectly attracting FDI inflows to central and eastern Europe because trade with Western Europe was so low under socialism.

FDI can be viewed as an alternative to exports and contractual resource transfers as it is done by Dunning (1981) within his Ownership-Location-Internalization (OLI) approach. In Dunning's eclectic theory multinationals are assumed to have some owner-specific advantages - e.g. patents - that allow the would-be foreign investor to successfully compete with indigenous producers abroad who enjoy certain natural advantages, e.g. the familiarity with the domestic economic and political system.[5] If only O-advantages of the MNC are present licensing could be a suitable strategy to serve a foreign market indirectly. If the firm also enjoys internalization advantages - in the sense that specific organization skills or peculiarities of the sector or the product allows a profitable substitution of pure market transactions by intra-firm transactions into which setting up at least a network of sales representatives abroad can be included - then exports are the best way to serve the foreign market unless there are particular locational advantages relevant to local production. If in addition to ownership and internalization advantages there are attractive conditions in host countries the firm would establish production abroad and serve both local and third-country markets (possibly including at some date the home market of the parent company). East European economies have to develop locational advantages in order to attract foreign direct investment.

A receptive policy for foreign investors is only visible in Hungary, and, to some extent in Poland, but in Poland as in other ex-CMEA countries the population or influential political parties strongly resist foreign investment. People are afraid that foreign firms could buy assets at below long-term market prices, that foreign owners will be less willing to save jobs in outdated factories and will be able to keep wages relatively low for many years. From a microeconomic point of view, that is in the case of an individual firm, these reservations might in some cases be substantiated. However, the macroeconomic aspects and the evolutionary dynamics are totally neglected in such a view. If workers want to have rising net real wages one would have to support productivity growth in firms and competition in goods markets and labour markets which will help to check price increases and to raise wages

---

5 Intangible assets could be important for successful foreign investment projects, too (Caves, 1982); tariff discrimination is likely to play a major role in the ex-USSR.

across all sectors; and one would have to keep tax rates low by avoiding a rising burden of subsidies allocated to unprofitable state firms and reducing the burden of foreign debt by a gradual improvement of the terms of trade. Moreover, one would have to promote economic growth, and for this the role of MNCs is vital; the transfer of technologies is dominated worldwide by intra-firm transactions. Foreign investors' willingness to pay relatively high prices for acquiring firms in former CMEA countries depends positively on the expected profitability and the perceived uncertainty of investment conditions and the degree of political risk. Profitability will be increased if there is local private industry with firms that can supply intermediate products and specific inputs for production. Here privatization is important for successful foreign investment policies. Employee share ownership participation (ESOP) could be specifically encouraged in firms in which foreign investors have a high stake, and in general one may consider introducing a moderate capital gains tax which would split the gains from transformation between the firm and society.

	Ownership (O)	Location (L)	Interna-lization (I)
a) FDI	+	+	+
b) Exports	+	-	+
c) Contractual Re-source Transfer	+	-	-

Source: Dunning, 1981, Figure 5.1, ch. 5.

Figure E1: The Dunning Approach to FDI

The infrastructure and hostile bureaucratic attitudes *vis-à-vis* foreign investors are still an impediment to foreign investment inflows in most ex-CMEA countries. Only if a critical minimum mass of FDI can be mobilized would people in the host country probably be more aware of the positive economic impact of MNCs. Finally, the new private firms of central and eastern Europe will have to learn for themselves that exports and local production abroad or contractual services are alternatives that should be considered in a long term business strategy. International investment could be as much an engine of economic growth as international trade has been for a long time.

If a country - such as Poland - mainly attracts small joint venture investment, the supply-side effects from FDI will on average be lower than in the case that the world's leading MNCs invest. MNCs normally will organize the training of local staff and management on the one hand, and, on the other hand, integrate local subsidiaries into the international network of the multinational company which should stimulate exports of host countries in the long run. While many small firms might bring as much capital to a host country as the investment of a few MNCs the transfer of skills is likely to be higher in the case of big MNCs. Absence of MNCs suggests that political risks are considered to be prohibitive. Host countries can only try to reorganize the political system in a way that supports stability. Sometimes external help could be useful, too; for example the EC supports joint ventures of small firms within the Phare program; but it may indeed be interesting to encourage EC MNCs by transitory tax incentives in the source countries to contribute to building market economies in central and eastern Europe. If the economic reconstruction in that area fails the negative external effects will be strongly felt in Western Europe; and there is indeed some risk that Europe may fall back into the chaotic and protectionist interwar period of 1919-1939. Positive external effects of FDI flows could indeed justify EC subsidies for FDI outflows.

3.2.1 Long Term Aspects of FDI Inflows and Welfare Effects

While FDI inflows are likely to remain modest in the short term, they might become significant in the long term. First reform steps such as price liberalization, introducing current account convertibility and trade liberalization as well as adopting new tax laws have to be completed before MNCs can be expected to plan major investments. However, once a critical minimum number of investors have made a firm commitment rival firms are likely to also consider FDI engagements; this is particularly true in industries with international oligopolies. But even countries with big home markets, such as Poland, the Ukraine or Russia cannot expect investors to be eager to invest if political stability does not hold.

The developments in Russia, Belarus and the Ukraine are still uncertain; however, German investors can be expected to play a relatively strong role together with Canadian, US and some West European investors.[6] Scandinavian investors could play an important role in the new Baltic states which are economically in a very difficult situation. It remains doubtful that the absolute amount of FDI inflows into the CIS will be significant in the early 1990s. Where expectations of foreign investors first have to be influenced favourably by successful reorganization and restructuring, it seems crucial that expectations of domestic consumers and voters not be raised too fast since otherwise the disappointment will be extreme and political extremism could spread.

Foreign Direct Investment and Trade

The socialist East European countries had most of their trade among themselves. One might argue that this is in line with trading patterns in Western Europe.[7] Even in the smaller countries export-GNP ratios were in the range of 20-30 per cent - low when compared to Spain, the Netherlands or Belgium with ratios of 22, 60 and 65 per cent (or Korea with 40 per cent) in the late 1980s.

Moreover, in centrally planned economies with rigid quantitative targets world market impulses could not affect the whole array of tradables and non-tradables via substitution effects or complementary goods; and there were no multinational companies (MNCs) which account in Western market economies for about 30 per cent of all international trade. Not allowing foreign direct investment implied not only foregoing multinationals' intra-firm trade and hence having a different trading pattern and a lower trade level than otherwise; it also implied that international technology transfers were low which in the OECD countries mostly go through the network of MNCs or cross-licensing arrangements between MNCs.

Most East European countries are heavily indebted and require the inflow of foreign capital for modernization needs, so that high (net) export growth is vital for these economies. Only if the production potential can be modernized and the tradables sector enlarged can one expect sustaining economic growth.

Foreign investors can support trade liberalization, but they might also impair it. In the medium term they are likely to contribute to higher import tariffs which help to achieve a greater amount of profitable investment, but in

---

[6] On conclusions from the transformation process for the success states of the USSR see Welfens (1993d); experiences from privatization and FDI inflows in smaller ex-CMEA countries can be used only *mutatis mutandis* for Russia and the Ukraine.
[7] In the CMEA there was bilateralism as opposed to multilateral trade relations in the EC; there was almost no intra-industry trade but monopolistic specialization among CMEA countries, and all countries were relatively less open than their Western counterparts. See Csaba (1990).

the long term MNCs typically are interested in free trade (not necessarily in free competition in the host country market - a closer look at Brazil is most interesting in this context).

The relative share of benefits from FDI will be critical for organizing a sustaining and significant share of foreign investment in Eastern Europe. In the MacDougall diagram major FDI aspects can be covered, where we assume a given stock of capital in the home country (K) and abroad (K*, starred variables), so that the length of the box is the world capital stock in a two-country model; both countries use a neoclassical production function with labour and capital, and firms are assumed to maximize profits such that the marginal product of capital (Y_K, Y_K*) will be equal to the interest rate r (at home) and r*, respectively. At first, both countries are assumed to be in a situation of complete capital flow restrictions, and the MacDougall diagram makes clear what happens with the removal of capital flow barriers.

The MacDougall diagram portrays the marginal product schedule Y_K, assuming given labour inputs, for the home country and the rest of the world (assuming given inputs of labour L) such that the area under the marginal product schedules is equal to output; since factors are assumed to be rewarded in accordance to marginal products, rK is capital income at home and r*K* capital income abroad before capital mobility is established; the rest of the area under the marginal product schedule of the home country and the foreign country is, of course, labour income. From O to the right we measure K, from O' to the left we measure K* so that the length of the box is the world capital stock. Initially, we assume that K_1 is employed in the home country (ex-CMEA country), K_1* is employed abroad (OECD country group). Optimal world capital allocation with capital mobility occurs in the intersection of the two marginal product schedules (point B in which $Y_K = Y_K$* = r = r*).

The traditional argument is as follows. If initially marginal products diverge, the move towards the intersection of both Y_K schedules will raise world income by the triangle EBD. Under profit maximization the real interest rate r = Y_K and r* = Y_K*, but with FDI there will be a unique real interest rate (= Y_K abroad and at home). The MacDougall diagram suggests that capital will flow from the capital rich Western Europe to the capital poor Eastern Europe, where labour income will increase (the integral under the Y_K schedule represents total output, and output minus capital income rK is real wage income). However, FDI will bring not only an inflow of capital but also a transfer of technology and entrepreneurship, and this means that the marginal product would rotate upwards; hence income gains from inward FDI will increase over time as the domestic Y_K curve will rotate upwards (additional worldwide gain: area BB'GG'). If there were positive backtransfers of know how and technology even the Y_K schedule in the parent company country could rotate upwards in the long term (however, while EC firms might benefit from FDI in the US in this way, there is not much reason to believe that EC firms could reap similar benefits in the ex-CMEA area).

Both in the host country and in the capital exporting country there might be some long term positive spill-over effects in the tradables sector so that indirect FDI benefits should be included in a long term analysis (Welfens, 1992b). The basic problem of a political risk premium can be easily demonstrated with the MacDougall diagram. If the risk premium R is as high as the initial difference between the marginal product of capital at home - the transforming economies - and abroad (distance DE), there would be no FDI inflows into central and eastern Europe. Moreover, if the risk premium would further increase and reach the equivalent of the distance D'E' capital outflows to Western Europe would be the result provided that capital outflows are not restricted; restrictions will result in capital flight. The worldwide welfare loss from a risk premium of D'E' would be an opportunity cost equivalent to the triangle D'E'B plus the area BB'GG'.

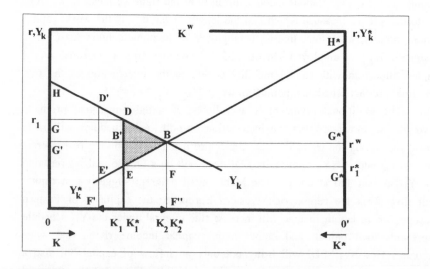

Figure E2: FDI Effects in the MacDougall Diagram

3.2.2 Risk Spillovers as Negative Externalities for International Investment

A major problem in eastern and southeastern Europe concerns the political uncertainty and the potential for ethnic problems and renewed nationalism in many countries of the region. For would-be host countries in central Europe this could imply negative externalities for foreign investment. In economics externalities are normally defined as technical externalities in the sense that the costs of firm B are affected by firm C's production - say, in a negative manner via emissions that raise water treatment costs in firm B which uses water as an input in production. One might consider at least one specific non-pecuniary externality, namely if political uncertainty in country C raises the risk premium in country B - either because there are negative political spill-overs or because investors face a regionalization syndrome of the type already observed in the Latin American debt crisis of 1982 when the illiquidity of Mexico reduced the trust and faith in all Latin American debtor countries.[8] In an implicit three country model in which country A is the source country of investment and C (with no capital inflows or outflows for whatever reasons) is a neighbouring country of B we can interpret the rise of the risk premium (R** > 0 and therefore R* > 0) analogous to Figure E2. More capital in the rich OECD country A will be employed than otherwise and country B will realise lower FDI inflows or - worse - higher capital outflows than otherwise. If political uncertainty would also induce migration from B to A then B's marginal product schedule will shift downward, while that of country A will shift upwards in Figure E3. Vertical integration between B&C (&A firms) could become unfeasible, too.

---

[8] In 1983-86 resource transfers to OECD countries became positive in the case of Mexico and Brazil; both countries suffered at the same time from a reduction of the investment/GNP ratio. The swing of this ratio was minus 7 percentage points compared to 1975-82. See on this Dittus *et al.*, 1991. Mexico benefited from the accession to GATT and the switch to export promotion in the second half of the 1980s. The reversal of capital flight helped Latin American countries, but the Baker plan also was important for managing the debt crisis and restoring confidence of both domestic and foreign investors.

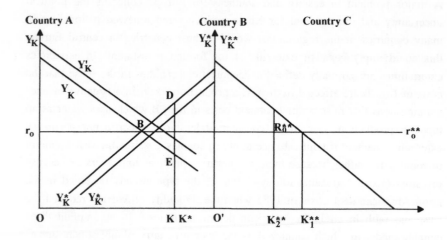

Figure E3: Political Risk as a Negative Externality for International Investment

Relative Benefits for Producers and Consumers as a Short-Term Sequencing Criterion

A crucial question with respect to FDI concerns the relative benefits of FDI inflows for the host country and the source countries (or the parent companies). In the following we draw on Welfens (1992b) where it is argued that international conflicts over income distribution in the context of FDI can be analyzed in terms of the ratio of consumer surplus to producer surplus - the latter might fully accrue to foreign investors if they acquire all firms in a certain industry.

Figure E4 shows a downward-sloping standard demand schedule D_0 and an upward-sloping supply curve S which represents the aggregate marginal cost curves of the industry's firms. That is, demand reduces as the price increases and the supply will rise as the price is increasing. Under competition the intersection of the two curves determines the market-clearing equilibrium price at which each firm will sell its output and at which each consumer will buy. However, as indicated by the demand curve most consumers had been willing to pay more than the market price, and the triangle F_1 is an indicator of this extra benefit from market allocation - the consumer surplus triangle. A similar reasoning holds with respect to producers; as indicated by the supply curve it holds that at least some producers had been willing to supply their products even at prices lower than the actual market-clearing price - the triangle F2 indicates the so-called producer surplus which is a true residual income. In the long term when firms can realize the optimum plant size (or choose the optimal amount of the fixed factor), the aggregate supply curve will be less steep which is crucial in the context of FDI. If one can assume that foreign investors can transfer their experience internationally in choosing the optimal plant size and thereby switching to an output at the minimum of the total cost curve the conclusion can be drawn that the supply curve of the respective industry will become more elastic than in the presence of - inexperienced - domestic producers only. This is crucial for the relative share of benefits from FDI in the non-tradables sector (a generalized analysis is possible).

To stay as simple as possible one may assume that the whole industry is owned by foreign investors such that the producer surplus fully goes to them. The ratio of the consumer surplus F1 to the producer surplus F2 is given by the relation of the slope of the demand curve (b) and that of the supply curve (g). Eastern European countries would like to have as much consumer surplus relative to the producer surplus as possible, and therefore they should open up for FDI industries with a low demand elasticity (high value of b, relative to the slope of the supply curve, (g). R&D policies and competition policies that encourage product innovation would help to raise (b) over time, and, possibly, to reduce (g) - until process innovations raise (g) again. Taking into account the modified Tirole analysis presented before, one could argue that import liberalization and domestic competition for eliminating monopolies are particularly important in industries with a high elasticity of demand, while FDI liberalization should occur in industries with a high ratio of b/g.

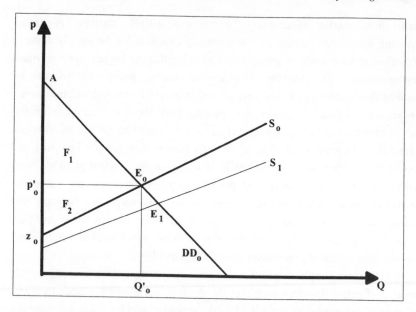

Figure E4: Welfare Effects with Foreign Direct Investments in Industry

A similar reasoning holds if FDI occurs in the tradables industry. One only has to take into account the broken supply curve S_1 in Figure E4.[9] If FDI makes supply more elastic the amount of goods exported will be higher than in the case of domestic ownership only. A different question, however, is the rate of technological progress in the case of no foreign ownership vs. full (or strong) foreign ownership of an industry.

Given the increasing role of intra-company trade and international technology flows as well as the surge in international R&D cooperation in the 1980s (UNCTC, 1988; Klein and Welfens, 1992) one may also emphasize that foreign direct investment is an engine of economic growth. Murrell (1990, 1991) argued that the absence of FDI largely explains the distorted trade patterns and slow economic growth in socialist economies and that rebuilding the institutional network under new political and economic rules is a time-consuming task which should not be solved in a shock therapy approach. If one adopts this view the conclusion is that Eastern Europe needs not only institutional liberalization, but positive incentives for exports and FDI. The

---

[9] With g declining, the international conflicts over gains from FDI - in the sense of the ratio F1/F2 - would reduce provided that workers/voters do not dislike profits accruing to foreign capital owners much more than in the case of domestic ownership.

integration of eastern Europe into the global economy indeed can not be accomplished within a few years because on the one hand so many elements of an economic system determine the economy's orientation, flexibility and responsiveness, and on the other hand the socialist links with the capitalist world were thin and fragile in most CMEA countries (Csaba, 1990; 1991).

3.2.3 FDI, Privatization and the Exchange Rate

FDI inflows and privatization will shift the supply curve of Eastern Europe to the right (ESSo to ESS1 in Figure E5). If Eastern Europe's import demand is EDD_0 and the world market price level is $p*_0$ and import prices are $p_0 = p*_0(1+z)$ - that is the transforming countries apply similar or identical import taxes to imports from outside the region - Eastern European output will be equal to I before privatization and FDI, but I' after systemic transition. There is a positive welfare effect equal to the area ACDB plus DEF. While rising output of Eastern Europe is equivalent to regional trade cration in Eastern Europe the rightward shift of the supply curve ESS will reduce imports from third countries: With a regional demand curve EDDo the import from third countries (including the CIS) will be equal to M minus I before privatization and FDI, but it will be M minus I' after transition. The biggest loser will be the ex-USSR since it not only will lose its role as a preferred trading partner for the smaller East European economies; moreover, it can hardly replace exports by FDI in Eastern Europe. Third countries will not suffer from trade diversion if regional transformation would boost aggregate demand and thus imports; trade creation would also occur if Eastern Europe would enjoy market power so that falling imports would go along with positive terms of trade effects (a fall of p*). Only Poland, Hungary and the ex-CSFR are likely to show some modest growth in the 1990s, and this will be mainly to the benefit of Western Europe. While economic transformations in the smaller countries of the ex-CMEA may temporarily show pitfalls and a standstill these economies enjoy the advantage of being relatively small so that observation and careful analysis will bring about learning by doing in the long term. By contrast, Russia is much too big for a comprehensive reform with fast learning steps. However, if Russia cannot be stabilized the whole of Eastern Europe could face sustained uncertainty and slow FDI inflows. Promoting FDI will then become even more necessary in the smaller ex-CMEA countries which might consider US FDI inflows as the best insurance against Russian interference.

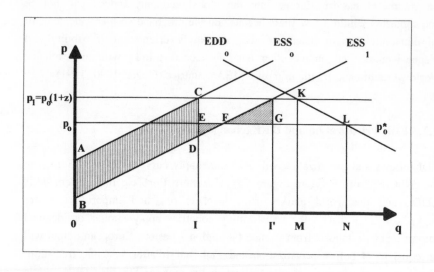

Figure E5: Trade Effects of Privatization and FDI

Two Sector Perspective

Privatization, FDI and competition can be expected to reinforce the growth of factor productivity via positive diffusion effects. In a simple two country model of structural privatization one may distinguish between the tradables (T-)sector and the nontradables(N-)sector. Labour is mobile between sectors and profit maximization results in the conditions that the marginal product of labour is equal to the respective real product wage rate (T_L, N_L = marginal product of labour in the T-, N-sector; in the COBB-DOUGLAS case is proportional to average products).

(A1) $W/P^T = T_L$
(A2) $W/P^N = N_L$

Hence $P^T = W/T_L$ and $P^N = W/N_L = P^T(T_L/N_L)$ so that the general price level, defined by $P = P^T \exp b \ P^N \exp (1-b)$ will lead to the expression:

(A3) $P = P^T \exp b \ [P^T(T_L/N_L)] \exp (1-b)$

and, similarly in the foreign country (starred variables):

(A4) $P^* = P^{T*} \exp b^* \ [P^{T*}(T_L^*/N_L^*)] \exp (1-b^*)$

If purchasing power parity holds in the tradables sector in the long term, the equilibrium exchange rate $\underline{e}$ is given by:

(A5) $\underline{e} = P^T/P^T*$

We obtain after logarithmization and using (3) and (4), while assuming for simplicity $b=b*$:

(A6) $d\ln\underline{e}/dt = dp/dt - dp*/dt + (1-b)[(d(n_L/n_L*)/dt)-(d(f_L/f_L*)/dt],$

where $p=\ln P$, $n_L=\ln N_L$, $f_L=\ln T_L$

Equation (A6) is a familiar result from modern exchange rate economics and suggests how the long term equilibrium exchange rate $\underline{e}$ is affected by certain key variables. Indeed, equation (A6) suggests that the real exchange rate in the sense of $eP*/P$ will show a real appreciation if labour productivity growth in the nontradables sector abroad is higher than in Eastern Europe and if productivity growth in Eastern Europe's tradables sectors exceeds that abroad. Here modern growth theory with its emphasis on dynamic scale economies can be used. One can also argue that only significant FDI inflows will allow Eastern Europe to realise productivity growth rates that exceed those in Western Europe. FDI will result in sustaining technology inflows whose economy-wide effect, however, could be smaller in former CMEA countries if diffusion-stimulating competition does not match the intensity in the technology source countries, say the EC. A real appreciation which would reduce the real burden of debt and hence generate positive wealth effects would, of course, be most welcome in transforming economies - the higher the foreign debt-output ratios the more important this could be.

International Price Discrimination
If there is international price discrimination, (A5) would have to be replaced by (5'):

(C5') $P^T(1-1/\epsilon) = P^T*(1-1/\epsilon*),$

where ϵ is the price elasticity of the demand for tradables

(A6') $d\ln\underline{e} = dp - dp* + (1-b)[(dn_L-dn_L*) -(df_L-df_L*)] +d[(1/\epsilon)-(1/\epsilon*)]^{10}$

---

[10] We make use of the approximation $\ln(1+1/\epsilon) = 1/\epsilon$ which is appropriate if ϵ is relatively high.

The last term on the RHS of (A6') says that there will be a nominal and a real depreciation if the demand elasticity in the domestic tradables sector falls or if the elasticity abroad is rising. The elasticity of demand can be assumed to fall if the intensity of product innovation is rising, if the availability of substitutes from domestic sources or abroad is falling, if the information costs for consumers are increasing and if market access is reduced. Privatization should generally increase the range of available product substitutes. Import liberalization could transitorily raise ϵ in those transforming economies which so far have had few links with the capitalist world; that is, in the first transformation period they are facing a foreign wave of new products offered. FDI inflows could reduce the demand elasticity in Eastern Europe (and open up opportunities for price discrimination), namely to the extent that investments in exclusive distribution channels, product-specific after-sales service and advertising (representing sunk costs) are creating and reinforcing brand loyalties. The foreign tradables' demand price elasticity ϵ^* - that in the OECD countries - can be assumed to be given because no significant impact of East European transformations is be expected in the short run.

3.2.4 FDI in the Open Economy Macro Model

Systemic transition to a market economy can survive only if economic growth can be restored. The loss in social status, real income and wealth suffered by many groups during the first transition stage calls for a strong growth of future real income; only then would individuals be willing to support the transformation process. The growth of output Y depends on the development of the production function (scale factor a and technological progress rate z) and the increasing availability of improved domestic and foreign inputs; $Y = (H+K^*)^{\beta}L^{(1-\beta)}\acute{e}^{z(J,x^*,Z)t}$, where H denotes the domestic capital stock, K^* is the stock of foreign direct investment, L is labour input, J the stock of knowledge, x^* the ratio of imported intermediary goods to output (a proxy for modernization accruing through relative imports), and α the relative scope of market institutions developed (could be scaled to fall between 0 and 1); $\acute{e}$ is the Euler number, z is the rate of technological progress, β is the elasticity of real capital output and t is the time index; in reality β for K^* could be higher than the respective elasticity for H. With profit maximization the growth rate of output g_Y therefore is given by (B1)

(B1) $g_Y = (rK/Y)(g_K) + (1-ß)g_L + z(J,x^*,\alpha,\Sigma X)$

Whether a rapid output growth can be achieved will mainly depend on three economic aspects:
- Growth of the capital stock g_K which contains domestic and foreign capital flows;
- efficiency of investment which will depend on positive (!) real interest rates;
- successful technological catching-up, namely the rate of technological progress z. It is assumed here that know-how J, the exploitation of international technological progress as proxied by x^*, the relative scope of market institutions acting as the basis for the propagation of technological information and the accumulated amount of exports ΣX - partly reflecting impulses from world market competition - positively influence the rate of technological progress; accumulated know-how from exports can be assumed to erode over time. Accumulated export output and hence the degree of export orientation will be the more important for raising the rate of technological progress the greater the role of dynamic economies of scale is. A growing presence of MNCs is likely to positively influence all determinants of z.

Foreign investors are expected to augment the capital stock, to introduce less costly technologies and to contribute to higher product quality. At first sight these effects are mainly supply-side effects, and - as is well-known - the supply side is not well covered in the familiar Keynesian IS-LM model. The situation in central and eastern Europe, however, still makes a modified IS-LM-ZZ model of an open economy with underemployment an interesting model setting; the ZZ curve is the balance of payments equilibrium locus.[11] Inflation can be incorporated by distinguishing the nominal interest rate i relevant for the money market equilibrium line LM and the real interest rate r as one of the important factors shaping the goods demand curve IS via the influence of r on investment - and even the supply-side can be incorporated (Welfens, 1992b). The expected rate of inflation will be the difference between i and r.

A major transformation aspect associated with the slope of the ZZ curve that portrays equilibrium in the foreign exchange market is that both

---

[11] To the right of the ZZ curve the import demand induced by Y is bigger than the amount of net capital imports generated by the going interest rate. Hence to the right of the ZZ curve there is an excess demand for foreign exchange which will lead to a depreciation of the currency if flexible exchange rates characterize the international system. With fixed exchange rates a point to the right of the ZZ curve - reflecting the intersection of the IS curve and the LM curve - will force the central bank to run down its foreign exchange reserves. Intervention in the foreign exchange market will reduce the nominal money supply so that the LM curve would then shift to the left.

privatization and FDI will tend to raise the elasticity of net capital inflows Q which depend on the difference between the domestic rate and the foreign interest rate (i-i*) and the expected devaluation rate a; under perfect capital mobility and if domestic and foreign bonds were perfect substitutes one could assume interest parity i-i*=a;[12] but since political risk R can be expected to play an important role we will use modified interest parity in the form i-i*= a+R.

As suggested by Froot and Stein (1992) part of capital inflows, namely, FDI depends upon the real exchange rate q=eP*/P; e denotes the nominal exchange rate, P* (P) the foreign (domestic) price level. Note here that if the devaluation a would reflect purchasing power parity (a=π-π*), net capital inflows Q can be written as Q'(r-r*,q,R). In the short term one, of course, can not assume that PPP will hold, but in the long term net imports can be written as Q'(...) and as soon as expectations are forward-looking one would have to consider even within a short term analysis the implied long term equilibrium values for Y and r. For the foreign exchange market to clear equation (B2) must hold, namely that the net import of goods and services -T (T is therefore net exports) will equal net capital inflows Q(...). Net exports are conventionally assumed to be a positive function of real income abroad Y*, a negative function of domestic demand Y and a negative function of the real exchange rate q; in addition to this we also assume that net exports are a positive function of the production potential Z which in turn depends on the stock of domestic capital H, the stock of FDI inflows K* and labour employed L. We take into account an improved product quality in the form of the variable W which is positively influenced by K* and the intensity of competition v; the latter could be proxied by the share of output produced in the private sector, and one could take into account the effective import tariff as a negative determinant of v. If foreign demand shifts in favour of the country's output or export potential both the ZZ curve and the IS curve will shift to the right. A balance of payments surplus would result from this.[13] A specific element of the net export function T(...) is therefore that a change of the supply potential as well as competition are taken

---

[12] If the nominal interest rate i is equal to r plus the expected inflation rate, while the depreciation rate a is determined by the modified purchasing power parity (a=inflation rate differential) a world with perfect foresight would imply real interest rate parity: r=r*.

[13] This is unlikely in reality because foreign economic liberalization will mainly imply reducing import barriers: imports will then sharply increase. It could also mean reducing export barriers, but becoming a successful exporter will be rather difficult to learn. Eastern Europe will have to accept current account deficits if a net resource transfer is to occur. Such a transfer is necessary if Western aid is to result in a real resource transfer that helps to raise investment and consumption beyond the level that would be feasible without foreign aid.

into account in a straightforward formulation. If government expenditure is increased the IS curve will shift to the right (IS_1); point B is below the ZZ_1 schedule and capital will be flowing out. In a system of flexible exchange rates the currency will suffer a depreciation which shifts the ZZ_1 curve and the IS_1 to the right - assuming that the Robinson condition would hold (implying a normal reaction: a current account surplus). If the Robinson condition does not hold the depreciation will create a balance of payments deficit.

(B2) $-T(q,Y,Y^*,Z(K^*,H,L),W(K^*,v)) = Q(...)$; ZZ curve

For a normal reaction of the trade balance the Robinson condition (with $D_x=$ elasticity of export demand; E_x supply elasticity of exports, X=exports; X*=imports or exports of country 2) states:
$X[D_x(1+E_x)]/(-E_x +D_x)] > X^* [E_{x^*}(1+D_{x^*})/(E_{x^*}-D_{x^*})]$
In the small country case E_x approaching infinity and D_x approaching minus infinity a normal reaction will occur if initially there was a current account surplus. If there was a current account deficit a normal reaction is the more likely the greater the supply elasticity and the greater the demand elasticity (in absolute terms) is. Privatization and FDI will crucially affect supply elasticities. In the first stage of systemic transformation - with most firms still state-owned and few managers willing to take any risks - one might assume that supply elasticities are zero.

Under profit maximization and assuming a Cobb-Douglas function the supply side of the economy is given by the production function $Y = K^{\beta}L^{(1-\beta)}$ which implies under competition $Y^S = rK + (1-\beta)Y$; K is comprised of the domestic capital stock H plus the stock of inward FDI (K^*): $K=H+K^*$. Hence the goods market equilibrium condition is given by equation (B3) in which C represents private consumption, I investment demand, G government consumption and T net exports. Investment is assumed to depend not only upon the real interest rate r at home and abroad (r^*), but also on the terms of trade (Froot and Stein argument). This formulation of the investment function implicitly considers FDI inflows as greenfield investments. In reality foreigners acquire part of the existing capital stock. C is assumed to positively depend on real income Y, government net transfers V, and wealth $A=M/P+(B/P)+H-qF^*$, where M/P denotes the real money stock, B/P the real value of the stock of (short term) domestic bonds, H the domestically owned capital stock and F^* the stock of (indexed) foreign debt. Increasing competition - through privatization - will improve product quality and therefore shift both the IS curve and the ZZ curve to the right.

(B3) $rK + (1-ß)Y = C(Y,A,V) + I(r,r^*,q) + G + T(...)$; IS curve

If we integrate the supply side as suggested here (Welfens, 1992b), one immediately recognizes that the supply-augmented goods market equilibrium curve IS is less steep than suggested by the traditional IS curve in the pure demand setting. An exogenous increase in the capital stock K - regardless of whether stemming from H or K^* - will reduce the slope of the IS curve such that the new intersection point with the LM curve would indicate a higher real GNP Y.

The demand for money can conveniently be written as follows:

(B4) $M/P = Yé^{-\sigma i}$;   é=Euler number;

(B4') $\ln(M/P)/Y = -\sigma i$;   LM curve

where i= nominal interest rate, and $i = r + E(\pi)$; the expected inflation rate $E(\pi)$ can be treated as exogenous in the short run (a monetarist view would suggest that actual inflation π is determined by the difference between the growth rate of the money supply and the growth rate of the productive potential); σ= semi interest elasticity; the elasticity of the real demand for money is assumed, for simplicity, to be unity.

A rising degree of capital mobility means - as is well known from the standard analysis - that the ZZ curve will become more flat. Its slope di/dY = $x^*/(\delta Q/\delta j)$, where x^* is the marginal propensity to import and $\delta Q/\delta j$ denotes the marginal reaction of Q with respect to the net interest rate differential. Progress in privatization and a rising stock of FDI inflows will not only increase $\delta Q/\delta j$, but will also raise x^*. If government deliberately impairs the switch to rising capital mobility the rise of x^* could dominate in the medium term so that the ZZ curve will remain steeper than the LM curve. If privatization helps to reduce the budget deficit and thereby facilitates anti-inflationary policies one may indeed expect that capital mobility is indirectly reduced. It is well known from Western countries that the higher the inflation rate the lower the average maturity of bonds; to put it differently, with a low inflation rate more financial investments will be long term which should reduce the average responsiveness of capital flows to changing average international interest rate differentials.

If the LM curve is less steep than the ZZ curve (here ZZ_1) an expansive fiscal policy or an exogenous increase in exports of goods and services will establish point B in Figure E6; from the initial general equilibrium in A the economy would move towards B in which real income is higher than before.[14] So far we have neglected inflation, but we will introduce it later.

Since point B is below the ZZ_1 curve B reflects a trade balance deficit which implies that foreign indebtedness will increase. The latter will tend to reduce domestic (per capita) wealth A so that the IS curve will shift back towards its original position in point A. If, however, the trade deficit goes along with a corresponding net FDI inflow the long term result will be an improved quality of export goods which implies in the case of a small country - facing no restrictions for raising exports to the rest of the world - that both the IS curve and the ZZ curve will shift to the right such that B could indeed be a long term solution of the model (intersection of ZZ_1' and LM_0 and IS_1). In the very long term in which the ZZ curve is assumed to be rather flat (see ZZ_0 as an extreme case) point B would indicate a current account surplus. If exchange rates are flexible there will be a currency appreciation; if, however, the ZZ curve were steeper than the LM curve one would witness a currency depreciation. (i) In the presence of growing FDI one may assume that capital mobility will increase because the presence of MNCs means that information about international financial markets as well as access to these markets are increasing; (ii) it will become technically more difficult to control capital outflows if domestic firms have the option to form joint ventures with a growing pool of foreign investors; (iii) foreign investors will build up political pressure for capital import liberalization because they are used to and interested in taking loans wherever the costs of borrowing are lowest. Moreover, domestic firms will argue that MNCs' subsidiaries enjoy an unfair advantage if they can effectively borrow - even in the presence of official restrictions - in international markets (e.g. through the parent company) while local competitors are not allowed to use the cheapest sources of capital.

---

[14] We disregard dynamics here. The traditional view is that stability requires that the ZZ curve is less steep than the LM curve.

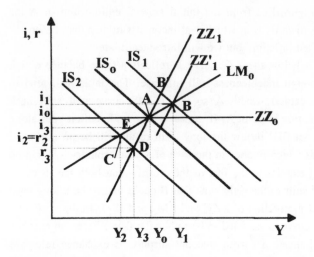

Figure E6: Systemic Transformation in the Supply-Augmented Macro Model

In the very first stage of systemic transformation employment and the number of firms is reduced, wealth is falling and government consumption is typically reduced (partly under external pressure, e.g. from the IMF). Point C in Figure E5 will be realized such that the real interest rate and output are falling. Assuming a steep ZZ curve (ZZ_1) there will be a trade balance surplus. This was indeed the situation observed in Hungary, Poland and the CSFR in 1990/91. So far we have disregarded inflation. One could easily take inflation into account if one assumes for simplicity that purchasing power parity would hold. This implies that the equilibrium value of r is determined by the intersection of the IS curve and the ZZ curve (point D), while the nominal interest rate i is determined on the LM curve. The real interest rate is r_3 and is lower than in a situation of zero inflation; output is higher (Y_3). The distance DE would reflect the inflation rate.[15] We disregard here currency substitution which could become increasingly important in the presence of MNCs.

---

[15] In a more elaborate analysis non-neutrality of inflation could also occur by an inflation-induced shift of the IS curve and the ZZ curve.

4. Conclusions for Transformation Policies

Privatization raises a series of problems in systemic transformation. The often observed insufficient momentum might be raised by an adequate privatization strategy. Combining privatization and FDI inflows could be an interesting option, but FDI inflows require political stability and the achievement of some minimum privatization progress. Without a competitive supplier industry few MNCs will consider major investment in central and eastern European economies. This holds especially because the locational advantages of host countries are thin and because economic growth is moderate at best. Foreign indebtedness need not be a major impediment to mobilizing FDI inflows as the Hungarian case shows, but monetary instability, complex regulations and bureaucratic inflexibility can prevent FDI inflows.

We have shown that one can identify certain criteria that suggest where and when privatization should be accelerated. FDI should generate positive external effects, but for reasons of conflict over profit income transforming economies might find it difficult to fully accept FDI inflows. Policies that encourage parallel inflows and thereby create competition, while possibly broadening the group of source countries, could be useful. Moreover, industries in which the ratio of the elasticity of demand to that of supply is high could be opened up to foreign investment first. Foreign investment and privatization will have major effects on the exchange rate, the current account development and economic growth.

While MNCs' activities have developed over decades in OECD countries and some NICs - which themselves have become source countries of FDI recently - the East European economies face the need for a rapid international investment catching up process which will last for decades. FDI inflows, however, are rarely openly welcomed in Eastern Europe where socialist ideology has always argued that foreign capitalists would only exploit people and countries. Main prospective source countries for capital are the EC countries and the US. Non-European FDI inflows are dominating in Hungary, while the CSFR and Poland are dominated by European investment inflows, mostly from Germany.

There have been three major shortcomings in the privatization process in ex-CMEA countries: West European demarcation lines between the private sector and the public sector have been followed too closely; the formation of new firms has been neglected; and emphasis was not placed early on in creating a functional capital market in which private banks and other financial intermediaries could guide a market-oriented investment policy. A gradual and sustaining transformation strategy is required, and supply-side effects and aspects of growth promotion should prominently figure in such an approach. Only if positive growth expectations can be generated will people be willing to politically accept the sharp reductions in real income and the rising risk of unemployment in a period of transition. Capitalism generates sustained income growth through a dynamic process of innovation, capital formation and adjustment. Moving from the safe but stagnant world of socialism to capitalism therefore requires that people can expect to obtain extra income gains in return for greater uncertainties and higher market risks.

A long term policy which is outward-oriented and stability-oriented seems to be the most promising avenue towards high investment, sustainable growth and prosperity. Finally, if the OECD countries do not further liberalize their imports and if the EC economies fail to resume high economic growth, the transformation of central and eastern European economies could come to a halt because the external environment - already difficult for the smaller countries when looking to the ex-USSR - has deteriorated in a period in which positive external impulses have been needed most. Without stabilizing the ex-USSR there is little prospect to achieve political and economic stability in the ex-CMEA area.

Mobilizing sustaining foreign investment in all major source countries (including Asian NICs such as Korea and Taiwan) will be one important element for economic catching up in central and eastern Europe. However, it will be only one major element because even substantive quantitative and qualitative impacts of FDI inflows leave the problem of how to reorganize the domestic sector of the economy unsolved. Sustainable and credible privatization processes are required as is a strong focus on encouraging the establishment of new business ventures. Market economy allocation under competition is a positive sum game whose yield is increased if a stable institutional framework has been developed. Hence the restructuring of the supply side via privatization from above and from below has to be accompanied by the building of credible institutions in transforming economies. As they gain reputation and credibility economic policy interference can be reduced since the announcement of policy measures of a credible actor already influence expectations and actions of the private sector. The example of successful Asian NICs suggests that political stability, outward oriented economic policies and functional domestic capital markets (with positive real interest rates and socially accepted high profit rates) as well as continuous human capital formation plus R&D promotion are vital ingredients for moving up the technological ladder and realising high economic growth rates.

Bibliography

Acs, Z. and D. Audretsch (1990), *Innovation and Small Firms*, MIT Press, Cambridge, Mass

Acs, Z. and D. Audretsch, eds (1991), *Innovation and Technical Change. An International Comparison*, UP, New York

Aghion, P. (1992), Comment on Eric S. Maskin, "Auctions and privatisation", in: Siebert, H., ed. (1992), 137 - 139

Ahlbrecht, R. (1973), Efficiency in the provision of fire services, *Public Choice*, 16:1-15

Akerlof, G.A. and J.K. Yellen (1990), The Fair Wage-Effort Hypothesis and Unemployment, *Journal of Economics*, 105:255-283

Aliber, R.Z. (1992), Comment on O. E. Williamson, "Private Ownership and the Capital Market", in: Siebert, H., ed., *Privatization*, Mohr, Tübingen, 55-67.

Armstrong, M. and J. Vickers (1990), *Competition and Regulation in the British Telecommunication Industry*, IES, Oxford, unpublished manuscript

Arrow, K. (1968), Economic equilibrium, *International Encyclopedia of the Social Sciences*, vol. 4, Macmillan, New York

Ascher, K. (1987), *The Politics of Privatisation. Contracting out Public Services*, Macmillan Education, London

Aslund, A. (1991), Principles of privatisation, in: Csaba (1991), 17 - 32

Atkinson, S.E. and R. Halvorsen (1986), The relative efficiency of public and private firms in a regulated environment: the case of U.S. Electric Utilities, *Journal of Public Economics*, 29:281-284

Averch, T.L. and L.L. Johnson (1962), Behaviour of the firm under regulatory constraint, *American Economic Review*, 52:1052-1069

Ayub, M. and H. Hegstad (1987), Management of public industrial enterprises, *World Bank Research Observer*, 2:79-102

Bailey, M.J. and G.S. Tavlas (1991), Exchange Rate Variability and Direct Investment, *Annals of the American Academy of Political and Social Science*, 1991/516, July, 106-116

Bajt, A. (1985), Trideset godina privrednog rasta: problemi efikasnosti i drustvenih odnosa, *Ekonomist*, 38

Balassa, B. (1978), Exports and Economic Growth: Further Evidence, *Journal of Development Economics*, 181-189

Balcerowicz, L. and P.J.J. Welfens, eds (1988), *Innovationsdynamik im Systemvergleich*, Physica, Heidelberg

Bardhan, P. (1991), *Risktaking, capital markets, and market socialism*, Working Paper No 91-154, University of California, Berkley

Barone, E. ([1908], 1935), The ministry of production in the collectivist state, in: Hayek, F. A. (1935), 245-290

Bays, C. (1979), Cost comparisons of for profit and nonprofit hospitals, *Social Science and Medicine*, 13C:219-25

Becker, E.R. and F.A. Sloan (1985), Hospital ownership and performance, *Economic Inquiry*, 23:21-36

Beksiak, J. et al. (1990), Outline of a programme for stabilisation and systemic changes, in: *The Polish Transformation: Program and Progress*, Center for Research into Comunist Economy, 19-59

Berck, P. and K. Sydsaeter (1992), *Economist's Mathematical Manual*, Heidelberg: Springer

Berg, A. (1992), *The logistics of privatisation in Poland*, Paper for the conference on "Transition in Eastern Europe", NBER, Cambridge, Mass., 26 - 29 February

Berg, A. and J. Sachs (1992), Structural Adjustment and International Trade in Eastern Europe: The Case of Poland, *Economic Policy*, April 1992, 14:118-173

Berle, A. and G. Means (1933), *The Modern Corporation and Private Property*, Macmillan, New York

Bilson, J.F.O. (1979), Recent Developments in Monetary Models of Exchange Rate Determination, *IMF Staff Papers*, 26:201-223

BIS (Bank of International Settlements, 1991), *61st Annual Report*, Basle

BIS (Bank of International Settlements, 1992), *62nd Annual Report*, Basle

Bishop, C. (1980), Nursing home cost studies and reimbursement issues, *Health Care Financing Review*, 1:47-64

Bishop, M.R. and J. Kay (1992), Privatization in Western Economies, in: SIEBERT, H., ed. (1992), 193-209

Blanchard, O. and R. Layard (1990), *Economic Change in Poland*, Centre for Economic Performance, 3, LSE, London

Blanchard, O.J., A. Shleifer and L.F. Katz (1991), *Reform in Eastern Europe*, The MIT Press, Cambridge, Mass.

Blommestein, H. and M. Marrese, eds. (1991), *Transformation of Planned Economies. Property Rights Reform and Macroeconomic Stability*, OECD, Paris

BMF (BUNDESMINISTERIUM DER FINANZEN, 1991), *Schnelle Privatisierung, Entschlossene Sanierung, Behutsame Stillegung*, Bonn 1991

Boardman, A. and A. Vining (1989), Ownership and performance in competitive environments: a comparison of the performance of private, mixed and state-owned enterprises, *Journal of Law and Economics*, 19:1-33

Bolton, P. and G. Roland (1992), Privatisation policies in Central and Eastern Europe, *Economic Policy*, 15:275-310

Borcherding, T. E., ed. (1977), *Budgets and Bureaucrats*, Duke University Press, Durham, N.C.

Borensztein, E. and M.S. Kumar (1991), Proposals for privatisation in Eastern Europe, *IMF Staff Papers*, 38:300-326

Bornstein, M. (1992), Privatisation in Eastern Europe, *Communist Economies and Economic Transformation*, 3(4): 283-320

Bornstein, M., ed. (1985), *Comparative Economic Systems*, Irwin, Homewood

Brabant, J.M. van (1992), *Privatizing Eastern Europe. The Role of Markets and Ownership in the Transition*, Kluwer Academic Publishers, Dordrecht

Bradley, K. and A. Nejad (1989), *Managing Owners. The National Freight Consortium in Perspective*, Cambridge University Press, Cambridge

Brittan, S. (1983), Privatisation: a new approach, *Financial Times*, 4 March

Brittan, S. (1984), The case for capital ownership for all, *Financial Times*, 17 November

Brown, C. and J. Medoff (1989), The Employer Size-Wage Effect, *Journal of Political Economy*, 97:1027-1959.

Brugging, T.H. (1982), Public versus regulated private enterprise in municipal water industry: a comparison of operating costs, *Quarterly Review of Economics and Business*, 22:111-125

Bruno, M. (1988), Opening Up: Liberalization with Stabilization, in: Dornbusch, R., F. Leslie and C.H. Helmers, eds, *The Open Economy Tools for Policymakers in Developing Countries*, Oxford University Press/The World Bank, New York, 223-248.

Brus, W. (1986a), Postwar reconstruction and socio-economic transformation, in: Kaser, M. C., ed. (1986), II:564-641

Brus, W. (1986b), Institutional change within a planned economy, in: Kaser, M. C., ed. (1986), III:3-249

Brus, W. (1988), The Political Economy of Reform, in: Marer, P. and W. Siwinski, eds (1988), 65-80

Brus, W. and K. Laski (1989), *From Marx to the Market. Socialism in search of an economic system*, Clarendon Press, Oxford

Caillaud, B., R. Guesnerie and J. Tirole (1988), Government intervention in production and incentives theory: a review of recent contribution, *Rand Journal of Economics*, 19:1-26

Caves, D. and L. Christensen (1980), The relative efficiency of public and private firms in a competitive environment: the case of Canadian railroads, *Journal of Political Economy*, 88:958-76

Caves, D.W. *et al.* (1982), Economic performance of U.S. and Canadian railroads, in: Stanbury, W.T. and F. Thompson, eds (1982), 123-51

Caves, R.E. (1982), *Multinational Enterprise and Economic Analysis*, Cambridge University Press, Cambridge

Ciechocinska, M. (1992), Development of the private sector in Poland in 1989 - 90, *Communist Economies and Economic Transformation*, 2(4):215-236

Clague, C. and G.C. Rausser, eds (1992), *The Emergence of Market Economies in Eastern Europe*, Blackwell, Oxford

Clarkson, K.W. (1972), Some implications of property rights in hospital management, *Journal of Law and Economics*, 15:363-84

Clegg, J. (1992), Explaining Foreign Direct Investment Flows, in: Buckley, P.J. and M. Casson, eds, *Multinational Enterprises in the World Economy*, Edward Elgar, Aldershot, 54-74

Coase, R. (1937), The Nature of the Firm, *Economica*, 4:368-405.

Coase, R. (1960), The problem of social cost, *Journal of Law and Economics*, 3(1):1-44

Coe, D.T. and T. Kruger (1990), Wage Determination, the Natural Rate of Unemployment, and Potential Output, in: Lipschitz, L. und D. McDonald, eds, German Unification. Economic Issues, *Occasional Paper*, Washington, D.C., 75:115-129.

Collins, J. and B. Downes (1977), The effect of size on the provisions of public services: the case of solid waste collection in smaller cities, *Urban Affairs Quarterly*, 12:333-345

Collins, S.M. (1990), Lessons from Korean Economic Growth, *American Economic Review, P&P*, 80:104-107

Collins, S.M. (1990), Lessons from Korean Economic Growth, *American Economic Review, P&P*, 80:104-107

Collins, S.M. and D. Rodrick (1991), *Eastern Europe and the Soviet Union in the World Economy*, Washington DC: Institute for International Economics

Cooter, R.D. (1989), The Coase Theorem, in: Eatwell, J., M. Milgate and P. Newman, eds, 64-70

Corbo, V., F. Coricelli and J. Bossak, eds (1991), *Reforming Central and East European Economies. Initial Results and Challenges*, The World Bank, Washington D.C.

Corden, W.M. (1987), Protection and Liberalization: A Review of Analytical Issues, *IMF Occasional Paper* No. 54, Washington, DC.

Cousins, C. (1990), The contracting-out of ancillary services in the NHS, in: Jenkins, G. and M. Poole, eds (1990), 97-111

Crain, W.M. and A. Zardkooh (1978), A test of the property rights theory of the firm: water utilities in the United States, *Journal of Law and Economics*, 21:398-408

Crain, W.M. and A. Zardkoohi (1980), Public sector expansion: stagnant technology or attenuated property rights, *Southern Economic Journal*, 46:1069-82

Crane, K. (1991), Property rights reform: Hungarian country study, in: Blommestein, H. and M. Marrese, eds (1991), 69-94

Csaba, L. (1990), *Eastern Europe in the World Economy*, Cambridge University Press, Cambridge

Csaba, L., ed. (1991), *Systemic Change and Stabilization in Eastern Europe*, Dartmouth, Aldershot

Cubbin, J., S. Domberger and S. Meadowcroft, (1987), Competitive tendering and refuse collection: identifying the sources of efficiency gains, *Fiscal Studies*, 8:49-58

Dabrowski, J.M., M. Federowicz, and A. Levitas (1991), Polish state enterprises and the properties of performance: stablilization, marketization, privatisation, *Politics and Society*, 19:403-437

Dabrowski, M. (1990), *Reforma, rynek, samorzad*, PWE, Warszawa

Davies, D. (1971), The efficiency of public versus private firms: the case of Australia's two airlines, *Journal of Law and Economics*, 14:149-65

Davies, D. (1977), Property rights and economic efficiency: the Australian airlines revisited, *Journal of Law and Economics*, 20:223-26

Davies, D. (1981), Property rights and economic behaviour in private and government enterprises: the case of Australia's banking system, *Research in Law and Economics*, 3:111-42

De Alessi, L. (1974), An economic analysis of government ownership and regulation: theory and the evidence from the electric power industry, *Public Choice*, 19:1-42

De Alessi, L. (1977), Ownership and peak-load pricing in the electric power industry, *Quarterly Review of Economics and Business*, 17:7-26

De Alessi, L. (1980), The economics of property rights: a review of the evidence, *Research in Law and Economics*, 2:1-47

De Alessi, L. (1983), Property rights, transaction costs, and X-efficiency: an essay in economic theory, *American Economic Review*, 73:64-81

De Alessi, L. (1987), Property rights and privatisation, in: Hanke, S.H., ed. (1987)

Demsetz, H. (1966), Some aspects of property rights, *Journal of Law and Economics*, 11:61-70

Demsetz, H. (1968), Why regulate utilities?, *Journal of Law and Economics*, 11:55-65

Dinopoulos, E. and T.D. Lane (1991), Market Liberalization Policies in a Reforming Socialist Economy, IMF working paper WP 91/119, forthcoming in *IMF Staff Papers*.

Dittus, P., P.S. O'Brien, P.S. and H.J. Blommenstein (1991), International Economic Linkages and the International Debt Situation, *OECD Economic Studies*, 16:134-168.

Dixit, A.K. (1980), Investment and entry deterrence, *Economic Journal*, 90:95-100

Domberger, S., S. Meadowcroft and D. Thompson (1986), Competitive tendering: the case of refuse collection, *Fiscal Studies*, 7:69-87

Dornbusch, R. (1976), Expectations and Exchange Rate Dynamics, *Journal of Political Economy*, 84:1167-1176

Dosi, G. (1988), Institutions and Markets in a Dynamic World, *The Manchester School of Economic and Social Studies*, LVI:119-146

Dreze, J.H. (1990), *Labour Management, Contracts and Capital Market. A General Equilibrium Approach*, Basil Blackwell, Oxford

Dunn, L.F. (1986), Work Disutility and Compensating Differentials: Estimation of Factors in the Links Between Wages and Firms Size, *Review of Economics and Statistics*, 68:67-73

Dunning, J.H. (1981), *International Production and the Multinational Enterprise*, Allen & Unwin, London

Dworzecki, Z., (1988), Innovationsmanagement in sozialistischen Staaten, in: Welfens, P.J.J. and L. Balcerowicz, eds (1988), 288-299

Eaton, B.C. and R.G. Lipsey (1981), Capital, commitment and entry equilibrium, *Bell Journal of Economics*, 12:593-604

Eatwell, J., M. Milgate and P. Newman, eds (1989), *Allocation, Information and Markets*, Macmillan, London

EBRD (1993), *Annual Economic Review 1992*, London

Economist (1992), *Fear of Finance. A Survey of the World Economy*, Economist, September 19th, London

Economist (1992c), *The Yen Block Breaks Open*, Economist, May 8, 1993, London, 64-70

Economist (1993), *A Survey of Multinationals*, Economist, March 27, 1993, London

Economist (1993a), *East European Privatisation. Making it Work*, Economist, March 13, 1993, London, 88

Edwards, F. and B. Stevens (1978), The provision of municipal sanitation by private firms: an empirical analysis of the efficiency of alternative market structures and regulatory arrangements, *Journal of Industrial Economics*, 27:133-47

Eggertsson, T. (1990) Economic Behaviour and Institutions, *Cambridge Studies of Economic Literature*, Cambridge University Press, Cambridge

Estrin, S. (1983), *Self-management: economic theory and Yugoslav practice*, Cambridge University Press, Cambridge

Eurostat (1990), *Provisional Report by Christine Spanneut on Direct Investment in the European Community*, Luxembourg, August 1990

Fallenbuchl, Z.M. (1991), Polish Privatization Policy, *Comparative Economic Studies*, 33:53-70

Fama, E. (1980), Agency problem and the theory of the firm, *Journal of Political Economy*, 88:288-307

Fama, E.F. and M.C. Jensen (1983a), Agency problems and residual claims, *Journal of Law and Economics*, 26:301-326

Fama, E.F. and M.C. Jensen (1983b), Separation of ownership and control, *Journal of Law and Economics*, 26:327-350

Färe, R., S. Grosskopf and J. Logan (1985), The relative performance of publicly owned and privately owned electric utilities, *Journal of Public Economics*, 26:89-106

Farrell, M.J. (1957), The measurement of productive efficiency, *Journal of the Royal Statistical Society*, Series A, 120:253-266

Feige, E. (1990), A message to Gorbatchev: redistribute the wealth, *Challenge*, 33:46-53

Feigenbaum, S. and R. Teeples (1983), Public versus private water delivery: a hedonic cost approach, *Review of Economics and Statistics*, 65:672-78

Feinstein, C.H., ed. (1969), *Socialism, Capitalism and Economic Growth: Essays Presented to Maurice Dobb*, Cambridge University Press, New York

Fershtman, C. (1990), The Interdependence Between Ownership Status and Market Structure: The Case of Privatisation, *Economica*, 57: 319-329

Fershtman, C. (1990), The interdependence between ownership status and market structure: the case of privatisation, *Economica*, 57:319-329

Finsinger, J. (1982), *The Performance of Public Enterprises in Insurance Markets*, Paper presented at a conference on the performance of public enterprises, Liege, Sart Tilman

Firth, M. (1979), The profitability of takeovers and mergers, *Economic Journal*, 89:316-328

Firth, M. (1980), Takeovers, shareholders returns and the theory of the firm, *Quarterly Journal of Economics*, 94:235-260

Fischer, S. (1992), Privatisation in East European Transformation, in: Clague, C. and G.C. Rausser, eds (1992), Blackwell, Oxford, p. 227-243

Fischer, S. and A. Gelb (1990), Issues in Socialist Economy Reform, The World Bank, *PRE working paper* WPS 565, Washington DC, 1990

Forsyth, P.J. and R.D. Hocking (1980), Property rights theory of the firm in a regulated environment: the case of Australian airlines, *Economic Record*, 56:182-85

Franks, J. and C. Mayer (1990), Capital markets and corporate control: a study of France, Germany and the UK, *Economic Policy*, 10:189-232

Franz, W. (1991), *Arbeitsmarktökonomik*, Springer, Heidelberg

Fraser, R., ed. (1988), *Privatisation: the UK Experience and International Trends*, Keesing's International Studies, Longman, London

Frech, H.E., III. and P.B. Ginsburg (1981), The cost of nursing home care in the United States: government financing, ownership and efficiency, in: Gaag, J. van der and M. Perlman, eds, 67-81

Frech, H.E., III., (1976), The property rights theory of the firm: empirical results from a natural experiment, *Journal of Political Economy*, 84:143-52

Frech, H.E., III., (1980), Property rights, the theory of the firm, and competitive markets for top decision-makers, *Research in Law and Economics*, 2:49-63

Frey, B.S. and F. Schneider (1985), Economic and Political Determinants of Foreign Direct Investment, *World Development*, 13:161-175

Friedman, M. (1976), How to denationalize?, *Newsweek*, 27 December

Frydman, R. and A. Rapaczynski (1991), Markets and institutions in large-scale privatisation: an approach to economic and social transformation in Eastern Europe, in: Corbo, V., F. Coricelli and J. Bossak, eds (1991), 253-274

Funkhauser, R. and P.W. MacAvoy (1979), A sample of observations on comparative prices in public and private enterprises, *Journal of Public Economics*, 11:353-68

Furubotn, E. (1974), Bank credit and labour-managed firm: the Yugoslav case, *Canadian-American Slavic Studies*, reprinted in: Furubotn, E. and S. Pejovich, (1974), 257-276

Furubotn, E. and S. Pejovich (1970), Property rights and the behaviour of the firm in a socialist state: the example of Yugoslavia, *Zeitschrift für Nationalökonomie*, 30:431-454

Furubotn, E. and S. Pejovich (1971), The role of the banking system in Yugoslav economic planning, *Revue Internationale D'Historie De La Banque*, 4

Furubotn, E. and S. Pejovich, eds (1974), *The Economics of Property Rights*, Ballinger Publishing Company, Camibridge, MA.

Gaag, J. van der and M. Perlman, eds (1981), *Health, Economics, and Health Economics*, North-Holland, New York

Gandolfo, G. (1980), *Economic Dynamics: Method and Models*, 2nd rev. edition, Amsterdam: North-Holland

GATT (1992), *Trade Policy Review Mechanism. The Republic of Poland*, Geneva

Gayle, D.J. and J.N. Goodrich, eds (1990), *Privatisation and Deregulation in Global Perspective*, Pinter Publisher, London

Gerschekron, A. (1962), *Economic Backwardness in Historical Perspective*, Harvard UP, Cambridge, MA.

Gomulka, S. (1989, [1992]), How to create a capital market in a socialist country for the purpose of privatisation, in: Prindl, A.R., ed. (1992)

Gomulka, S. and A. Polonsky, eds (1990), *Polish Paradoxes*, Roultledge, London and New York

Greene, J. and P. Isard (1991), *Currency Convertibility and the Transformation of Centrally Planned Economies*, IMF Occasional Paper No. 81, Washington DC.

Grosfeld, I. and P. Hare (1991), *Privatisation in Hungary, Poland and Czechoslovakia*, CEPR Discussion Paper 544, London, April

Grossman, G.M. and E. Helpman (1991), *Innovation and Growth in the Global Economy*, Cambridge: MIT Press, Cambridge, Mass.

Grossman, S. and O. Hart (1980), Takeover bids, the free-rider problem and the economics of the firm, *Bell Journal of Economics*, 11:42-64

Group of Thirty (1987), *Foreign Direct Investment*, 1973-87, New York

Gruszecki, T. (1987), *Przedsie biorstwo w we gierskiej reformie gospodarczej*, PAN, Warszawa

Gruszecki, T. (1990), *Privatisation. Initial conditions and analysis of the government programme (August 1989 - mid-April 1990)*, Stefan Batory Foundation, Warsaw

GUS (Glowny Urzad Statystyczny, 1991), *Statystyczny portret Polski na tle EWG*, Warsaw

Guski, H.-G. (1988), *Privatisierung in Großbritannien, Frankreich und USA*, Deutscher Instituts-Verlag, Köln

Hanke, S.H., ed. (1987), *Prospects for Privatisation*, Academy of Political Science, New York

Hare, P. and G. Hughes (1991), Competitiveness and Industrial Restructuring in Czechoslovakia, Hungary and Poland, London: *CEPR Discussion Paper* No. 543.

Hausman, J.M. (1976), *Urban Water Services Pricing: Public vs. Private Firms*, unpublished Ph.D.thesis, George Washington University, Department of Economics

Hay, D.A. and D.J. Morris, (1991), *Industrial Economics and Organization. Theory and Evidence*, Oxford University Press, Oxford

Hayek, F.A., ed. (1935), *Collectivist Economic Planning*, George Routledge and Sons, London

Hayek, F.A. (1935), The nature and history of the problem, and The present state of debate, in: Hayek, F.A., ed. (1935), 1-40.201-243

Hayek, F.A., ([1940], 1948), The competitive solution, *Economica*, reprinted in: Hayek, F.A., (1948), 181-208

Hayek, F.A., ([1945], 1984), The price system as a mechanism for using knowledge, *American Economic Review*, 35:519-530, reprinted as The use of knowledge in society, in: Nichiyama, C. and K.R. Leube, eds (1984), 211-224

Hayek, F.A. (1948), *Individualism and Economic Order*, Chicago

Hayek, F.A. von (1968), *Der Wettbewerb als Entdeckungsverfahren*, Mohr, Tübingen

Hayek, F.A. ([1978], 1984), Competition as a Discovery Procedure, in: *New Studies in Philosophy, Politics, Economics and the History of Ideas*, Chicago University Press, Chicago, 179-190, reprinted in: Nichiyama, C. and K.R. Leube, eds (1984), 254-265

Heald, D. and D. Stell ([1982], 1986), Privatising public enterprise: an analysis of the government's case, *Political Quarterly*, 1982:53, reprinted in: Kay, J. *et al.*, eds (1986)

Hellwig, M. (1991), Banking, Financial Intermediation and Corpoarate Finance, in: Giovannini, A. and C. Mayer, eds, *European Financial Integration*, Cambridge UP, Cambridge, 35-63

Herer, W. and W. Sadowski (1990), The incompatibility of system and culture and the Polish crisis, in: Gomulka, S. and A. Polonsky, eds (1990), 119-138

Hessen, R. (1983), The modern corporations and private property: a reappraisal, *Journal of Law and Economics*, 26:273-290

Hirsch, W.Z. (1965), Cost functions of an urban government service: refuse collection, *Review of Economics and Statistics*, 47:87-92

Holzmann, R. (1991), Budgetary Subsidies in Central and Eastern European Economies, *Economic Systems*, 15: 149-176

Hunya, G. (1992), Foreign Direct Investment and Privatisation in Central and Eastern Europe, *Communist Economies and Economic Transformation*, 4:501-511

Inotai, A. (1991), Liberalization and Foreign Direct Investment, in: Köves, A. and P. Marer, eds, *Foreign Economic Liberalization*, Westview, Boulder, Co., 99-111

Inotai, A. (1992), Foreign Direct Investments in Reforming CMEA Countries: Facts, Lessons and Perspectives, in: Klein M.W. and P.J.J. Welfens, eds, *Multinationals in the New Europe and Global Trade*, Springer, Heidelberg, 129-138

Instytut Gospodarki Narodowej (IGN), Metody kierowania rozwojem i funcjonowaniem gospodarki, *Zycie Gospodarcze*, 20 and 24/91

Jakubowicz, S. (1989), *Bitwa o Samorzad 1980 - 1981*, Aneks, London

Jasinski, P. (1990a), Two Models of Privatisation in Poland. A Critical Assessment, *Communist Economies*, 3(2):373-401

Jasinski, P. (1990b), Prywatyzacja, cz.1, *Zycie Gospodarcze*, 17/90

Jasinski, P. (1990c), Prywatyzacja, cz. 2, *Zycie Gospodarcze*, 19/90

Jasinski, P. (1990d), Kon u wodopoju. Od komunizmu do wolnego rynku, *Tygodnik Powszechny*, 42/90

Jasinski, P. (1991a), Wlasnosc, konkurencja i regulacje, *Przeglad Powszechny*, 1(833):36-53

Jasinski, P. (1991b), Prywatyzacyjne nieporozumienia, *Tygodnik Powszechny*, 49/91

Jasinski, P. (1992), The transfer and redefinition of property rights: theoretical analysis of transferring property rights and transformational privatisation in the post-STEs, *Communist Economies and Economic Transformation*, 2(4), forthcoming

Jasinski, P. and J. Lisiecki (1990), Czy to juz jest liberalizm?, *Tygodnik Powszechny*, 30/90

Jenkins, G. and M. Poole, eds (1990), *New Forms of Ownership. Management and Employment*, Routledge, London and New York

Jensen, M.C. and W.H. Meckling (1976), Theory of the firm: managerial behaviour, agency costs and ownership structure, *Journal of Financial Economics*, 3:305-60

Jensen, M.C. and W.H. Meckling (1979), Rights and production functions: an application to labour-managed firms and codeterminations, *Journal of Business*, 52:469-506

JETRO (1992), *JETRO White Paper on Foreign Direct Investment 1992*, Tokyo

Jones, L.P., Pankaj Tandon and Ingo Vogelsang (1990), *Selling Public Enterprises. A Cost - Benefit Methodology*, MIT, Cambridge MA.

Jordan, W.A. (1982), Performance of North American and Australian airlines, in: Stanbury, William T. and Fred Thompson, eds (1982), 161-99

Junker, J.A. (1975), Economic performance of public and private utilities: the case of U.S. electric utilities, *Journal of Economics and Business*, 28:60-67

Kaser, M.C., ed. (1986), *The Economic History of Eastern Europe*, vol. I - III, Clarendon Press, Oxford

Kawalec, S. (1989), Privatisation of the Polish Economy, *Communist Economies*, Vol.1, No. 3: 241-256

Kay, J., C. Mayer and D.J. Thompson, eds (1986), *Privatisation and Regulation: the UK Experience*, Clarendon Press, Oxford

Kemper, P. and J. Quigley (1976), *The Economics of Refuse Collection*, Ballinger, Cambridge MA.

Kim, K.S. (1981), Enterprise performance in the public and private sectors: Tanzanian experience, 1970-75, *Journal of Developing Areas*, 15:471-84.

Kiss, Y. (1991), *Privatisation in Hungary - wishful thinking or economic way-out?*, Paper for the conference on "International privatisation: strategies and practices", University of St. Andrews, Scotland, 12 - 14 September

Kiss, Y. (1992), *Privatisation paradoxes in East Central Europe*, Paper for the 2nd EACES conference on "Problems of transforming economies", Groningen, 24 - 26 September

Kitchen, H. (1976), A statistical estimation of an operating cost function for municipal refuse collection, *Public Finance Quarterly*, 4:56-76

Klein M.W. and P.J.J. Welfens, eds (1992), *Multinationals in the New Europe and Global Trade*, Heidelberg

Klein, B. (1983), Contracting costs and residual claims: the separation of ownerhsip and control, *Journal of Law and Economics*, 26:367-374

Kolodko, G.W. (1987), *Polska w wiecie inflacji*, Ksiazka i Wiedza, Warszawa

Kolodko, G.W. (1989), *Kryzys, dostosowanie, rozwój*, PWE, Warszawa

Kolodko, G.W. (1990), *Inflacja, reforma, stabilizacja*, Studencka Oficyna Wydawnicza ZSP, Warszawa

Kolodko, G.W. and W.W. McMahon (1987), Stagflation and shortageflation. A comparative approach, *Kyklos*, 40, reprinted in: Bornstein, M., (1989), ch. 26

Kolodko, G.W., D. Gotz-Kozierkiewicz and E. Skrzeszewska-Paczek (1991), *Hiperinflacja and stabilizacja w gospodarce postsocjalistycznej*, PWE, Warszawa

Kolodko, G.W., ed. (1991), *Polityka finansowa, stablizacja, transformacja*, Instytut Finansów, Warszawa

König, H., ed. (1990), *Economics of Wage Determination*, Springer, New York

Kornai, J. (1980), *Economics of Shortage*, North-Holland, Amsterdam, New York, Oxford

Kornai, J. (1986), The Hungarian reform process: visions, hopes, and reality, *Journal of Economic Literature*, 36:1687-1737

Kornai, J. (1990a), *The Road to a Free Economy. Shifting from a Socialist System: The Case of Hungary*, W. W. Norton, New York and London

Kornai, J. (1990b), The affinity between ownership and forms of coordination mechanisms: the common experience of reform in socialist countries, *Journal of Economic Perspectives*, 3(4):131-147

Kornai, J. (1990c), *The Road to a Free Economy. Shifting from a Socialist System: The Example of Hungary*, W. W. Norton, New York and London

Kornai, J. (1992), *The Socialist System. The Political Economy of Communism*, Oxford University Press, Oxford and New York

Kostrzewa, W. and H. Schmieding (1989), The EFTA Option for Eastern Europe: Towards an Economic Reunification of the Divided Continent, Institute fuer Weltwirtschaft, *Kiel Working Papers*, 297, October 1989

Köves, A. and P. Marer, eds (1991), *Foreign Economic Liberalization*, Westview, Boulder, Co.

Kowalik, T. (1990a and b), Froblematyka gospodarcza w porozumieniach sierpniowych: (1) W imie solidarnosci "robotniczej"; (2) Rozstrzygna 1 Szczecin, *Zycie Gospodarcze*, 34 and 35/90

Kravis, I. and R.E. Lipsey (1988), National Price Levels and the Prices of Tradables and Nontradables, *American Economic Review*, P&P, 78:474-478

Krawczyk, R. (1990), *Wielka przemiana. Upadek i odrodzenie polskiej gospodarki*, Oficyna Wydawnicza, Warszawa

Lange, O. ([1936], 1964), On the economic theory of socialism, *Review of Economic Studies*, 3, reprinted in: Lippincott, B. E., ed. (1964), 55-142

Lange, O. ([1964], 1985), The computer and the market, reprinted in: Bornstein, M., ed. (1985), 127-140

Larner, R.J. (1966), Ownership and control in the 200 largest nonfinancial corporations, 1929-1963, *American Economic Review*, 56:777-787

Lavoie, D. (1985), *Rivalry and Central Planning. The Socialist Calculation Debate Reconsidered*, Cambridge University Press, Cambridge

Lavoie, D. (1990), Computation, incentives, and discovery: the cognitive function of markets in market socialism, in: Prybyla, J.S., ed. (1990), 72-79

Lawrence, P. (1991), *Selling off the state: privatisation in Hungary*, Paper for the conference on "International privatisation: strategies and practices", University of St. Andrews, Scotland, 12 - 14 September

Leibenstein, H. (1966), Allocative efficiency vs. "X-efficiency", *American Economic Review*, 56:392-415

Leibenstein, H. (1978a), X-Inefficiency Xists - Reply to an Xorcist, *American Economic Review Proceedings*, 68:328-334

Leibenstein, H. (1978b), *General X-Efficiency Theory and Economic Development*, Oxford University Press, New York

Letwin, O. (1988), *Privatising the World. A Study of International Privatisation in Theory and Practice*, Cassel, London

Levitas, A. (1992), *The trials and tribulations of property reform in Poland: from state-led to firm-led privatisation, 1989-1991*, Paper for the conference on "The political economy of pirvatisation in Eastern Europe, Asia and Latin America", Brown University, 23 - 24 April

Lewandowski, J. and J. Szomburg (1989), Property rights as a basis for social and economic reforms, *Communist Economies*, 1:257-68

Lewin, A.Y. (1982), Public enterprise, purposes and performance, in: Stanbury, W.T. and F. Thompson, eds (1982), 51-78

Lindbeck, A. and D. Snower (1988), *The Insider-Outsider-Theory of Emplyoment and Unemployment*, MIT Press, Cambridge, MA.

Lindsay, C.M. (1976), A theory of government enterprise, *Journal of Political Economy*, 84:1061-77

Lippincott, B.E., ed. (1964), *On the Economic Theory of Socialism, Oskar Lange - Fred Taylor*, New York

Lipton, D. and J. Sachs (1990), Creating a market economy in Eastern Europe: the case of Poland, *Brookings Papers on Economic Activity*, 1:75-147

Lipton, D. and J. Sachs (1990), Privatization in Eastern Europe: The Case of Poland, *Brookings Papers on Economic Activity*, 2:293-341.

Lorenz, W. and J. Wagner (1988), Gibt es kompensierende Lohndifferentiale in der Bundesrepublik Deutschland?, *Zeitschrift für Wirtschafts- und Sozialwissenschaften*, 108:371-381

LUCAS, R.E., Jr. (1990), Why Doesn't Capital Flow from Rich to Poor Countries, *American Economic Review*, P&P, 80:92-96

Lydall, H. (1984), *Yugoslav Socialism: Theory and Practice*, Clarendon Press, Oxford

Lydall, H. (1989), *Yugoslavia in Crisis*, Clarendon Press, Oxford

MacAvoy, P.W., W.T. Stanbury, G. Yarrow and R.J. Zeckhauser, eds (1989), *Privatisation and State-Owned Enterprises. Lessons from the United State, Great Britain and Canada*. Kluwer Academic Publishers, Boston

Maj, H. (1991), Proces dostosowan mikroekonomicznych. Reakcje przedsie biorstw w warunkach polityki stabilizacyjnej, in: Kolodko, G.W., ed. (1991), 67-90

Mann, P.C. (1970), Publicly owned electric utility profits and resource allocation, *Land Economics*, 46:478-84

Mann, P.C. and J.L. Mikesell (1971), Tax payments and electric utility prices, *Southern Economic Journal*, 38:69-78

Marer, P. and W. Siwinski, eds (1988), *Creditworthiness and Reform in Poland. Western and Polish Perspectives*, Indiana University Press, Bloomington and Indianapolis

Maskin, E.S. (1992), Auctions and privatisation, in: Siebert, H., ed. (1992), 115-136

Mayhew, K. and P. Seabright (1992), Incentive and the management of enterprises in economic transition: capital markets are not enough, *Oxford Review of Economic Policy*, 8

McGuire, R.A. and T.N. Van Cott (1984), Public versus private economic activity: a new look at school bus transportation, *Public Choice*, 43:25-43

McKinnon, R. (1991), Liberalizing Foreign Trade in a Socialist Economy: The Problem of Negative Value Added, in: Williamson, J., ed. (1991), 96-115

Meeks, G. (1979), *Disappointing Marriage: A study of the gains from mergers*, Cambridge University Press, Cambridge

Meyer, R.A. (1975), Publicly owned vs. privately owned utilities: a policy choice, *Review of Economics and Statistics*, 57:391-99

Mihailovic, K. (1982), *Ekonomska Stvarnost Jugoslavije*, Boegrad

Mises, L. von ([1932], 1981), *Socialism. An economic and sociological analysis*, translation of 2nd. edition, Liberty Classics, Indianopolis

Mises, L. von ([1949], 1966), *Human Action. A Treatise on Economics*, 3rd revised edition, Contemporary Books, Chicago

Mises, L. von, ([1920], 1935), Economic calculation in the socialist society, reprinted in: Hayek, F.A., ed. (1935), 87-130

Mizsei, K. (1992), Privatisation in Eastern Europe: a comparative study of Poland and Hungary, *Soviet Studies*, 44:283-296

Molle, W. and R. Morsink (1991), Intra-European Direct Investment, in: Burgenmeier, B. and J.L. Mucchielli, eds (1991), *Multinationals and Europe 1992*, Routledge, London, 81-101

Monsen, R.J. and K.D. Walters (1983), *Nationalized Companies: A Threat to American Business*, McGraw-Hill, New York

Moore, J. (1986), Why privatise? and The success of privatisation, in: Kay, J., C. Mayer and D.J. Thompson, eds (1986), 78-98

Moore, T.G. (1970), The effectiveness of regulation of electric utility prices, *Southern Economic Journal*, 36:365-75

Morgan, W.D. (1977), Investor owned vs. publicly owned water agencies: an evaluation of the property rights theory of the firm, *Water Resource Bulletin*, 13:775-81

Morrison, S. (1981), *Property rights and economic efficiency: a further examination of the Australian Airlines*, Unpublished paper, University of British Columbia, Faculty of Commerce and Business Administration

Murphy, K.J. (1989), *Comment*, in: MacAvoy, P., et al., eds (1989)

Murrell, P. (1990), *The Nature of Socialist Economies*, Princeton University Press, Princeton

Murrell, P. (1991), *Evolution in Economics and in the Economic Reform of the Centrally Planned Economies*, University of Maryland, mimeo, May 1991

Myers, S.C. (1977), Determinants of Corporate Borrowing, *Journal of Financial Economics*, 5:14-175

Nelson, R.R. and S.G. Winter (1982), *An Evolutionary Theory of Economic Change*, Harvard University Press, Boston, Mass.

Neuberg, L.G. (1977), Two issues in the municipal ownership of electric power distribution systems, *Bell Journal of Economics*, 8:303-23

Newman, K. (1986), *The Selling of British Telecom*, Holt, Rinehart and Wiston, London

Nichiyama, C. and K.R. Leube, eds (1984), *The Essence of Hayek*, Hoover Institution Press, Stanford University, Stanford

Nove, A. (1983), *The Economics of Feasible Socialism*, Allen and Unwin, London

Nove, A. and D.M. Nuti, eds (1972), *Socialist Economics. Selected Readings*, Penguin, Harmondsworth

Nuti, D.M. (1991), Privatisation of socialist economies: general issues and the Polish case, in: Blommestein, H. and M. Marrese, eds (1991), 51-68

OECD (1991), *The Role of Tax Reform in Central and Eastern European Economies*, Paris

OECD (1992), *Industry in Poland*, Paris

OECD (1993), *Trends and Policies in Privatisation*, No. 1, Paris

Ostrom V. and R. Bish, eds (1977), *Comparing Urban Service Delivery Systems, Urban Affairs Annual Review*, Sage Publications, Beverly Hills, California

Paddon, M. (1991), *The Impact of UK CCT and EC Public Procurement Direvtives: Competition from European Contractors*, Paper presented at the conference: International Privatisation: Strategies and Practices, University of St. Andrews, 12 - 14 September 1991

Palmer, J.P., J. Quinn and R. Resendes, (1983), A case study of public enterprise: Grey Coach Lines, Ltd., in: Prichard, J.R.S., ed. (1983), 369-446

Panic, M. (1991), The Impact of Multinationals on National Economic Policies, in: Burgenmeier, B. and J.L. Mucchielli, eds (1991), *Multinationals and Europe 1992*, Routledge, London, 81-101

Papageorgiou, D., A.M. Choski, and M. Michaely (1990), *Liberalizing Foreign Trade in Developing Countries*, The World Bank, Washington, D.C.

Pashigian, B.P. (1973), Consequences and causes of public ownership of urban transit facilities, *Journal of Political Economy*, 84:1239-60

Pejovich, S. (1990), *The Economics of Property Rights: Towards a Theory of Comparative Systems*, Kluwer Academic Publishers, Dordrecht

Peltzman, S. (1971), Pricing in public and private enterprises: electric utilities in the United States, *Journal of Law and Economics*, 14:109-47

Peltzman, S. (1976), Toward a more general theory of regulation, *Journal of Law and Economics*, 19:211-240

Pescatrice, D.R. and J.M. Trapani, III., (1980), The performance and objectives of public and private utilities operating in the United States, *Journal of Public Economics*, 13:259-76

Picot, A. and T. Kaulmann (1989), Comparative performance of government-owned and privately owned industrial corporations - empirical results from six countries, *Journal of Institutional and Theoretical Economics*, 145:298-316

Pier, W.J., R.B. Vernon and J.H. Wicks (1974), An empirical comparison of government and private production efficiency, *National Tax Journal*, 27:653-56

Pindyck, R.S. (1991), Irreversible Investment, Capacity Choice, and the Value of the Firm, *American Economic Review*, 78:969-985

Pirie, M. (1988), *Privatisation. Theory, Practice and Choice*, Wildwood House, Aldershot

Pollitt, M. (1991), *The Relative Performance of Publicly Onwed and Privately Owned Electric Utilities*, unpublished M.Phil thesis, Brasenose College, Oxford University

Pommerehne, W.W. and B.S. Frey (1977), Public versus private production efficiency in Switzerland: a theoretical and empirical comparison, in: Ostrom V. and R. Bish, eds (1977), 221-241

Prichard, J.R.S., ed. (1983), *Crown Corporations in Canada: The Calculus of Instrument Choice*, Butterworths, Toronto

Prindl, A.R., ed. (1992), *Banking and Finance in Eastern Europe*, Woodhead-Faulkner, 56-64

Prybyla, J.S., ed. (1990), *Privatising and Marketizing Socialism. The Annals of the American Academy of Political and Social Science*, vol. 507, Sage Publications, London

Rasmusen, E. (1989), *Games and Information. An Introduction to Game Theory*, Basil Blackwell, Oxford

Redwood, J. (1990), Privatisation: a consultant's perspective, in: Gayle, D.J. and J.N. Goodrich, eds (1990), 48-62

Rees, R. (1988), Inefficiency, public enterprise and privatisation, *European Economic Review*, 32:422-431

Rey, P.P. (1969), Articulation des modes de dependance et des modes de production dans deux lineages, *Cahiers d'Etudes Africaines*, 35:415-40

Rieber, W.J. and Y. Islam (1991), Trade Liberalization in Asian Newly Industrialized Countries, *The International Trade Journal*, V:471-490

Riedel, J. (1990), The State of Debate on Trade and Industrialization in Developing Countries, in Pearson, C. and J. Riedel, eds, *The Direction of Trade Policy*, London: Basil Blackwell, 130-149

Romer, P.M. (1990), Are Nonconvexities Important for Understanding Growth, *American Economic Review, P&P*, 80:97-103

Rushing, W. (1974), Differences in profit and non-profit organisations: a study of effectiveness and efficiency in general short-stay hospitals, *Administrative Science Quarterly*, 19:474-84

Rychard, A. and A. Sulek, eds (1988), *Legitymacja. Klasyczne teorie i polskie doswiadczenia*, Polskie Towarzystwo Socjologiczne, Warszawa

Sachs, J. (1991), Accelarating privatisation in Eastern Europe: the case of Poland, Paper presented at the World Bank Annual Conference on Development Economics, Washington D.C., 25-26 April

Sadowski, Z.L. (1991), Privatization in Eastern Europe: Goals, Problems and Implications, *Oxford Review of Economic Policy*, Vol.7, No.4:46-56

Sajko, K. (1987), Enterprise organization of Eastern European socialist countries: a creative approach, *Tulane Law Review*, 61:1365-1382

Sappington, D.E.M. and J.E. Stiglitz (1987), Privatisation, information and incentives, *Journal of Policy Analysis and Management*, 6:567-82

Savas, E.S. (1977), Policy analysis for local government: public vs. private refuse collection, *Policy Analysis*, 3:49-74

Savas, E.S. (1987), *Privatisation: The key to better government*, Chatham House Publishers Inc., Chatham, NJ

Schaffer, M. (1991), *A note on the Polish state-owned enterprise sector in 1990*, Discussion paper, London School of Economics, London

Schanze, E. (1991), Evolution of Antitrust Policies in France, in: *Journal of Institutional and Theoretical Economics*, 147 (1991), 66-71

Scherer, F.M. (1992), Schumpeter and Plausible Capitalism, Harvard University, fortcoming in: *Journal of Economic Literature*.

Schipke, A. (1992), *Two Down - One to Go?: An Analysis of Two Years of Privatization in Germany*, Harvard University, mimeo.

Schlesinger, M. and R. Dorwart (1984), Ownership and mental health services, *New England Journal of Medicine*, 311:959-65

Schmidt, C.M. and K.F. Zimmermann (1990), Work Characteristics, Firms Size and Wages, *Review of Economics and Statistics*, forthcoming

Schmieding, H. (1992), Alternative approaches to privatisation: some notes on the debate, in: Siebert, H., ed. (1992), 97-108

Schnabel, C. (1990), *Privatisierung und Deregulierung in Großbritannien*, List Forum für Wirtschafts- und Gesellschaftspolitik, 16:148-166

Schneider, C.M. (1993), *Research and Development Management: From the Soviet Union to Russia*, forthcoming

Schneider, F. and B.S. Frey (1985), Economic and Political Determinants of Foreign Direct Investment, *World Development*, 13: 161-175

Schrenk, M. (1990), The CMEA System of Trade and Payments: Today and Tomorrow, *SPR Discussion Paper* No. 5, January 1990

Schumpeter, J.A., ([1942], 1954), *Capitalism, Socialism and Democracy*, 4th ed., Allen and Unwin, London

Sengupta, J.K. (1991), Rapid Growth in the NICs in Asia: Test of the New Growth Theory for Korea, *Kyklos*, 44:561-580

Shapiro, C. and J.E. Stiglitz (1984), Equilibrium Unemployment as a Worker Discipline, *American Economic Review*, 74:433-444

Shapiro, C. and R.D. Willig (1990), Economic rationales for the scope of privatisation, in: Suleiman, E.N. and J. Waterbury, eds (1990)

Sharkey, W.W. (1982), *The Theory of Natural Monopoly*, Cambridge University Press, Cambridge

Shepherd, W.G. (1966), Utility growth and profits under regulation, in: Shepherd, W.G. and T.G. Gies, eds (1966)

Shepherd, W.G. and T.G. Gies, eds (1966), *Utility Regulation: New Directions in Theory and Practice*, Random House, New York

Siebert, H., ed. (1992), *Privatisation*, J.C.B. Mohr (Paul Siebeck), Tübingen

Singh, A. (1971), *Takeovers: Their Relevance to the Stock Market and the Theory of the Firm*, Cambridge University Press, Cambridge

Singh, A. (1975), Takeovers, Economic Natural Selection and the Theory of the Firm, *Economic Journal*, 85:497-515

Sinn, G. and H.W. Sinn (1991), *Kaltstarkt. Volkswirtschaftliche Aspekte der deutschen Vereinigung*, Mohr, Tübingen

Solow, R.M. (1990), *The Labor Market as a Social Institution*, Basil Blackwell, Cambridge

Song, B. (1991), *The Rise of the Korean Economy*, Oxford University Press, Oxford

Spann, R.M. (1977), Public versus private provisions of governmental services, in: Borcherding, T.E., ed. (1977), 71-89

Stanbury, W.T. and F. Thompson, eds (1982), *Managing Public Enterprises*, Praeger, New York

Staniszkis, J. (1984), *Poland's Self-limiting Revolution*, Princeton University Press, Princeton

Staniszkis, J. (1987), The political articulation of property rights: some reflection on the "inert structure", in: Koralewicz, J., I. Bialecki and M. Watson, (1987), *Crisis and Transition. Polish Society in the 1980s*, Berg, Oxford, 53-79

Staniszkis, J. (1988a), Socjalistyczny sposob produkcji, *Colloquia Communia*, 4-5:145-174

Staniszkis, J. (1988b), Stabilizacja bez uprawomocnienia, in: Rychard, A. and A. Sulek, eds (1988), 215-238

Staniszkis, J. (1989), *Ontologia socjalizmu*, In Plus, Warszawa

Staniszkis, J. (1990), Poland's economic dilemma: "de-articulation" or "ownership reform", in: Gomulka, S. and A. Polonsky, eds (1990), 180-197

Stehn, J. (1992), *Ausländische Direktinvestitionen in Industrieländern*, Mohr, Tübingen

Stehn, J. and H. Schmieding (1990), Spezialisierungsmuster und Wettbewerbsfähigkeit: Eine Bestandsaufnahme des DDR-Außenhandels, *Die Weltwirtschaft*, H. 1.

Stevens, B.J. (1978), Scale, market structure, and the cost of refuse collection, *Review of Economics and Statistics*, 60:438-48

Stigler, G.J. (1971), The theory of economic regulation, *Bell Journal of Economics and Management Science*, 2:1-21

Stigler, G.J. (1976), The Xistence of X-efficiency, *American Economic Review*, 66:213-216

Stigler, G.J. and C. Friedland (1983), The literature of economics: the case of Berle and Means, *Journal of Law and Economics*, 26:237-268

Stiglitz, J.E. (1991), Some theoretical aspects of the privatisation: applications to Eastern Europe, *Rivista di Politica Economica*, 12(81):179-204

Stiglitz, J.E. (1992), The design of financial systems for the newly emerging democracies of Eastern Europe, in: Clague, C. and G.C. Rausser, eds (1992), Blackwell, Oxford, 161-184

Strand, J. (1987), The Relationship between Wages and Firm Size: An Information Theoretic Analysis, *International Economic Review*, 28:51-68

Suleiman, E.N. and J. Waterbury, eds (1990), *The Political Economy of Public Sector Reform and Privatisation*, Westview Press, Boulder, San Francisco, Oxford

Svetlicic, M. (1992), *Foreign Direct Investment and the Transformation of Former Socialist Countries*, University of Ljubljana, Faculty of Social Sciences, mimeo

Swiatkowski, E. and L. Cannon (1992), *Privatisation strategy in Poland and its political context*, Paper for the conference on "Transition to Democracy in Poland", Stanford University, Palo Alto, 23 - 24 November

Swiscicki, M. (1988), *Reforma wiasnosciowe*, Paper for the seminar on "Transformation Proposals for Polish Economy", SGPiS, Warsaw, 17 - 18 November

Szirmai, P. (1991), *The Stage of Small Business in Hungary* (1981-90), Paper for the International Center for Economic Growth (Washington DC), First Central and Eastern European Correspondent Institutes Meeting, Warschau, 27.5.

Tanzi, V. (1992), Tax Reform and the Move to a Market Economy: Overview of the Issues, in: OECD, *The Role of Tax Reform in Central and Eastern European Economies*, OECD, Paris

Temkin, G. (1989), On economic reform in socialist countries: the debate on economic calculation under socialism revisited, *Communist Economies*, 1:31-60

The Polish Transformation: Programme and Progress, (1990), Centre for Research into Communist Economies, London

Tilly, R. (1989), Banking Institutions in Historical Perspective - Gemrany, Great Britain and the United States in the 19th and 20th Century, *Journal of Institutional and Theoretical Economics*, 145: 189-209

Tilly, R. (1992), *German Banks and Foreign Investment in Eastern and Central Europe Before 1939*, paper prepared for Conference "The Economic Future of Central Europe", University of Minneapolis, April 16-18, 1992, Universität Münster

Tilton, J.E. (1973), *The Nature of Firm Ownership and the Adoption of Innovations in the Electric Power Industry*, referat przedstawiony na Public Choice Society, Washington D.C.

Tirole, J. (1988), *The Theory of Industrial Organization*, MIT Press, Cambridge, MA.

Tirole, J. (1991), Privatisation in Eastern Europe: incentives and the economics of transition, *NBER Macroeconomics Annual*, 221-259

Tirole, J. (1992), *Ownership and Incentives in a Transition Economy*, Document de Travail 10, Institut D'Economie Industrielle, Universite des Sciences Sociales de Toulouse

Treuhandanstalt (1993), *THA bulletin Monatsinformation*, 1/1993, February, 1993, Berlin

UNCE (1992), *Economic Survey of Europe in 1991-1992*, New York

UNCTC (1988), *Transnational Corporations in World Development*, New York

UNCTC (1992), *World Investment Report 1992*, Transnational Corporations as Engines of Growht, Springer, New York

UNIDO (1992), *Industry and Development, Global Report 1992/93*, Vienna

Vaubel, R. (1992), Comment on Holger Schmieding, Alternative approaches to privatisation: some note on the debate, in: Siebert, H., ed. (1992), 112-114

Veljanovski, C. (1987), *Selling the State. Privatisation in Britain*, Wiedenfeld and Nicolson, London

Veljanovski, C., ed. (1989), *Privatisation and Competition. A Market Prospectus*, IEA Hobart Paperback 28, Institute of Economic Affairs, London

Vickers, J. (1991) *Privatisation and the Risk of Expropriation*, Paper presented at the Third Villa Mondragone International Economic Seminar on *Privatisation Processes in Easter Europe: Theoretical Foundations and Empirical Results*, Rome, 25 - 27 June 1991, published in: *Rivista di Politica Economica*, 81:115-146

Vickers, J. and G. Yarrow (1988), *Privatisation. An Economic Analysis*, MIT Press, Cambridge, MA.

Vickers, J. and G. Yarrow (1991), The British electricity experiment, *Economic Policy*, 12:187-232

Ward, B. (1957), Workers management in Yugoslavia, *Journal of Political Economy*, 65:373-386

Ward, B. (1958), The firm in Illyria: market syndicalism, *American Economic Review*, 48:566-589

Weitzman, M. (1991), How not to privatise, *Rivista di Politica Economica*, 12(81):249-269

Welfens, M.J. (1993), *Umweltprobleme und Umweltpolitik in Mittel- und Osteuropa. Ökonomie, Ökologie und Systemwandel*, Physica/Springer, Heidelberg

Welfens, P.J.J. (1985), *Theorie und Praxis angebotsorientierter Stabilitätspolitik*, Nomos, Baden-Baden

Welfens, P.J.J. (1990a), *Internationalisierung von Wirtschaft und Wirtschaftspolitik/Internationalization of the Economy and Economic Policies*, Springer, New York-Heidelberg

Welfens, P.J.J. (1990b), Economic Reforms in Eastern Europe: Problems, Options and Opportunities, paper prepared for testimony before U.S. Senate, Small Business Committee, March 23, 1990, in: *Intereconomics*, 1991, June

Welfens, P.J.J. (1990c), *Internationalisierung von Wirtschaft und Wirtschaftspolitik*, Springer, Heidelberg

Welfens, P.J.J. (1991), Creating a European Central Bank after 1992: Issues of EC Monetary Integration and Problems of Institutional Innovation, in: Welfens, P.J.J., ed., *European Monetary Integration*, Springer, Heidelberg and New York, 2nd enlarged edition, 1993

Welfens, P.J.J. (1992a), EC Integration and Economic Reforms in CMEA Countries: A United Germany as a Bridge Between East and West?, in: Welfens, P.J.J., ed., *Economic Aspects of German Unification*, Springer, Heidelberg and New York, 9-42

Welfens, P.J.J. (1992b), *Market-Oriented Systemic Transformations in Eastern Europe*, Springer, Heidelberg and New York

Welfens, P.J.J., ed. (1992c), *Economic Aspects of German Unification*, Springer, Heidelberg und New York

Welfens, P.J.J. (1992d), Privatization, M&As, and Interfirm Cooperation in the EC: Improved Prospects for Innovation?, in: Scherer, F.M. and M. Perlman, eds, *Entrepreneurship, Technological Innovation, and Economic Growth. Studies in the Schumpeterian Tradition*, University of Michigan Press, Ann Arbor, 119-140

Welfens, P.J.J. (1993a), *A Supply-augemented Macro Model*, Münster University (forthcoming)

Welfens, P.J.J. (1993b), *The Single Market and the Eastern Enlargement of the EC. National and International Aspects of European Economic Dynamics*, Springer, Heidelberg and New York

Welfens, P.J.J. (1993c), *Europäische Gemeinschaft - Bestandsaufnahme und Perspektiven*, Schriften des Vereins für Socialpolitik, NF Band 225, 135-188

Welfens, P.J.J. (1993d), *The Growth of of the Private Sector: Privatization and Foreign Direct Investment in Eastern Europe*, paper to be presented at the International Conference "Overcoming the Transformation Crisis: Lessons from Eastern Europe for the Successor States of the Soviet Union, Institute for World Economics, Kiel, April 21-23, 1993

Welfens, P.J.J. (1993e), Privatization and Foreign Direct Investment in Systemic Transformation,.in: Csaba, L., ed.,-, forthcoming.

Welfens, P.J.J. and L. Balcerowicz, eds (1988), *Innovationsdynamik im Systemvergleich. Theorie und Praxis unternehmerischer, gesamtwirtschaftlicher and politischer Neuerung*, Physica-Verlag, Heidelberg

Wells, L.T., Jr. and A.G. Wint (1990), *Marketing a Country. Promotion as a Tool for Attracting Foreign Investment*, FIAS Occasional Paper 1, International Finance Corporation, Washington D.C.

Wiles, P. (1975), *Communist International Economics*, Blackwell, Oxford

Williamson, J., ed. (1991), *Currency Convertibility in Eastern Europe*, Institute for International Economics, Washington, DC.

Williamson, O.E. (1983), Organization Form, Residual Claimants, and Corporate Control, *Journal of Law and Economics*, 26:351-366

Williamson, O.E. (1985), *The Economic Institutions of Capitalism: Firms, Markets, and Relational Contracting*, Free Press, New York

Wilson, G.W. and J.M. Jadlow (1982), Competition, profit incentives, and technical efficiency in the nuclear medicine industry, *Bell Journal of Economics*, 13:472-82

Winiecki, J. (1986), *Why economic reforms fail in the Soviet system: a property rights-based approach*, Seminar Paper No. 374, The Institute for International Economic Studies, Stockholm

Winiecki, J. (1988), *The Distorted World of Soviet-Type Economies*, Routledge, London

Winiecki, J. (1990), Obstacles to economic reform of socialism: a property rights approach, in: Prybyla, J.S., ed. (1990), 65-71

Winiecki, J. (1992), *Privatisation in Poland. A Comparative Perspective*, Kieler Studies 248, J.C.B. Mohr (Paul Siebeck), Tübingen

Winter, S.G. (1984), Schumpeterian Competition in Alternative Technological Regimes, *Journal of Economic Behavior and Organization*, 5:287-320

Witt, U. (1990), *Studien zur Evolutorischen Ökonomik I*, Duncker & Humblot, Berlin

Wolf, T.A. (1988) *Foreign Trade in the Centrally Planned Economy*, Harwood, New York

Wolpe, H. (1980), *The Articulation of Modes of Production*, Routledge and Kegan Paul, London

World Bank (1990a), *Poland: Economic Management for a New Era*, Washington, D.C.

World Bank (1990b), *World Development Report 1990*, New York

World Bank (1991), *Free Trade Agreements with the US: What's in it for Latin America?*, Washington D.C.

Yannopoulos, G.N. (1992), *Multinational Corporations and the Single European Market*, University of Reading Discussion Paper No. 45, Reading

Yarrow, G. (1986), Privatisation in Theory and Practice, *Economic Policy*, 2:324-377

Yarrow, G. (1989a), Privatisation and economic performance in Britain, *Carnegie - Rochester Conference Series on Public Policy*, 31:303-344

Yarrow, G. (1989b), Does ownership matter?, in: Veljanovski, Cento, ed. (1989), 52-69

Zukrowska, K. (1990), *Determinanty przemian systemowych w Polsce. Pieriestrojka, entente a próba systemowej rekonstrukcji w Polsce*, Polski Instytut Spraw Mie dzynarodowych, Warszawa

Index